This is Advertising

Eliza Williams

This is Advertising

Laurence King Publishing

Author's acknowledgements
A huge thank you to all the contributors and everybody who helped in putting this book together, in particular Jo and Zoe at LKP, Patrick, Mark and Gavin at CR, and Nathan at Intercity. Thanks too to Mum, Sean and Martha for all their support.

LAURENCE KING

Published in 2010 by
Laurence King Publishing Ltd.
361–373 City Road
London EC1V 1LR
United Kingdom
email: enquiries@laurenceking.com
www.laurenceking.com

A catalogue record for this book is available from the British Library.

ISBN: 978 1 85669 647 0

Printed in China

Design by Intercity
www.intercitydesign.com

Frontispiece
Sony Japan: Rec You – Dentsu/GT Tokyo.

Chapter openers
(Digital) Red Bull: Red Bull Flugtag Flight Lab – less rain; **(Branded) Honda: Jump** – Wieden + Kennedy London/4 Creative; **(Ambient) The National Gallery, London: The Grand Tour** – The Partners; **(Integrated) Sci Fi Channel: Adopt Sci Fi** – BETC Euro RSCG; **(Self-initiated) The Glue Society Art Projects** – The Glue Society.

Picture credits
Burger King: Simpsonize Me (p32); Whopper Freakout (p86); Xbox King Games (p182) – The BURGER KING® trademarks and advertisements are used with permission from Burger King Brands, Inc. /"THE SIMPSONS"™ & © 2010. Twentieth Century Fox Film Corporation. All rights reserved.

Sony Pictures: 30 Days of Night (p48) – Courtesy of Columbia TriStar Marketing Group, Inc.

Honda: Jump (p58–9 and p74–5) – Photograph courtesy of Tony Danbury

The National Gallery, London: The Grand Tour (p102–3 and p108) – Photograph: Matt Stuart.

Sci Fi Channel: Adopt Sci Fi (p134–5 and p158–9) – Photograph by Sebastien Rabany, taken in Le Sème Elément Coiffure, Blvd Bigo Danel, Lille.

WWF: Earth Hour (p137) – Photographs of posters: Tamara Fana, Leo Burnett.

BETC Design, Art and Music Projects (p203) – Panik poster: Photographer: Mathieu Deluc Art director: Aurelie Pyvka

Contents

Introduction

Advertising has changed. The job of an advertising agency was once a straightforward one: to persuade people to buy a brand's products. The public knew what to expect from advertising; they recognized the language used to speak to them, and knew what was being asked of them in return. Now the transaction is less clear. The end goal of advertising is still a sale, but almost as important is the ability to persuade people to build a relationship with a brand, to make them feel that it has some relevance in their lives beyond a purely consumerist impulse. Brands now want their audience to play with them, talk to them, and live with them.

Until recently advertisers approached customers either through print and poster campaigns or on TV. Their audience was a captive one, accustomed to flicking through advertising in magazines or newspapers and to sitting through TV commercial breaks. Advertising agencies repaid their patience by occasionally making brilliant commercials – ones that they actually wanted to see and to talk about with their friends. These ads became part of popular culture and, although few and far between, they maintained the position of advertising as a creative force in the world.

The internet changed everything. Media in general began to splinter, and it was becoming more difficult to reach audiences. YouTube and other online channels gave people the opportunity to broadcast themselves. Those with something (or even nothing at all) to say could film themselves, put it up online and – if they happened to catch the prevailing cultural mood – get an audience of millions. TV, previously a solid, reliable vehicle for advertising, also began to evolve, with hundreds of channels available to viewers. At the same time, increasingly sophisticated TV recording devices appeared, allowing viewers to fast forward easily over any advertising they weren't interested in – the captive audience was a thing of the past.

The advertising industry was slow to respond, and resistant to the changes brought by the internet. Initially there was little belief amongst the major agencies and brands that it would have any effect. People clung to the hope that the status quo would remain – that brands could continue making huge, expensive TV spots and audiences would continue to respond. Some still believe this even now.

Agencies also wrestled with how to approach people online. Would the old 'interruption model' – where advertising breaks are forced into content that people have chosen to watch, such as a TV show – still be possible online? The internet was a more personal space, and initially there was a lot of resistance to advertising coming into this arena. It had to be handled carefully, and required a different way of thinking from the blockbuster advertising used on the small screen. The ad industry realized that a new approach was required. 'There has been a wholesale redefinition of what "advertising" is and how we relate to the audience or consumer,' says John Jay, co-executive creative director/partner at Wieden + Kennedy Portland. 'With all of the available channels of communication and reach, it is important to think about the entire brand experience so that you do not waste money or time. You need to be more creative today.'

A breakthrough in online advertising came with the emergence of 'viral advertising', an expression used to describe an ad campaign, usually a film, that was released online and passed on 'virally' among viewers. By using word of mouth, viral advertising bypassed the problems of the interruption model, where people are often irritated by the distraction. It quickly became an attractive option for advertisers – to achieve the reach of a TV spot without having to commit to the media spend.

Initially, much viral advertising was centred around what could not be shown on TV – largely sex and violence – with online audiences titillated by brands taking a risqué and playful approach. This quickly opened the way for spoofs, however, and the potential for brands to be damaged by films placed online that incorporated their brand name but had in fact nothing to do with them. A famous example of this was the fake 'VW Suicide Bomber' ad of 2005, which played on the VW Polo Small But Tough campaign. It showed a suicide bomber blowing himself up inside a Polo while the car remained undamaged. The 'ad' was viewed by millions, a coup for the young directors who had made it, but embarrassing for the marketing department at VW. This was a glimpse of the future of advertising, where the customer has the potential to both infiltrate and interact with brands, to powerful effect.

Viral advertising satisfies the core requirement for advertisers in the digital age: the necessity to get people interested. Savvy audiences reject obvious attempts by brands to infiltrate their world. They demand quality, and the internet offers them a place to express their displeasure with brands that have disappointed them, using online forums to vociferously berate companies that have failed to live up to expectation. As a result, brands have discovered that they need to come up with increasingly sophisticated ways to encourage their audience to interact with them – they have to 'woo' them, rather than simply blast them into submission with a ubiquitous campaign as in the TV-dominated advertising days of old. 'Brands should spend less time worrying about what they're saying and actually start doing,' says Daniel Bonner, chief creative officer at AKQA. 'But also think about what other people are saying about them. We know they're all talking but we've got to harness it and make sure they're saying good things about the brand. Because it can be really cost effective, but also it's about groundswell, it's about influencing culture. Because that's what advertising has always been good at; when it was good it would influence culture. It would change people's opinions.'

As well as opening up a more interactive, playful relationship with consumers, digital advertising has influenced how advertisers are thinking about their brands. For a long time the aim of an ad agency has been to define the 'story' of a brand – how it has developed a certain style and tone that sets it apart from other products that may in fact be otherwise virtually identical. Until recently this narrative has been largely one-way, with the advertiser telling the audience what to feel about a product. Now it is developing into a more interactive, game-like experience, with advertisers encouraging consumers to help shape their brands alongside them, thus engaging on a deeper level. 'I'm not sure we create advertising at all, at least not in the traditional sense,' says Michael Lebowitz, founder and CEO at Big Spaceship, New York. 'We are certainly marketing, but it's more about providing value or essential information in the form of entertainment or function than pure awareness. We talk about what we do as telling stories or starting conversations on behalf of brands.'

This book gathers together some of the most exciting examples of recent campaigns that use these less traditional methods, and divides them into chapters that highlight some of the biggest advertising trends to emerge over the last decade. The first chapter, 'Digital', focuses on certain innovative campaigns that have played out exclusively online, pushing the boundaries of what is possible to achieve with advertising on the internet. It includes ad campaigns that incorporate online blogs, games and other interactive websites.

The second chapter, 'Branded', looks at branded content, a phenomenon that has been around for several decades, but that has taken on new meaning in the digital era, where an ad no longer has to be something that appears between content – it can now be the content. This chapter includes books, short films, and a feature-length movie, all funded by brands. It also includes ads that initially appeared on TV but found a new, more successful life online, where they are shared by millions and have engendered countless copies and remixes by fans.

'That's what advertising has always been good at; when it was good it would influence culture. It would change people's opinions.'

Daniel Bonner, chief creative officer, AKQA

Ad campaigns created to appear only in a specific, usually localized, setting, are covered in the third chapter, 'Ambient', which includes artworks created for brands, and even a branded city neighbourhood.

The fourth chapter, 'Integrated', looks at initiatives where all forms of advertising come together in campaigns that appear across a multitude of media, traditional and new.

The final chapter, 'Self-initiated', examines how the reinvigorated creative outlook in advertising has affected agency life, by looking at some of the projects created by ad agencies, but not for clients. These might be personal business ventures or contemporary artworks made for an exhibition, but in each case the agency involved has reached beyond the usual expectations of what people in advertising should deliver.

More than ever, audiences are demanding to be treated with intelligence and respect, and are beginning to reject the brands that fail to do this. They are new-media literate and adept at using the plethora of communication methods now available, so brands and advertising agencies need to work hard at finding ways to approach them. Inevitably these changes have required agencies and clients to adapt, find new business models and prove their creative capabilities. The advertising discussed in this book is still often seen as being outside of the mainstream, yet it has reached audiences of millions, has revitalized well-established brands and launched new ones. A new and exciting era of advertising has begun. 'People working in advertising at this time are immensely lucky,' says Rafael Soto, creative director of Herraiz & Soto agency in Madrid. 'More than ever before in the industry we now have the real opportunity to invent, to evolve the relationship between brands and consumers, to create a more interesting model, have more fun.'

> **'More than ever before in the industry we now have the real opportunity to invent, to evolve the relationship between brands and consumers, to create a more interesting model, have more fun.'**
>
> **Rafael Soto, creative director, Herraiz & Soto**

An Industry in Flux

As the brands and their audiences have changed, the ad industry has had to make some adjustments. For a long time viewed by those outside the industry (and occasionally inside) as a champagne-guzzling, arrogant business, which was increasingly placing a premium on making money rather than creative credibility, its self-assurance has begun to show some cracks. While the larger worldwide networks of agencies have found it hard to respond quickly to the rapid developments in media and communications, the younger, smaller companies have prospered. Agencies once described as 'maverick' or 'boutique' have begun to win the large brand accounts, as they show an ability to react effectively to the confusion of the times.

The evolution of these smaller companies can be traced over more than a decade, and they have introduced new ways of working to the wider industry. The creative department, previously kept in ivory tower seclusion from less rarefied areas of the company, now has to interact with technologists and other strategists directly. This development has been partly influenced by the rise of digital agencies. Appearing as a response to the larger agencies' reluctance to tackle the new possibilities offered by the internet, digital companies offer brands a different kind of proposition, with the advice of a technical expert often central to the development of a creative idea. This approach is now increasingly accepted by larger agencies. 'In the past, digital has been this bastard child,' says Dominic Goldman, digital creative director at BBH London. 'It was a dirty word a few years ago; people didn't really want to deal with it. They were either scared of it or didn't think it was very good. Nowadays people realize that they don't have to be that technically savvy; it's about ideas again.'

These shifts in the working life of an agency, particularly within the creative department, have wrought wider reaching changes. Previously the make-up of an agency's creative department would be largely copywriters or art directors. Now you are also likely to find technologists, PR people and event organizers, all playing a pivotal role in the development of a creative idea. Even the need to be part of a copywriter/art director team – the traditional model for creative teams stretching back to the 1960s and once seen as absolutely crucial – is beginning to seem unnecessary.

There are even examples of how one person can seemingly do everything. Koichiro Tanaka, co-founder and creative director of the small Tokyo-based ad agency/production company Projector, found himself thrust into the advertising industry spotlight in 2008, after his online branded clock, Uniqlock (page 16), for Japanese clothing company Uniqlo, won every award going. It was a brilliant idea – creating a web gadget so useful and charming that people would want to have it constantly ticking away on their computer desktops and blogs – but what was more interesting was Tanaka's way of working. He oversaw all aspects of the project, from briefing the directors making the films that appear on the clock, to leading the web development teams, to advising the PR company that promoted Uniqlock. 'If you look at each individual skill, I'm not a great technician, perhaps I'm just a very skilled amateur,' explains Tanaka. 'But I am able to keep an eye on everything, the totality of it.' It's difficult to imagine a traditional agency allowing one of its creative directors the time to oversee a single campaign in all its minutiae in this way, but it undoubtedly brought success here.

Elsewhere, agencies are actively encouraging new voices into the creative department. Realizing that one of the answers to the diverse demands now made upon the modern agency is to find a broader way of thinking than the traditional ad team structure can necessarily provide, Fallon in London has a number of 'creative associates' working in its ranks, who have joined the agency from other creative industries such as magazine publishing, the music business, TV and events promotion. Other companies regularly stretch beyond the usual creative expectations of an advertising agency. BETC Euro RSCG in Paris, for example, runs its own design arm, making products for its clients and others (page 202). It also holds regular music and fashion events and parties, and even has a successful contemporary art gallery in its basement. All these spin-off projects nurture the minds of BETC's creative department, while providing clients with ample proof of the company's ambitious ideas and capabilities. 'As far as advertising is concerned, things have always been simple and transparent, the deal with consumers clear,' explains Rémi Babinet, founder and chairman at BETC. 'All that has changed today are the means and the media of expression. Voice and gesture are no longer enough; to convey a message successfully, we need to find modern forms of eloquence, practise a new art of conversation, create images, compose music, make films, stage events, involve, dramatize and orchestrate the whole thing.'

Some agencies are even taking this nurturing to a formal level, by running their own in-house schools. Wieden + Kennedy in Portland runs a yearly school, WK12, which sees 12 trainees join the agency to work on real briefs for real clients, while getting a hands-on taste of all aspects of agency life, from creative to production to PR. Rather than the typical graduate trainee, applications are encouraged from people from all walks of life, and of all ages. All that is needed is some evidence of creative thought. An emphasis on creativity exists all across the Wieden + Kennedy network, with a number of innovative side projects often taking place alongside the usual client work, be it design projects, or even a successful record label (Tokyo Lab, run from Wieden + Kennedy's Tokyo offices, has been releasing CDs and DVDs for over five years, page 216). 'We don't always do enough playing,' says Tony Davidson, executive creative director at Wieden + Kennedy London, of the creative process. 'I know my best ideas come when I'm not always supposed to be thinking about ideas. That two-and-a-half pints, just before you go to bed, the subconscious time. It's why you'll always be more creative if you're not sitting in an office, if you're walking around a gallery.'

Likewise, at KesselsKramer advertising agency, which has its main offices in Amsterdam with a smaller offshoot in London, self-initiated creative projects are actively encouraged, and its London office even has a shop, selling the wares of KesselsKramer's employees. The products range from books to more eclectic propositions (page 200). While these kinds of quirky projects may not seem all that unusual for an advertising agency, what sets KesselsKramer apart is the seriousness with which they are taken within the company, and its emphasis on commerce. The ideas are not simply created as vanity projects to prove an agency's creative worth, but as objects and ideas to be proliferated outside the realm of advertising.

Other new agency models are also beginning to emerge. The Glue Society, based in Sydney and New York, has no permanent client accounts, but instead works on a project-by-project basis, allowing a level of creative freedom unknown in traditional set-ups. The agency operates as a solely creative proposition, with all the account handling side of its business managed by a separate company. A lack of permanent clients does mean that the agency has less financial security, but the return for this is the ability to work in a multitude of different ways, depending on the

'As far as advertising is concerned, things have always been simple and transparent, the deal with consumers clear. All that has changed today are the means and the media of expression.'

Rémi Babinet, founder and chairman, BETC Euro RSCG

requirements of each individual project. The Glue Society's portfolio includes everything from traditional TV campaigns to integrated projects for brands, and even contemporary artworks.

Agencies have also recognized the necessity of having an international team. This reflects both the multicultural make-up of most major cities around the world now, as well as the increased global focus of brands. While brands will usually always come from somewhere – Coca-Cola and McDonald's will always be seen as American, for example, despite their global ubiquity– it is now important to be recognized (and sold) all over the world, and often the same campaign will be rolled out across all markets. Despite this, there is also recognition of the success of localized campaigns, as well as targeting specific groups, offering something of particular use to them. 'Today, the smart companies who get it right understand that the power lies less with your money and more with your intelligence power,' says Carlos Bayala, creative director and partner at Madre, Buenos Aires. 'As a brand, the smarter you are, the more attractive to intelligent minds you are, the more powerful you will be. That has to do with the people you attract to your corporation and also the public with which you relate.'

'As a brand, the smarter you are, the more attractive to intelligent minds you are, the more powerful you will be.'

Carlos Bayala, creative director and partner, Madre

The Relationship with the Client

Of course none of these new approaches in advertising would be possible without backing from clients. The client is often the first to be blamed by agencies when bland advertising is sent out into the world. Usually market research will be held up as the main culprit for this, with nervous clients reacting to initial responses from research groups by removing anything that makes the campaign edgy and interesting. However, a brave client can also make a campaign. Behind all brilliant advertising ideas lies a confident and well-informed client – one who deeply understands the market the campaign is entering but is also willing to make a leap of faith by experimenting with new and untested ideas.

As the landscape of possibility for advertising increases, it is more necessary than ever for an agency to have a strong and trusting relationship with its clients, for it is from this backdrop that risks are taken and interesting work arises. 'It takes courage to do the best, most effective work,' says Kevin Proudfoot, co-creative director, Wieden + Kennedy New York. 'Consumers recognize and reward brands that are decisive and believe in what they have to say. And yet that type of work is incredibly rare.'

Many of the most innovative ideas of recent years have begun as cheap add-ons to a larger campaign, thus minimizing the gamble as well as the costs. The 2004 Subservient Chicken website for Burger King, for example, which became an early internet advertising phenomena, was initially viewed as peripheral to a much bigger TV launch. It has since entirely eclipsed the campaign it was part of and has entered advertising history on its own terms. The website (created by the Barbarian Group) formed part of a campaign from Crispin Porter + Bogusky for BK's TenderCrisp chicken sandwich entitled Have It Your Way. It is simple in design, showing a grown man dressed as a chicken pacing around a sparsely decorated room, and users are encouraged to 'have it their way' by interacting with the man by typing instructions on the site. While all the footage is pre-recorded, the website has the feel of an interactive webcam, with the chicken-man responding to over 300 different commands, including 'backflip', 'dance' and 'swim'. This mildly subversive premise caught the public mood and went on to be hugely successful, far outstripping the impact of the accompanying TV ad.

Another project seen to be something of a watershed moment for the development of advertising is Nike+ (page 188). Nike joined forces with Apple in 2006 to create a device that measures and records the distance and pace of a walk or run onto an iPod. These statistics can then be transferred easily from the iPod to the Nike+ website (created by R/GA in New York) where they can be shared with other runners all over the world, thus creating an international running community via the site. The idea is significant for two reasons –its tie-up between two major brands, which reveals a spirit of collaboration rarely seen in the corporate world (although Nike did go on to also create its own kit that didn't require the use of an iPod), and its generosity to its audience. Using the website is free, with Nike understanding the delayed monetary benefits that may come from this goodwill gesture. Also interesting was the specificity of the product, with Nike focusing its attention solely on runners, and creating something of genuine use to this audience.

Not all non-traditional advertising is about interaction, however, with some campaigns simply intending to make you think about the brand in a new way. When it came to promoting the third edition of the Xbox computer game Halo in 2007, Microsoft was keen to create a campaign that would appeal to previous Halo gamers, while also attracting a new audience to the series. To do this, the McCann and T.A.G. agencies in San Francisco created an elaborate integrated launch for the game, which introduced a fictional history to its story. This was documented within a museum exhibition, as well as within a series of beautifully shot short films, which played out online (page 180). Both methods were far removed from those normally associated with gaming, and neither included animated footage from the game. For the previous players of Halo, more subtle clues and stories were also fed online. The launch proved incredibly successful.

Such campaigns are successful for a number of reasons. Subservient Chicken, for example, presented something funny and unexpected, which tied in with a general interest in new ways of communicating online. If the base idea or product is not appealing or entertaining, the campaign is less likely to work. Also, to achieve a real breakthrough, the idea or strategy must be surprising. Once it has happened, no matter how many times the idea is re-used it is unlikely to achieve the same impact as the first time. Explaining that to the client is not always easy, however. 'I go into fits of rage with account people when they start telling me I've got to do a viral,' says James Hilton, chief creative officer at AKQA. 'Because viral is a consequence. It's such an assumption to get a brief that says "a viral film" at the top – it's like getting a scriptwriter saying "blockbuster film". You hope it's a blockbuster film, you hope it's viral. Making something that is enormously popular, because that's what "viral" is, is incredibly difficult.'

Of course, all of this makes life harder for both agencies and clients, as they are compelled to come up with ever more unusual and unexpected approaches. Unfortunately though, this can also lead to the major pitfall that surrounds all of this kind of advertising: the risk that the public may be put off a brand if they believe that it is using stealth, and trying to sneak advertising on them unawares. This dilemma came to light for Mother advertising agency in 2008 when it worked with Eurostar to create a feature film, *Somers Town* (page 90), funded by the rail company and directed by acclaimed British director Shane Meadows. Aside from requesting that the then-new St Pancras station, where the Eurostar trains from London depart, would make an appearance in the film, Eurostar supposedly had no influence on the script or storyline. However, when the backing of Eurostar was revealed it was difficult not to see certain scenes, which presented both the station and the London-to-Paris train journey in glowing terms, as being influenced by the company funding the film. The film received good reviews, but when Eurostar's involvement was discovered, it also provoked a number of more questioning articles both online and in the UK national press, discussing whether the 'purity' of cinema was being infiltrated by advertising.

While this sanctity is very much open to debate – product placement has appeared in films for decades, after all – it does highlight a problem for brands and agencies that are experimenting with new methods of promotion and advertising. For, despite the increasing prominence of branding in all aspects of life, there is still a strong drive for audiences to reject brands that overstep the mark, even when it is far from clear just where that mark may be. Perhaps the best approach is to be upfront with your intentions, however. 'It's about adding to what's there, not replacing it,' says David Droga, founder and creative chairman of Droga5 in New York. 'There is a place for a certain advertising that is much more conversational and transparent. Not all advertising has to be stealth.'

> 'There is a place for a certain advertising that is much more conversational and transparent. Not all advertising has to be stealth.'
>
> **David Droga, founder and creative chairman, Droga5**

The Future for Advertising Agencies

So what is required of the modern advertising agency? As the case studies in this book demonstrate, it must be flexible, creative and able to generate campaigns that work across the full range of media, both new and old. As clients are beginning to appreciate that advertising can take new and varied forms, the industry is entering into uncharted territory, with agencies now expected to offer – either in-house or through collaboration with specialist companies – an increasingly broad palette of creative solutions. What remains unchanged is that the root of great advertising is still having a great idea; the transformation has occurred in the multitude of forms that these ideas can now take. 'To the ranks of our traditional competitors, we must now add others,' says BETC's Rémi Babinet. 'On the one hand, the leading information and entertainment professionals (Disney, Time Warner or Google), and on the other the countless mass of creator-producers of amateur content, you and me.... The challenge that advertising agencies are called upon to meet can be simply put: we have to be as talented and interesting as the major content producers, and as reactive, fresh and nimble as the small fry.'

The limitations of TV and print are now becoming obvious, and clients are finally putting more and more of their budgets towards new types of advertising solutions. Some of these have seen the old, tried-and-tested methods of advertising simply remodelled for the digital world – banner ads on websites are an obvious example of this, where ads appear on popular sites in much the same way as they do in magazines, usually to the irritation of users. Similarly, audiences are already getting used to having to sit through ads in order to access video content on news and magazine websites. Certain areas of the web are particularly resistant to this kind of advertising, however. Social networking websites such as Facebook contain ads, but these are often criticized for being intrusive in what is seen by users to be a 'private' sphere, over which they have control. Advertisers are likely to receive short shrift in these worlds, unless they are specifically invited in by users or use passive techniques, such as setting up groups that people are then invited to join.

Despite these examples, the interruption model is increasingly being replaced by more innovative solutions and ideas, often incorporating other creative products such as films, books and events. There is a theory, or a concern, that this type of advertising is only appropriate for certain kinds of brands – particularly sport or leisure brands. But while the gaming or sport industries may be a natural fit for a more playful marketing approach, there are also examples of less predictable brands having success with the non-traditional model. If insurance – a notoriously difficult industry to make interesting advertising for – can see the benefits of creating an online community, which includes specially commissioned short films and blog debates (see the Responsibility Project, created by Hill Holliday in 2008 for US insurance firm Liberty Mutual, page 154), then it would appear that any business can prosper from taking a creative and brave approach to its advertising.

With advertising appearing across a wide range of media, budgets are increasingly tight. This is not necessarily an obstacle for non-traditional advertising, however, with its focus on creativity rather than media spend. These campaigns are often deliberately targeted to get free press attention, and to be included in the editorial pages of newspapers, magazines and websites, rather than in the expensive advertising sections. To achieve this, an inspiring, newsworthy idea is key. For example, when promoting the new series of *The Chaser's War on Everything*, an Australian satirical comedy show, in 2007, The Glue Society in Sydney decided to use the small budget available to buy space on the world's cheapest poster sites (page 160). Ads for the show appeared on billboards in Iraq, India, Estonia, Kenya and Iceland, and, while its audience were unlikely to witness the ads first hand, the ensuing media coverage of the campaign ensured that its message reached them regardless, while also providing an entertaining story for the press. Such campaigns require an understanding of the culture of the times, and of what will prove intriguing. 'Technology is the mechanism of all this angst and change in the advertising industry, but, to me, the issue is the lack of connection our industry has with culture and the fast pace of change in the lives of our audience, especially if you are dealing with youth,' says John Jay, Wieden + Kennedy Portland. 'Through our celebration of ourselves, we have lost touch with a broader, global, faster culture of change. Everything we do exists in context with time, society and culture, not other people's advertising. We are living in the most exciting moment of social change, so as creatives we must be somehow connected personally to the shifting landscape.'

While small budgets therefore do not automatically mean a lack of interesting advertising, they have meant that agencies are beginning to look at new ways to retain their financial security. One of these is to begin creating products themselves, rather than simply marketing other people's work. Droga5 advertising agency in New York, which has created a string of impressive campaigns for clients including UNICEF (page 138), clothing brand eckō (page 70) and the New York City

Department of Education (page 140), joined forces in 2007 with production company Smuggler to launch Honeyshed (page 201), an online shopping channel for the MTV generation. The website, which closed in 2009, demonstrated a model where an ad agency used its creative know-how for its own, rather than solely for its clients' gains. Anomaly, which has two offices in New York, takes this notion even further, by regularly creating intellectual property for the clients it works with, alongside supplying their branding and advertising needs. The company has helped design and release an eclectic range of products, from make-up lines and skin care products to a venture with chef Eric Ripert. Anomaly part-owns these initiatives, giving it a vested interest in the success of its advertising (page 214).

These kinds of developments have raised the question of whether the term 'advertising agency' is an appropriate description for many of the companies featured in this book. Some prefer to use 'creative company' or other vague terminologies, partly as an attempt to dissociate themselves from an industry that has for so long been tied to an image of greed and raging egos. Certainly there appears to be an increasing effort made by many to promote a more humble impression, where creative innovation and respect for audiences are seen as being more important than being able to lord it at the various international advertising festivals and awards events. 'People will have the chance to live without seeing advertising soon,' says Oliver Voss, partner and chief creative officer at Jung von Matt in Hamburg. 'So we need to do ads that interest people and ads that people want to see.'

As Voss implies, the future of advertising may actually be in a 'post-advertising world', where deliberately manipulative advertising is replaced entirely by content that users will want to engage and interact with. This may be hard to imagine when sitting through the average TV commercial break, but recent innovations and new ways of working suggest that in time our understanding of advertising and of what an advertising agency does will be startlingly different.

'People will have the chance to live without seeing advertising soon, so we need to do ads that interest people and ads that people want to see.'

Oliver Voss, partner and chief creative officer, Jung von Matt

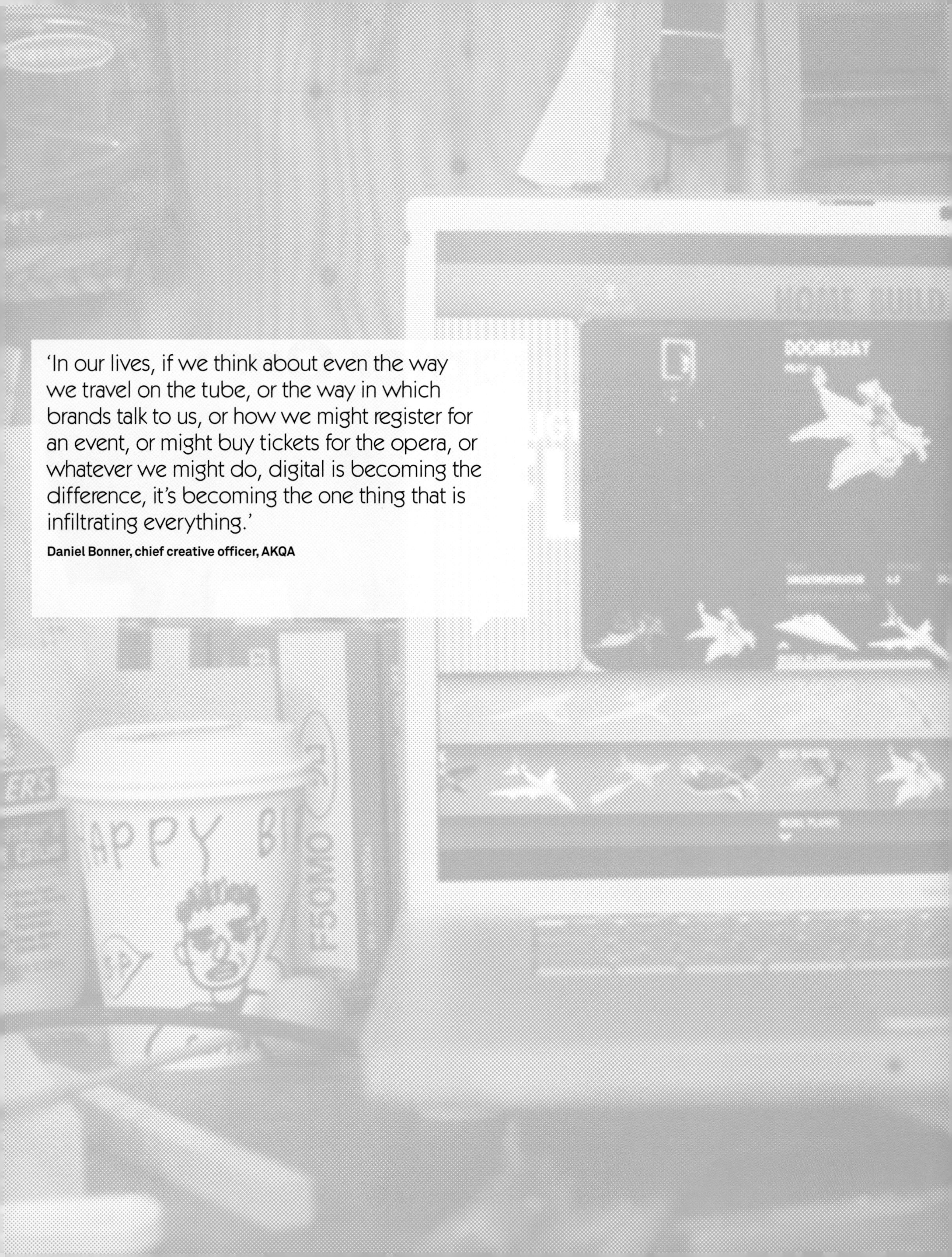
DOOMSDAY

'In our lives, if we think about even the way we travel on the tube, or the way in which brands talk to us, or how we might register for an event, or might buy tickets for the opera, or whatever we might do, digital is becoming the difference, it's becoming the one thing that is infiltrating everything.'

Daniel Bonner, chief creative officer, AKQA

HANGAR

Chapter One:
Digital

Since the internet first came into widespread use, the advertising industry has been struggling to come up with ways in which it might be used to promote brands. Although online marketing has spawned many buzz words, sometimes it seems that there has been much talk but little action in this area, and it is only relatively recently that advertising agencies have begun to use the internet and digital advertising effectively. This chapter contains case studies of some of the most successful recent online campaigns, which demonstrate just how central a role the internet will play in the future of advertising.

Projector, Tokyo

Uniqlo: Uniqlock

Uniqlock (www.uniqlock.jp) is a downloadable clock that can be placed on blogs. The clock combines films of Uniqlo-wearing dancers with a digital clock face that counts down each second. Its genius lies in the fact that, rather than viewing it just once or twice, as in a normal ad, users will make it, and Uniqlo, a continuous presence on their computer. Uniqlock contains over 100 different films of the dancers, who change clothes depending on the season, and are shown asleep at midnight. It also has special hourly films, as well as an alarm option. Uniqlock can be set to the time in any one of 282 cities in the world, and its website displays a map of current users, so fans can see where else Uniqlock is being used at any one time. The Uniqlock website has attracted over 68 million views (and counting) from 209 countries.

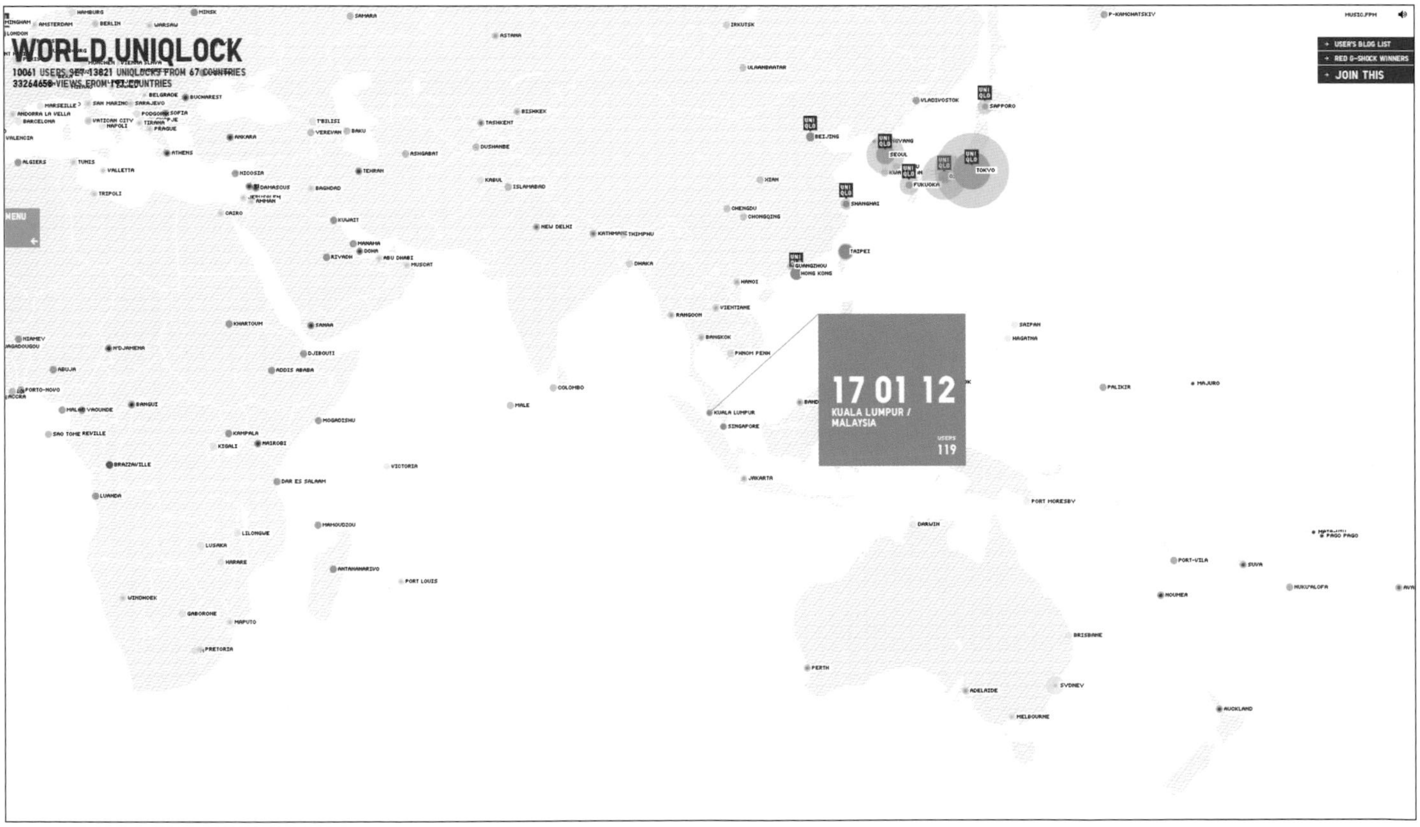
WORLD UNIQLOCK
USER'S BLOG LIST
RED G-SHOCK WINNERS
JOIN THIS
MENU
17 01 12
KUALA LUMPUR / MALAYSIA
USERS
119

05 17 04
TOKYO / JAPAN

UNIQLOCK
BLOG PARTS
WORLD.UNIQLOCK

UNIQLOCK
BLOG PARTS
WORLD.UNIQLOCK

UNIQLOCK
BLOG PARTS
WORLD.UNIQLOCK
SCREENSAVER

'I wanted to create a new path to connect Uniqlock and consumers across the world.... I focused on the blog, because everyday I read blogs. One thing I realized is that when there is interesting content, it spreads across the world very, very quickly.'

Koichiro Tanaka, co-founder and creative director, Projector

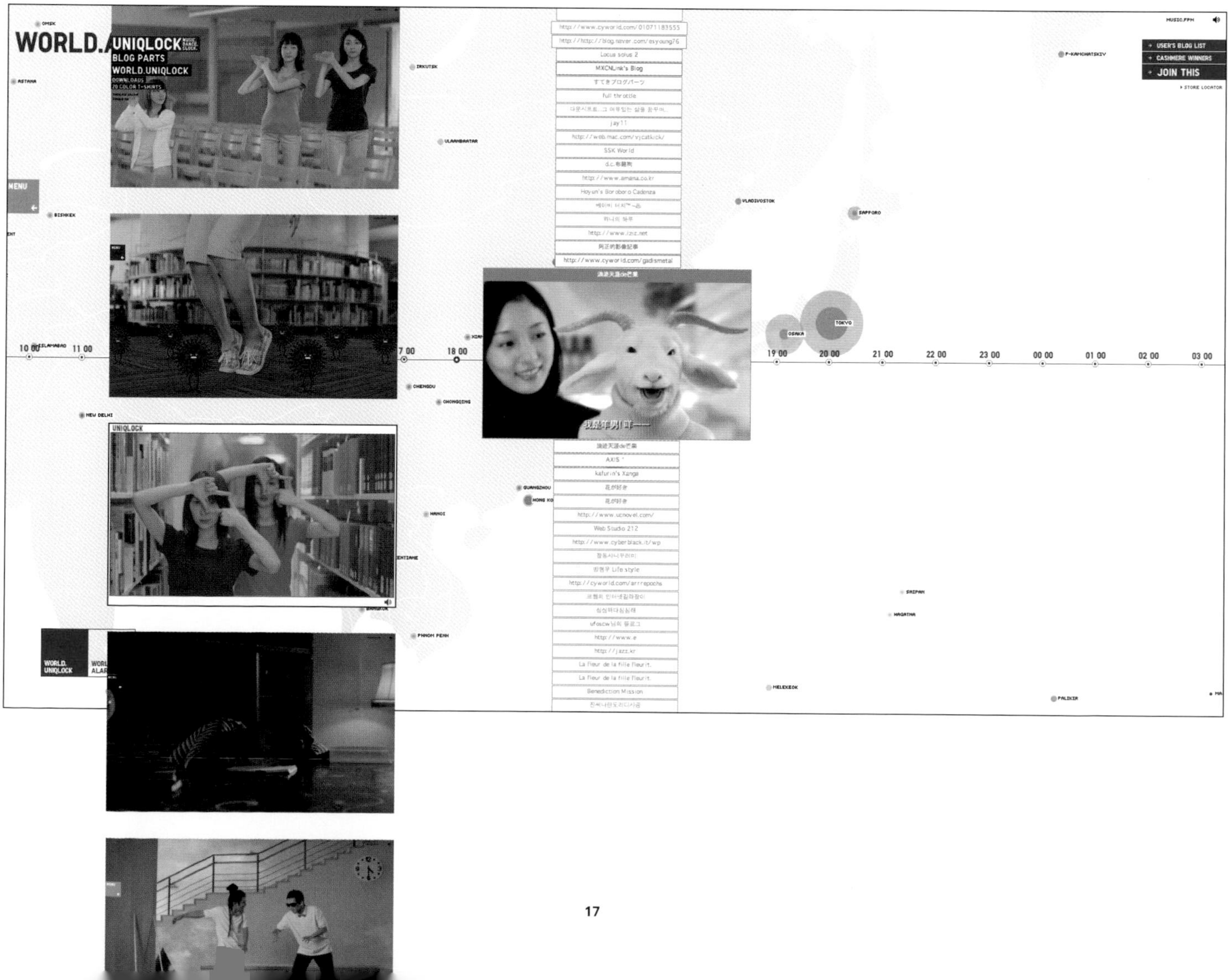
WORLD.
UNIQLOCK
BLOG PARTS
WORLD.UNIQLOCK
MENU
USER'S BLOG LIST
CASHMERE WINNERS
JOIN THIS
TOKYO
OSAKA
19 00
20 00
21 00
22 00
23 00
00 00
01 00
02 00
03 00
WORLD.
UNIQLOCK

Poke, London

Orange: Unlimited

The Orange Unlimited website (www.unlimited.orange.co.uk) formed part of a campaign for the Orange mobile phone brand, titled 'Good Things Should Never End'. Poke took that sentence literally and created a website that features a never-ending scrolling page. At the centre of the site is a strand of rainbow, created by generative maths artist Marius Watz, which can be programmed to change direction, speed and inertia, and to respond to instructions from the content around it. The rainbow guides users down the page where they find things to interact with, including characters, games, downloads, giveaways, toys and mobile goodies. Users can also share items from the Unlimited site on their own blogs and MySpace pages, and leave messages for friends on the rainbow.

Orange - Good Things Should Never End
www.goodthingsshouldneverend.co.uk
orange
good things
should never end

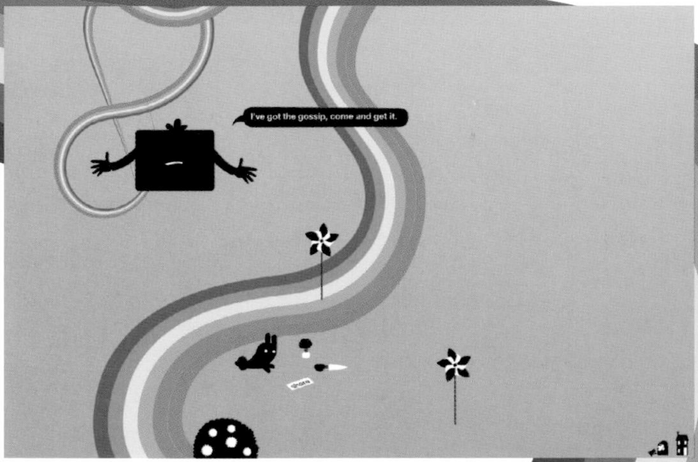
I've got the gossip, come and get it.

READ
MY
MIND

Nicolas
StrangeMuffin
Sophie
yum yum supprise
Sophie
SockSmells
paulo
paulos suprise
Vu
strawvilla
hannoffe raspberry
strawberry cheesecake
Charlotte
creamilicious
what is your name?

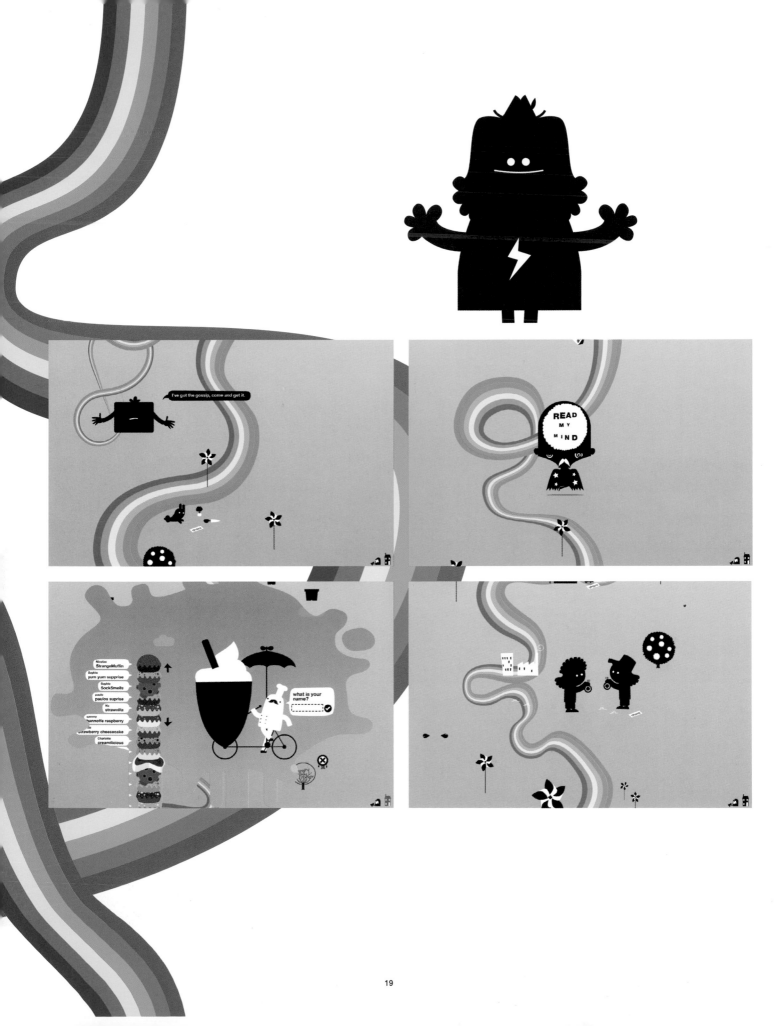

Layer Tennis match between Marian Bantjes (left) and Armin Vit (right), which took place online on 2 November 2007 with commentary by Heather Armstrong. Bantjes was the winner.

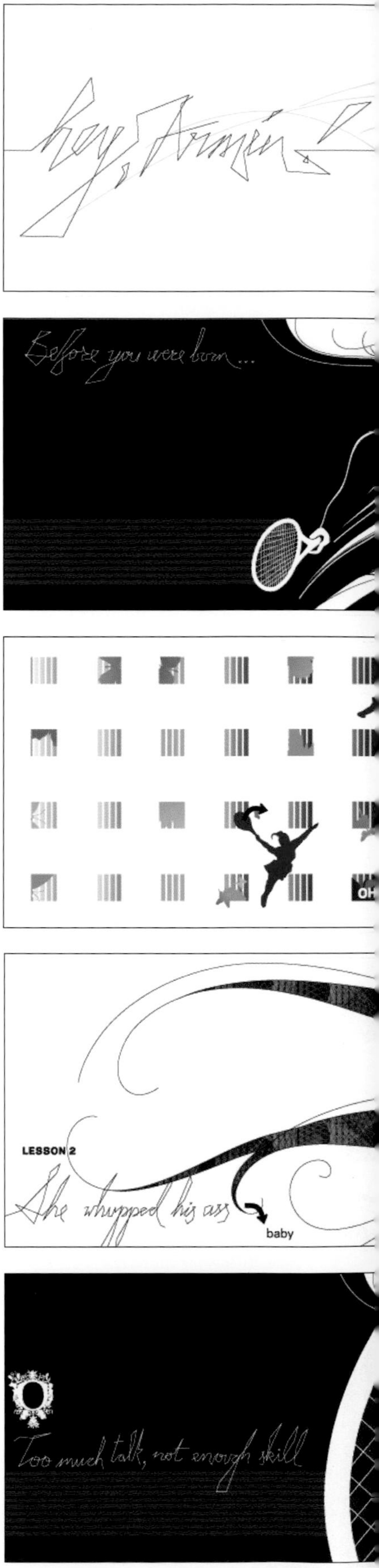
Before you were born...
LESSON 2
She whipped his ass
baby
Too much talk, not enough skill

Coudal Partners, Chicago/Goodby, Silverstein & Partners, San Francisco

Adobe: Layer Tennis

Layer Tennis (www.layertennis.com) was an innovative game created to get designers, photographers, animators and advertising creatives excited about Adobe's Creative Suite 3 (CS3) software. Rather than simply taking out ads for the software in traditional media, Coudal Partners and Goodby, Silverstein & Partners created a sport. The game was simple yet brilliant: Player One had 15 minutes to create a single layer of art. This was placed on the 'web stadium', where Player Two then had 15 minutes to manipulate it creatively, using only Adobe tools. The manipulated image would be 'volleyed' back to Player One, who would re-manipulate it. Each player had five turns, creating a ten-volley match. Every match also featured a commentator, who gave witty play-by-play analysis live and explained the Adobe features being used. Viewers could participate by leaving comments, and by voting to decide which player was the winner. No money was spent promoting Layer Tennis but word of mouth attracted an audience of 500,000 over the course of a season of 14 matches.

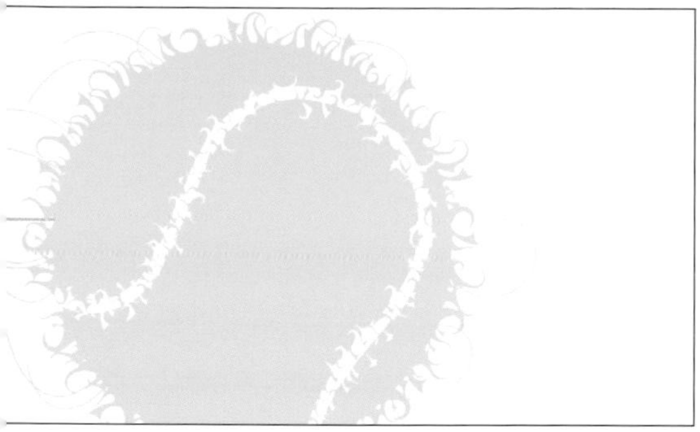

hey, Armin
WHY SO HARSH?
LESSON 1 IN WEB GRAPHICS: A study has shown that rounded corners and heavier weight strokes lead to more traffic and better clickthrough rates on advertising.

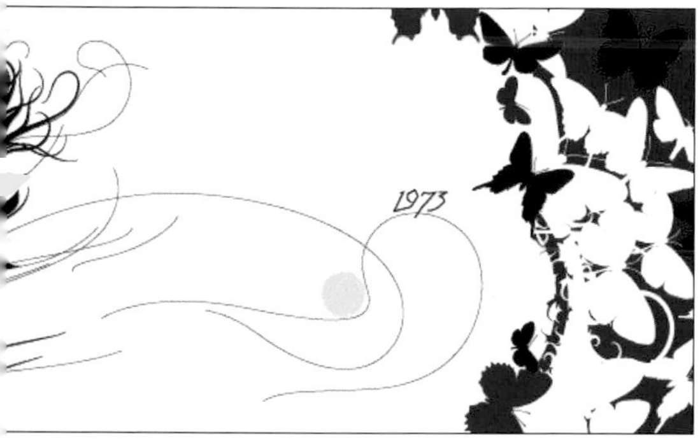
1973

MANY THINGS HAPPENED BEFORE I WAS BORN, INCLUDING ABBA. THIS IS NOW, MAN...
ONL
Let u
Walk
This
Way

bet
er
stro
kes
Billie Jean King vs. Bobby Riggs
RA
SH

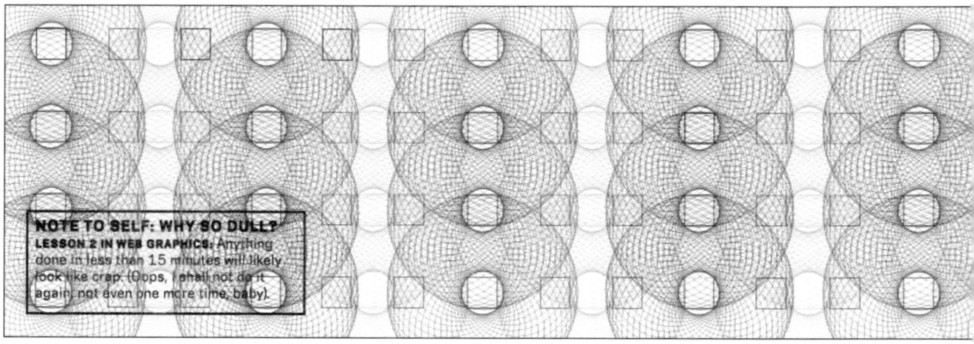
NOTE TO SELF: WHY SO DULL?
LESSON 2 IN WEB GRAPHICS: Anything done in less than 15 minutes will likely look like crap. (Oops, I shall not do it again, not even one more time, baby).

LESS IS MORE
ORNAMENT IS WANTED DEAD OR ALIVE

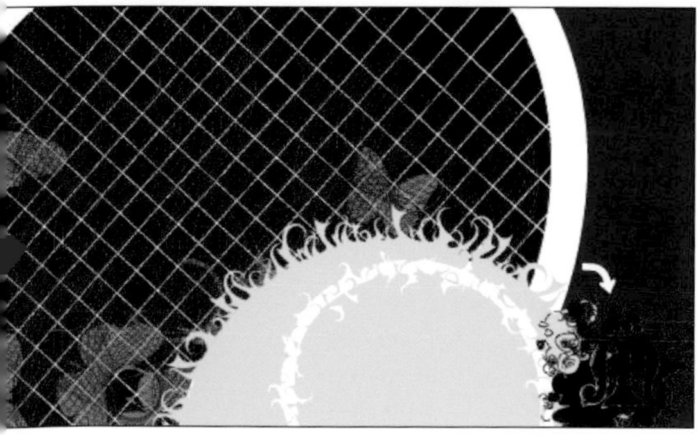

friends?

Layer Tennis match between Scott Hansen (left) and Rob Cordiner (right), which took place online on 9 November 2007 with commentary from Alissa Walker. Hansen won the match.

MOVIN
ON
VER
SUS
COLOUR
COLOR
EVOLVE!

Layer Tennis match between Aaron Draplin (left) and David Nakamoto (right), which took place online on 16 November 2007 with commentary from Steven Heller. Draplin emerged as the victorious one.

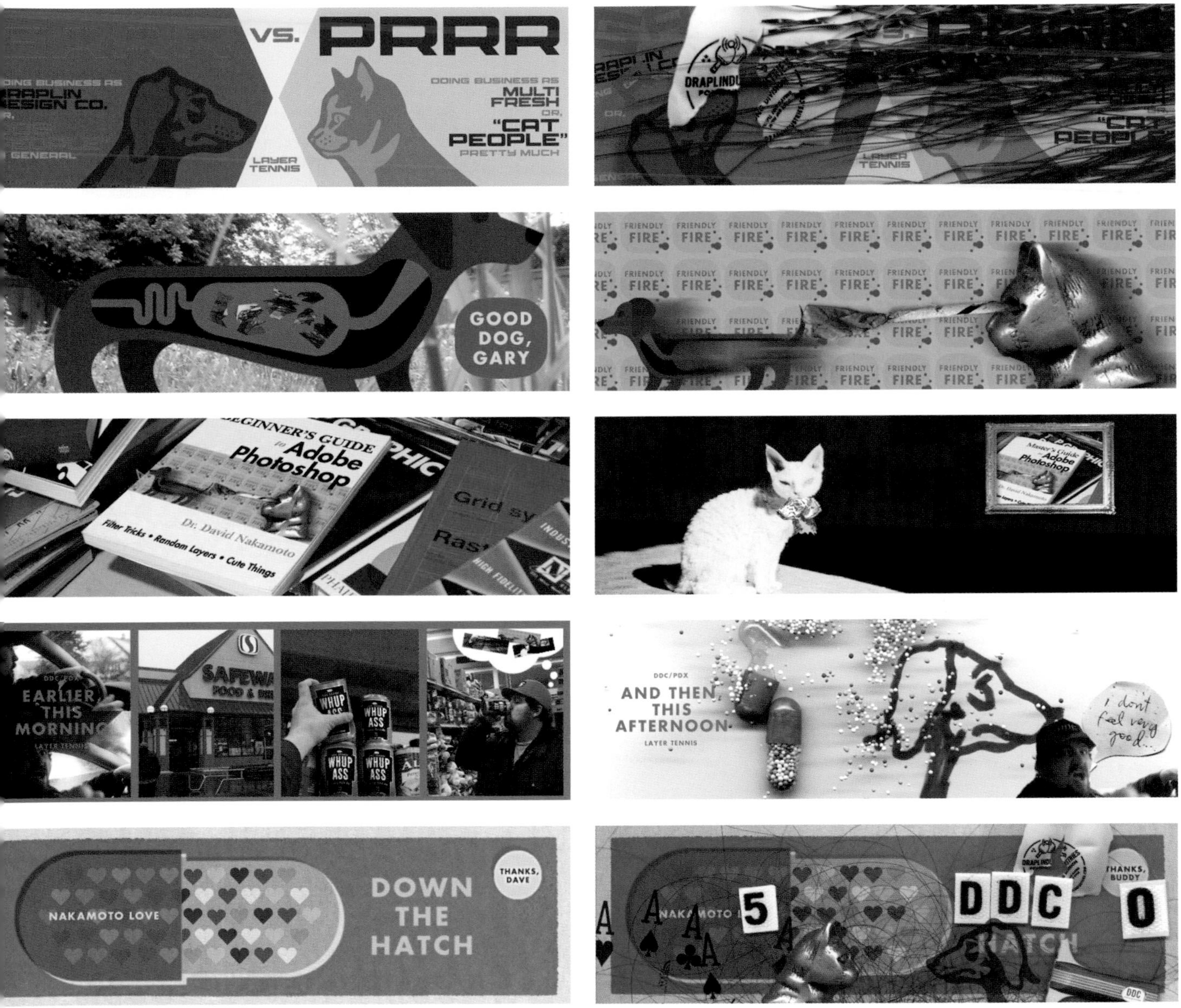

VS. PRRR
DOING BUSINESS AS MULTI FRESH OR, "CAT PEOPLE" PRETTY MUCH
LAYER TENNIS
GOOD DOG, GARY
FRIENDLY FIRE
BEGINNER'S GUIDE to Adobe Photoshop
Dr. David Nakamoto
Filter Tricks • Random Layers • Cute Things
EARLIER THIS MORNING
SAFEWAY FOOD & DRUG
WHUP ASS
DDC/PDX
AND THEN, THIS AFTERNOON
LAYER TENNIS
i don't feel very good...
NAKAMOTO LOVE
DOWN THE HATCH
THANKS, DAVE
THANKS, BUDDY
5 DDC 0

Big Spaceship, New York

Adobe: Flash on

The Adobe Flash on website, www.adobe.com/flashon, was created by Big Spaceship to demonstrate the vast amount of information online that would be impossible to access without the use of Flash. Big Spaceship's approach was simple – just highlight a small selection of the 14 trillion Flash video streams that appear online each year. The website uses a mosaic interface system that shows still images from the films on its home page, and the films are available to watch in full when clicked upon. Users are encouraged to explore and see which films they will chance upon.

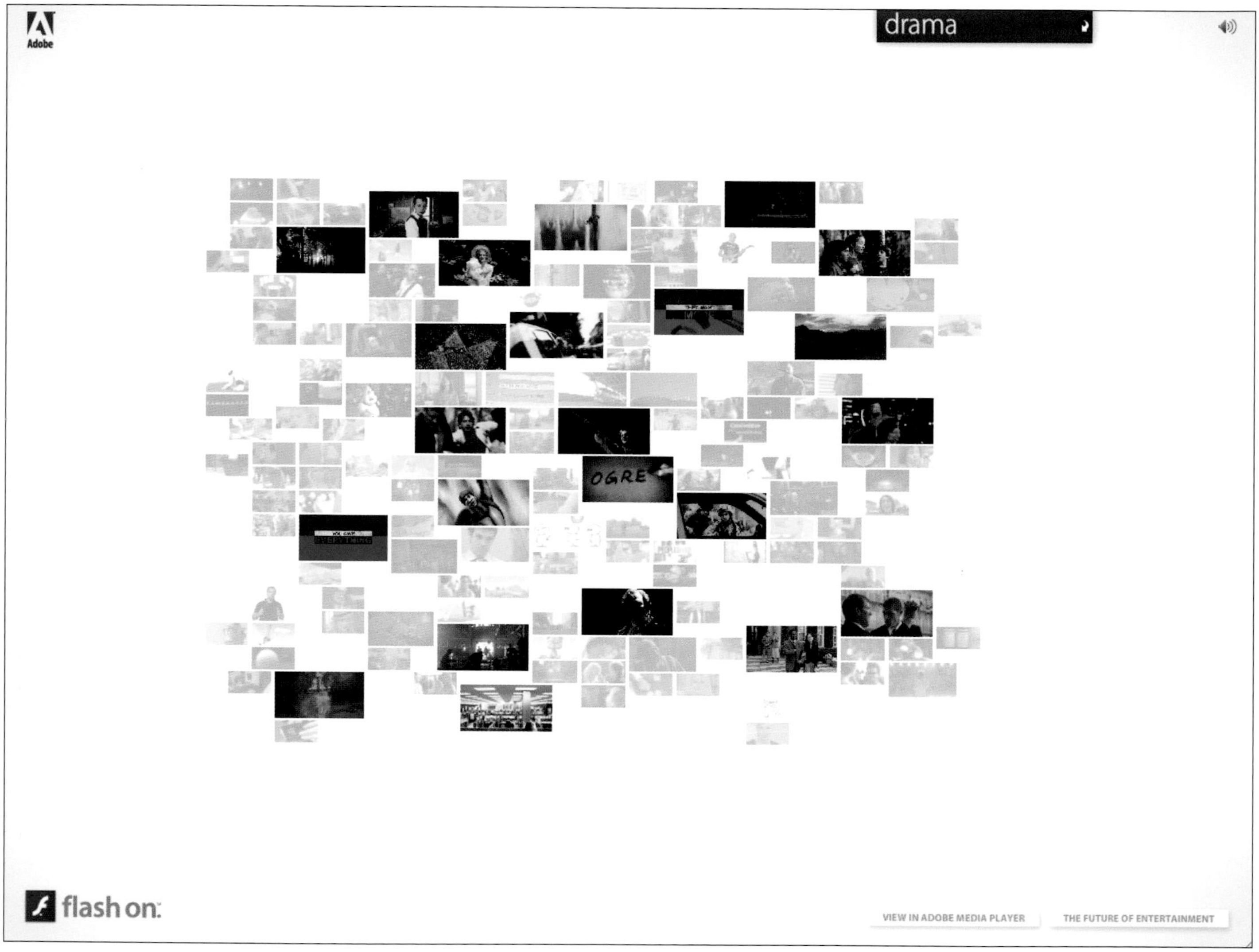
Adobe
drama
OGRE
flash on
VIEW IN ADOBE MEDIA PLAYER
THE FUTURE OF ENTERTAINMENT

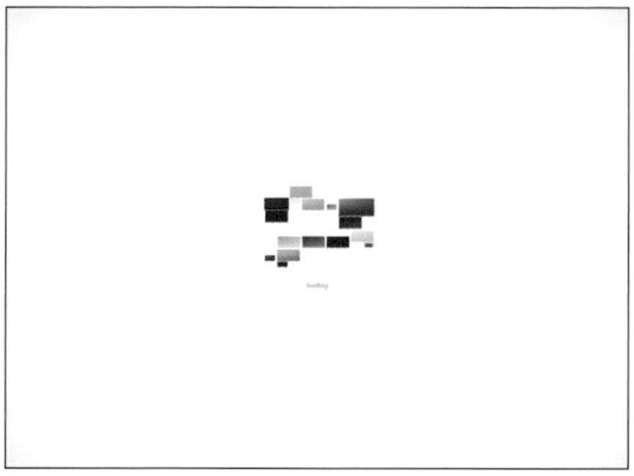

Adobe
lifestyle
Yahoo!
Mashed Potatoes
LINK TO THIS VIDEO:
flash on.
VIEW IN ADOBE MEDIA PLAYER
THE FUTURE OF ENTERTAINMENT

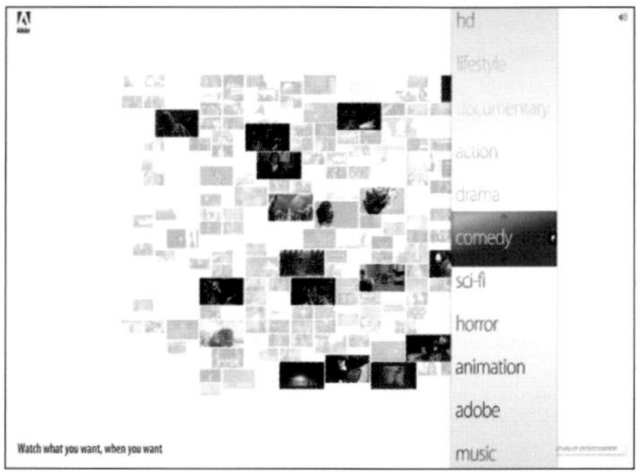
hd
lifestyle
documentary
action
drama
comedy
sci-fi
horror
animation
adobe
music
Watch what you want, when you want

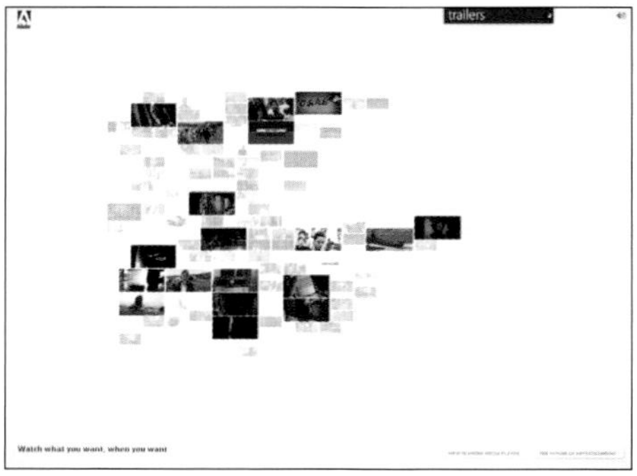
trailers
Watch what you want, when you want

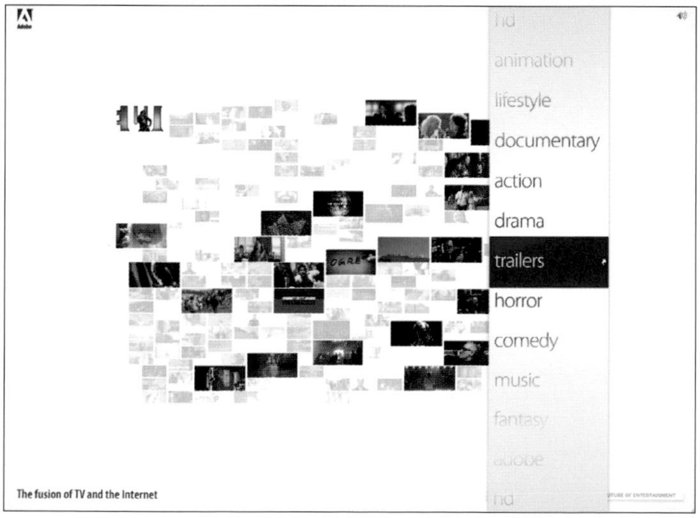
hd
animation
lifestyle
documentary
action
drama
trailers
horror
comedy
music
fantasy
adobe
hd
The fusion of TV and the Internet

Dentsu/GT Tokyo

Sony Japan: Rec You

To advertise a new model Sony Walkman, which contains a TV programme recording function, Sony Japan launched the Rec You campaign, which placed the consumer at the centre of the campaign. Conceived by ad agencies Dentsu and GT Tokyo, the site (www.recyou.jp) encouraged users to upload photographs of themselves, which were then animated so that they appeared to headbang and sing along to music.

Hundreds of thumbnails of the participants were then shown on the website, all appearing to sing in harmony. The photographs were also used on banner ads and were projected onto buildings around Tokyo, including Sony HQ. Over 10,000 people contributed to Rec You.

REC
YOU.
WALKMAN
写真を撮る。送る。
動き出す。
"ウォークマン"で歌う。
テレビでデビュー。
日本中に、ネット中に、氾濫。
そんな自分を、RECする。
ENTER

'We aimed to create a new advertising style in which the consumer exacts a major role. The consumer is the nucleus of the advertising rather than just being featured as a bonus.'

Naoki Ito, creative director, GT Tokyo

MENU
メニューへ戻る

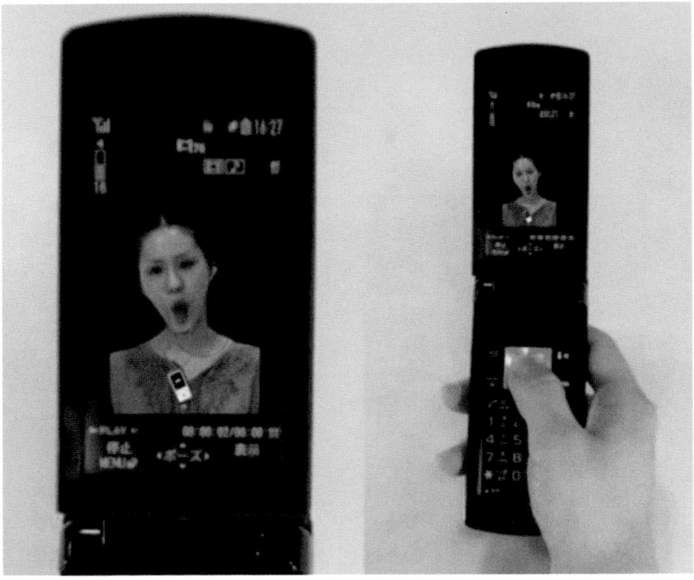

Interview: Alex Bogusky

Alex Bogusky is co-chairman of Crispin Porter + Bogusky, which has offices in Miami, Boulder, Los Angeles and London. CP+B is behind some of the most recent innovative advertising, particularly in its work for Burger King (pages 86, 182).

EW: **Do you think that the emphasis of advertising is moving more towards non-traditional work?**

AB: Usually the US is behind in a lot of things, but in terms of the fracturing of media, we experienced that a little bit earlier, with 500 television stations and things like that. Then the internet came along and added to that, so media became so fractured that broadcast didn't really exist anymore. We call it broadcast because it was broadly cast but the notion of something getting to a broad audience merely because you pay for it can't really happen. Or it's very difficult and very, very, very expensive so there's only a handful of advertisers that can do it. So the non-traditional stuff was a reaction to that. We as an agency grew up with small clients and usually the number two or number three brand at best, if we were lucky. We tended to be a bit more scrappy and have more limited budgets. It's not a preference thing, it's more just out of necessity.

EW: **When you did Subservient Chicken [a Burger King website where users could order around a man dressed as a chicken] did you feel like you were breaking new ground?**

AB: We didn't really think about it that way. At the same time we did that site we were launching a network campaign with the same character, so there was broadcast advertising too, not a huge budget, but way more was spent on commercials with the chicken. The website was something we did in the evening with a little bit of money we had left over, we just snuck off and did that on the side.

EW: **But that's the thing that's remembered now.**

AB: Yeah, it got much, much bigger. Even at the time it got much, much bigger. Sometimes advertising has these phenomena, like when Bud did 'Wassup' for example – it was beyond popular and well-liked, it was a phenomenon. The chicken was like that. There aren't really the proper conditions for it to happen again quite like that because at the time microsites were pretty novel. There was very little marketing within the internet and I remember a lot of the commentary within the internet was: 'Hey, do we even want marketing in this space?' Which you wouldn't have anymore because it's sort of accepted. So the return on investment for things like that... that's the thing about doing stuff that's non-traditional – any time you invent something you tend to increase the fractures within media. So Subservient Chicken created thousands of Subservient Chicken-like marketing things out there and that really limits the potential return on investment. So we're really sceptical of microsites now, we're really careful about using them and how we use them and why we're doing them.

EW: **There must be quite a pressure to come up with new strategies for approaching people on top of new campaign ideas.**

AB: It doesn't feel so much like pressure because as technologies collide and people's behaviours change, new things just make themselves visible and new combinations arrive, and you realize, 'Oh, we can do this now'. Usually you have a sense of something that you want to do for a while before you get the opportunity to do it.

EW: **How are clients reacting to this? Are they putting more budget towards non-traditional work?**

AB: For sure, they are putting a lot more budget towards it. I'm not sure that it's the kind of thing you just put budget to, though. Because when you put budget in this area, where does it go? It goes into banners basically. And here's the other thing – a banner is not a banner is not a banner, right? So you can do very dynamic, really interesting things that I guess begin with a banner, or are based on a banner – you can do amazing things. But a lot of what gets bought, as the money just pours in, is the least technically inspiring banners, so you can't really do anything interesting with them.... In a way the money that's coming in is actually hindering the creativity now because it's being bought in the same way that network TV was bought. Instead of having an idea for, let's call it a banner-inspired piece of creative, which maybe becomes much more, the agencies are inheriting these media plans, with banners in them. Suddenly you can't really do anything really interesting.

EW: **Does it vary from client to client as to how interested they are in doing more experimental work?**

AB: Burger King are passionate about breaking new ideas into new areas, and so every few months we do something that's a lot of fun. Other clients are probably reacting more to the news of a client like BK, and then realizing 'everyone's allocating budget here, so let's allocate budget here'. I think it's a little dangerous to allocate budget before you know what you're doing, right? One of the things that we've talked about for a while now is not to lose the ability to make good 30- and 60-second films because I think those films are reasserting themselves online now, too. The forum seems to be surviving all the turmoil.

EW: **How about something like the Burger King games [a series of computer games for BK created in collaboration with Xbox] – how did that come about?**

AB: The games came through another partner, who put together a deal and it was about a year in the making. It sort of fell to us to develop the games. We designed all the games and strategized about what kind of games to make and, knowing that we would be making them, in the traditional advertising we were doing we started introducing other characters that would be characters in the game. Sometimes a year seems like a long time but it's actually not very long and it was great to get everything in order, so the same time we were creating characters, we were digitizing characters and at the end of the year they were all together.

EW: **Did you have to employ people in the agency who knew how to do games stuff?**

AB: It was a little bit of both. We had probably a broader group to create the concepts of the games, and then in execution there were some people out of the interactive department that finalized all that creative. There were also gamers – not everybody is a big gamer. It was helpful to know gaming culture because some of the games were going to be more elaborate than others, just because of what was possible. So if we're doing a really simple game, what's the white space for a simple game that hasn't been created – is there a bumper-car game out there? So, as we put together those strategies, we needed people well-versed in the gaming world.

EW: **The reason I ask that is I'm curious as to how your creative department is set up now – are all the creatives in together, regardless of their specialities?**

AB: Well, what we've got is about 150 people who work solely in interactive, and by that I mean they specialize in it. So some of them are programmers and information architects, and they work only in that area. Others are art directors and writers – they'll work in that area but they'll also work on the traditional side and they get briefed at the same time. We've talked about when there will be no specialization on the creative side, but still the technology moves so fast that it's pretty difficult to keep up with it, unless you specialize in it. I think in the next couple of years ... the other thing is we have old folks, who aren't any good at the digital side so we let them specialize in TV and print. They're still really good creatives so you don't want to put them out to pasture yet. So there's that tension too. A little over half of the young people that we hire could easily move back and forth, and they can program a little Flash, they're really well-versed and comfortable in that world.

EW: **Do you think in the future it will be that agencies have everything in house?**

AB: I think there's room for people to work with other people, but it depends on how. Conceptually I think it would be really weird if it's not in house. I think for broadcast you go out and you bring in directors and you bring in production specialists and stuff like that, so I could see that a portion of it could exist outside the agency, but I wouldn't like the idea of the creative not existing in the agency – it seems odd to me. We actually believe that so much of the creativity in this space is happening with the programmers, so that's why we've got 150 people here that do that. We just bet on it a long time ago.

In our experience what you want is your creative team – let's say they're working on web ideas – you want them to be sitting really close to the programmers and the information architects. Because although they may not be charged with creative, they're going to have ideas and influences that the creatives are not going to get unless they're sitting adjacent to those folks. So you're not necessarily looking for it out of one person – but even if you had all the creative in house and you shipped out for production, it's a little weird to not know how to do that stuff, because the knowing of how to do it really influences the execution of it. We were working on an online game and we try to do a thing now called 'quick prototyping', where the programmers put together a fast, wire-frame prototype of a site and of this game, so, without all the graphics and everything, we could look at the game play. And through that I would have ideas and all of them would have been good for the game, but some of them were really easy to accomplish without making the file enormous, and others would have ruined the game play because the file would have gotten so big that it couldn't stream. I can't tell the difference, and even the web team can't tell the difference but the programmer's right there going 'Ooohh'. And then I'd give them another idea and they'd be 'that would be awesome, we should do that'. And to me they're the same. So it's really critical to have the technical people nearby.

EW: **What do you think will begin to become more prominent in advertising? Do you think it will be branded content?**

AB: I get confused by branded content – it could mean so much. Is product placement branded content? It really is so broad. So, product placement, just as one example of that, I don't care for it. There are people who specialize in it, who are passionate about it. I like working with them but it's not something that necessarily turns us on, so we would probably always work through partners in terms of that. I'm sceptical that if I see a Coke on a desk in a movie, that that makes me want Coke. Plus I'm old enough that I remember when they'd pay us to have our brands in the movie. And now somehow they were smart enough to flip it and we're giving them millions of dollars to put them in there. So, then, in terms of do we need to create things that are interesting enough and relevant enough that consumers come to the brand to experience it? I agree with that in some way. When I hear 'branded content' it kind of sounds like films made by brands – that I'm more sceptical of, because why compete there?

I think for advertisers the bar's a bit higher than that – you've got to make something that's generally so fresh or relevant that it's important that I know about it. We did a BK campaign here recently where we did this social experiment and pulled the Whopper out of a BK, and filmed the whole thing. It created a lot of consumer generated content, which is another way of looking at this idea of branded content. But we didn't seed that notion and we didn't kickstart that, it just happened because we'd got something relevant enough that consumers want to play. Our execution online was actually very, very specific – we wanted to prove that it was real so the only thing that happened if you went to the URL was that a film played, an eight-minute documentary. The client was pushing to do a more elaborate website with different films and toys and an interactive game and things like that, and we were just careful about that return on investments with those microsites and just thought 'What does this microsite really need to do? It needs to make it real – it needs to make everyone realize that the thing they saw that seemed like it's maybe real, it's real.' And the effect there is that it launched it into the cultural dialogue, and that makes it viral. Sometimes people get too caught up in creating a tool that can make something viral, and it doesn't work because you either have the right relevant cultural cocktail or you don't. It doesn't matter how great the tool is if you don't have the goods.

EW: **Do blogs and other user-generated content related to brands bother your clients? Is that an issue for them?**

AB: It's really interesting because I think we're beginning to move past that. It depends on the client. That instantaneous feedback that never existed before – you had the luxury of sending your work out on a TV spot and never having to hear a consumer complain about it, or talk about it. Also, I always say that consumers, when they play with your brand – if you do the right thing, and they play – they play rough. They play very, very rough and the first few times a brand experiences that, it feels more like criticism, even when it is play. The parodies that they make of the work, they're crazy – we wish we could do stuff like that. And it does take a certain intestinal fortitude to realize that that's OK and in fact a good thing.

The whole notion of play and gaming within brands is something that, at least for us, is really critical. We really look at a lot of the campaigns as a game that we're playing with consumers. We've spent time studying game theory and what makes a good game, and have had lectures from game designers. Video games sales have passed the revenue of movies in Hollywood in the US and that's a major cultural shift that I don't know that people are thinking about. We've been such a narrative society and our understanding of brands is narrative – how we learn about ourselves is through narrative generally. But there's a whole generation that's preferring to be entertained, and even learn, through gaming. It's so fundamental, because for so long we've said 'What's the story of your brand?', 'What's the narrative of your brand?'. But also now it's 'What's the game of your brand?', 'How does your brand play?' – I think those are the kinds of question that we might hear more often down the road.

Crispin Porter + Bogusky/Pitch, USA

Burger King: Simpsonize Me

Crispin Porter + Bogusky created www.simpsonizeme.com in collaboration with Pitch as part of a campaign for Burger King that tied in with the release of *The Simpsons Movie* in 2007. The site allows users to upload photographs of themselves and watch as they are turned into cartoons. The Simpsons-esque caricatures can then be fine-tuned to get hairstyles and accessories just right. In its first week of launch, the website received in excess of 150 million hits, with over four million visitors uploading their photographs to be Simpsonized.

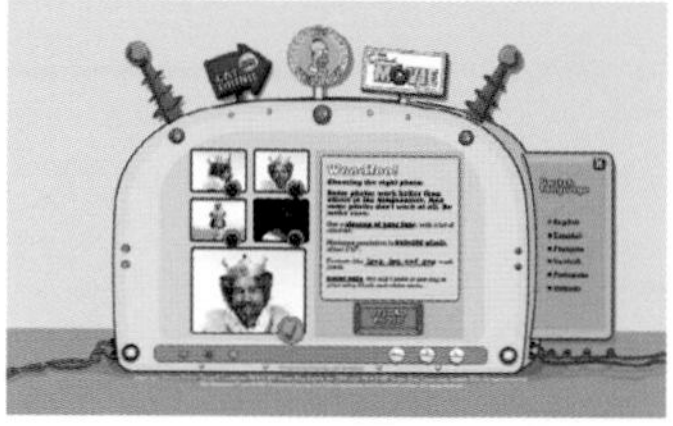

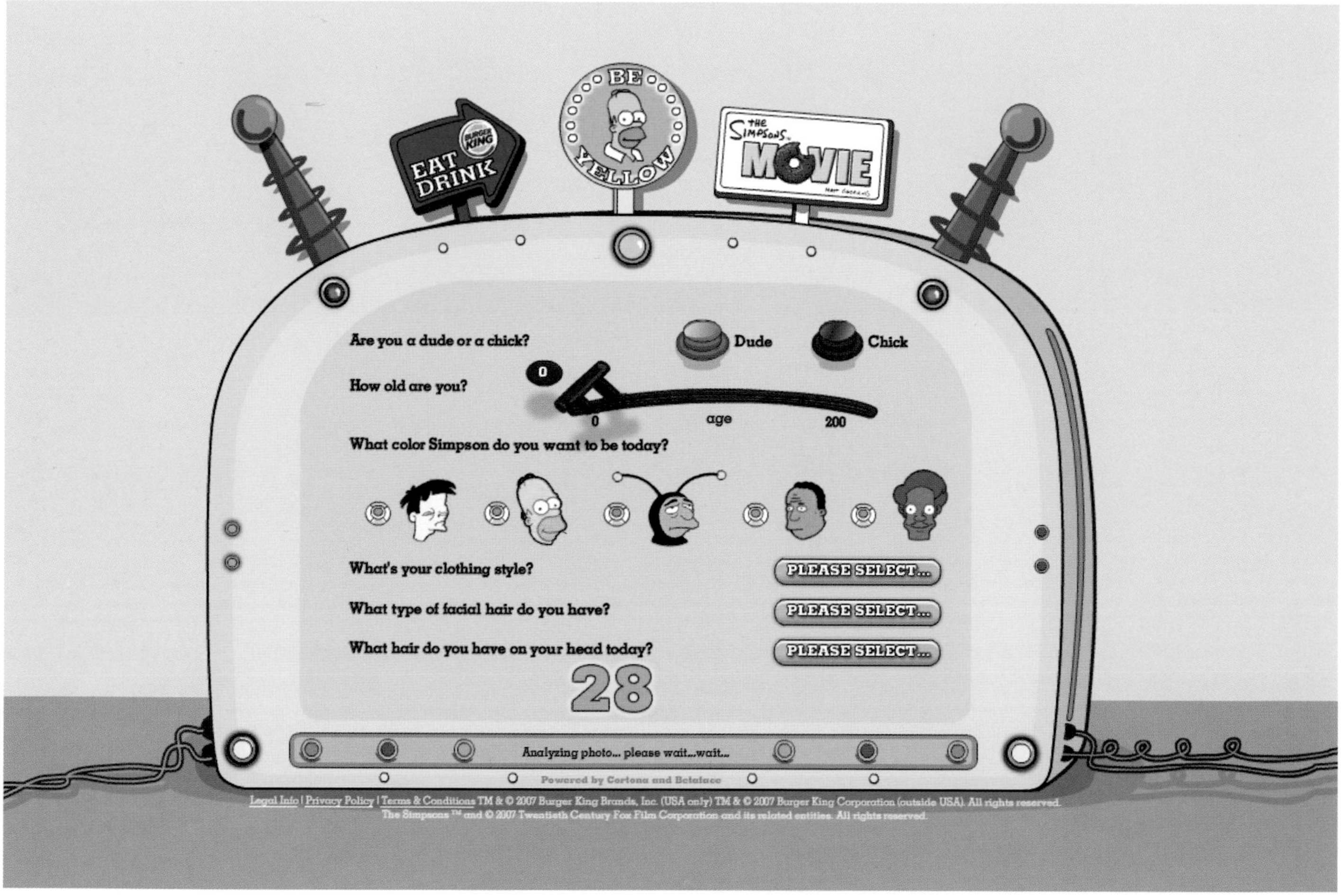
BURGER KING
EAT DRINK
BE YELLOW
THE SIMPSONS MOVIE
Are you a dude or a chick?
Dude
Chick
How old are you?
0
0
age
200
What color Simpson do you want to be today?
What's your clothing style?
PLEASE SELECT...
What type of facial hair do you have?
PLEASE SELECT...
What hair do you have on your head today?
PLEASE SELECT...
28
Analyzing photo... please wait...wait...
Powered by Cortona and Betaface
Legal Info | Privacy Policy | Terms & Conditions TM & © 2007 Burger King Brands, Inc. (USA only) TM & © 2007 Burger King Corporation (outside USA). All rights reserved.
The Simpsons ™ and © 2007 Twentieth Century Fox Film Corporation and its related entities. All rights reserved.

Agency Republic, London

BBC Radio 1: Musicubes

The BBC Radio 1 Musicubes website (www.radio1musicubes.co.uk) aims to promote the eclectic range of music that is played by the station by allowing users to assemble 'towers' of their favourite music, whether it be hip hop or dance music, indie or pop. Once an individual tower has been built, it leads users to information about BBC Radio 1 programmes that specialize in their preferred sounds. 'Musicubes is a digital first; it allows each user to express their individual music taste – or "Musical DNA" – in a simple and visually striking way, and allows easy access to the BBC Radio 1 DJs on BBC iPlayer,' says creative director Gavin Gordon-Rogers.

The towers can also be pasted into blogs, and, as a by-product, provides vital feedback for BBC Radio 1 about which genres of music are most popular with their listeners. The campaign was a runaway success, with over 40,000 Musicubes towers built so far, resulting in millions of impressions.

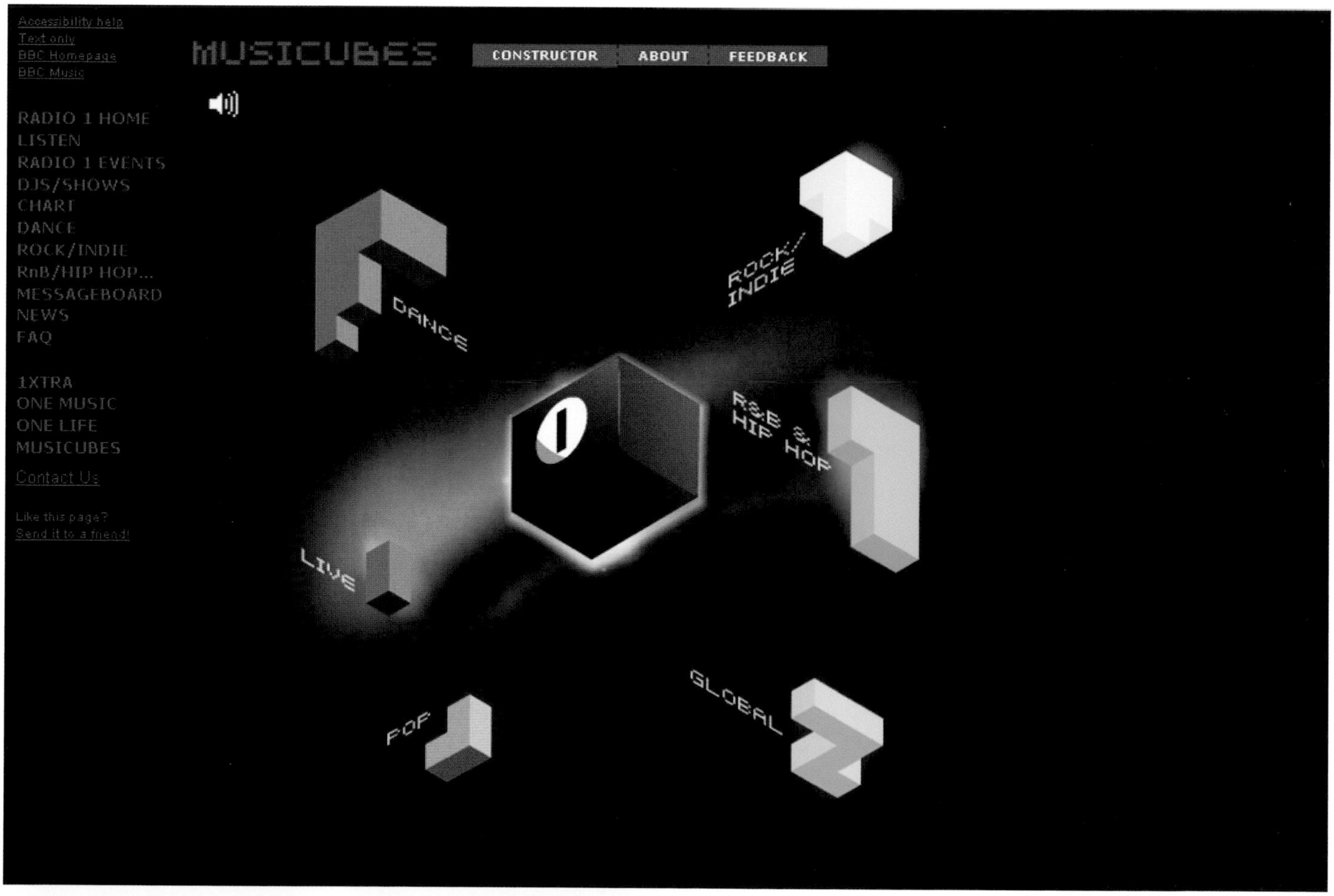
Accessibility help
Text only
BBC Homepage
BBC Music
MUSICUBES
CONSTRUCTOR
ABOUT
FEEDBACK
RADIO 1 HOME
LISTEN
RADIO 1 EVENTS
DJS/SHOWS
CHART
DANCE
ROCK/INDIE
RnB/HIP HOP...
MESSAGEBOARD
NEWS
FAQ
1XTRA
ONE MUSIC
ONE LIFE
MUSICUBES
Contact Us
Like this page?
Send it to a friend!
DANCE
ROCK/INDIE
R&B & HIP HOP
LIVE
POP
GLOBAL

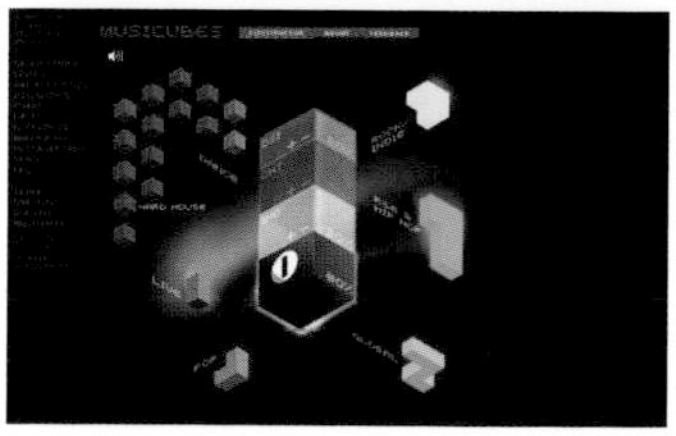

JOGA BONITO

LBi, Copenhagen

Nike: The Chain

The Chain campaign was kicked off, literally, by Ronaldinho. The football star was filmed kicking a ball out of the camera frame, and then viewers were encouraged to film the following link in the chain. The rules were very simple – the ball must enter from the left and exit to the right. Beyond this the participants could show off their footballing skills any way they liked. Over 40,000 films were uploaded to the website, with 2,000 of those selected for use in *The Chain*, a two-hour football video that has been viewed by more than 20 million people.

HOME BUILD FLY HANGAR
DOOMSDAY
SMOOTHOPERATOR
34.0
MORE PLANES
BEST RATED
VISIT RED BULL.COM IMPRINT SOUND ON OFF
HAPPY BI
3M
ワンタッチ ユニ
F50MO

less rain, Tokyo

Red Bull: Red Bull Flugtag Flight Lab

The Red Bull Flugtag Flight Lab is a 3D model game with flight simulator that was created by less rain for energy drink Red Bull. The website (www.redbull.com/flightlab) is based on the Red Bull Flugtag, an event where participants launch their homemade aircraft from a high ramp, to see if they will fly. Around 70 Flugtags have already taken place in 52 cities across the world.

less rain took this do-it-yourself spirit for their website game, which allows users to cut out a virtual model online from polystyrene, cardboard, wood or scrap metal. The pieces are then assembled automatically into a 3D aeroplane and you can customize your plane by uploading photographs or designs, or paint the plane using the colours available in the game. Your personal plane is then launched in the flight simulator and you can see how successful you are at aerodynamics. Points are given for the distance travelled and for piloting style, with loops, rolls and other manoeuvres rewarded. Other users can also rate the design of your plane, and the planes can all be saved online and developed further at a later date.

HOME
LOGIN REGISTER
Red Bull
FLUGTAG FLIGHT LAB
VISIT RED BULL.COM IMPRINT SOUND ON OFF

HOME BUILD FLY HANGAR
LOGIN REGISTER
VISIT RED BULL.COM IMPRINT SOUND ON OFF

HOME BUILD FLY HANGAR
LOGIN REGISTER
Red Bull
MORE PLANES
3...
0.0
BEST RATED
MORE PLANES
VISIT RED BULL.COM IMPRINT SOUND ON OFF

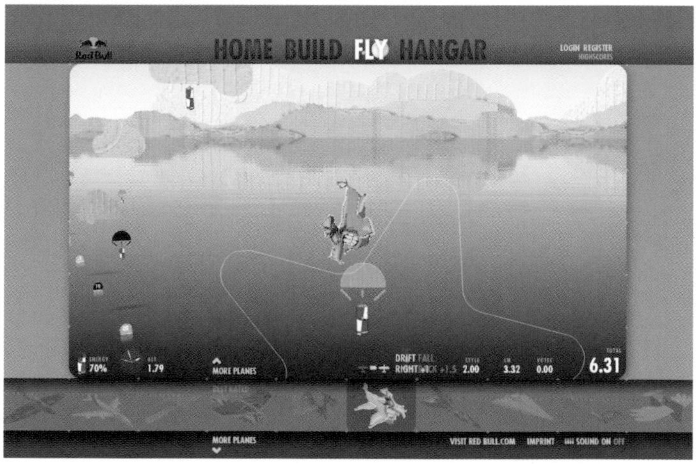
HOME BUILD FLY HANGAR
LOGIN REGISTER
70%
1.79
MORE PLANES
DRIFT FALL
2.00
3.32
0.00
6.31
MORE PLANES
VISIT RED BULL.COM IMPRINT SOUND ON OFF

HOME BUILD FLY HANGAR
LOGIN REGISTER
FLUGTAG
FLIGHT LAB
VISIT RED BULL.COM IMPRINT SOUND ON OFF

HOME BUILD FLY HANGAR
LOGIN REGISTER
DOOMSDAY
PILOT
SMOOTHOPERATOR
6.0
24.0
★★★★★
34.0
MORE PLANES
BEST RATED
MORE PLANES
VISIT RED BULL.COM IMPRINT SOUND ON OFF

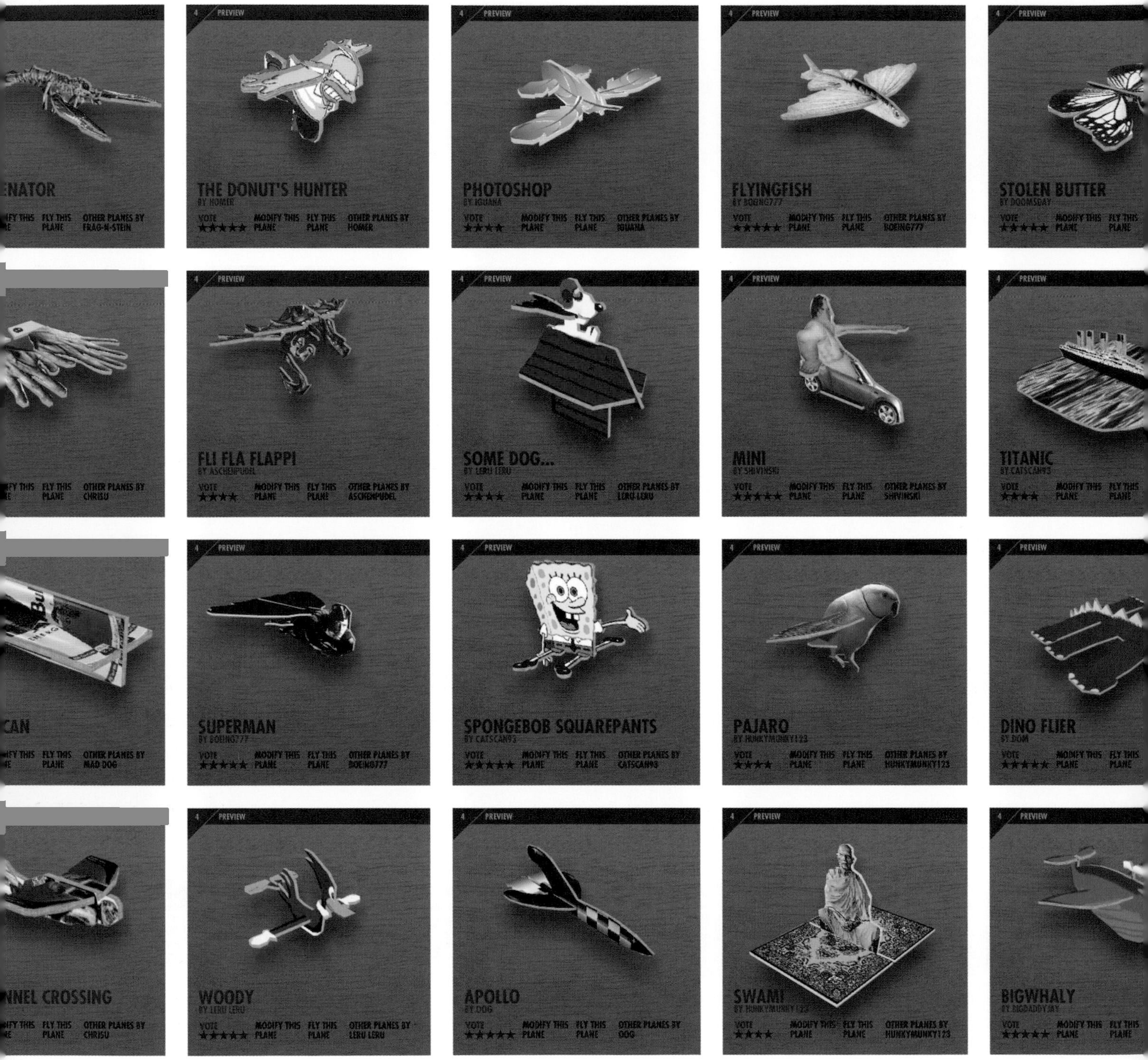

ENATOR
THE DONUT'S HUNTER
PHOTOSHOP
FLYINGFISH
STOLEN BUTTER
FLI FLA FLAPPI
SOME DOG...
MINI
TITANIC
CAN
SUPERMAN
SPONGEBOB SQUAREPANTS
PAJARO
DINO FLIER
NNEL CROSSING
WOODY
APOLLO
SWAMI
BIGWHALY

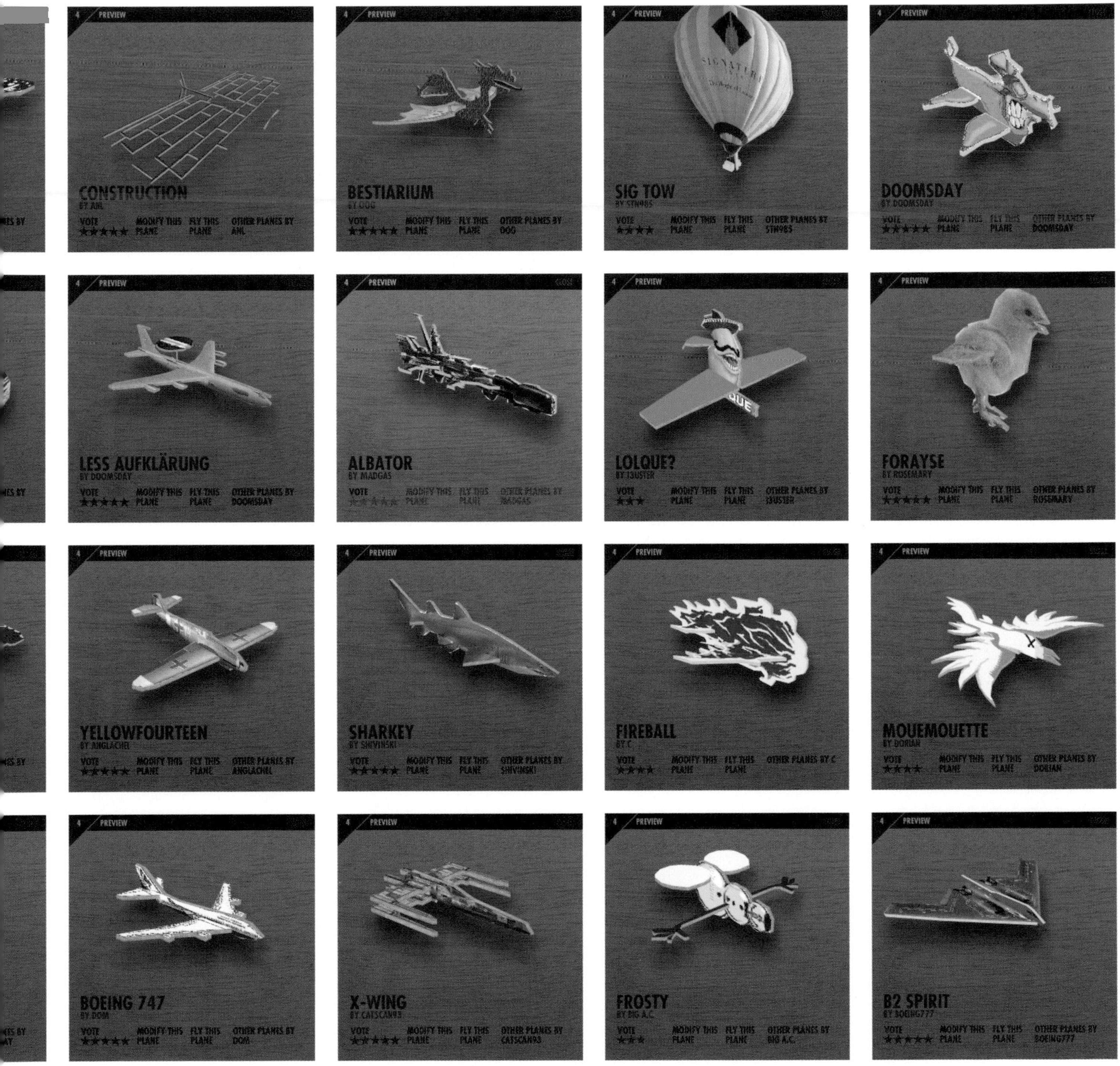
CONSTRUCTION
BY ANL
BESTIARIUM
SIG TOW
BY STN983
DOOMSDAY
BY DOOMSDAY
LESS AUFKLÄRUNG
BY DOOMSDAY
ALBATOR
BY MADGAS
LOLQUE?
BY 13USTER
FORAYSE
BY ROSEMARY
YELLOWFOURTEEN
BY ANGLACHEL
SHARKEY
BY SHIVINSKI
FIREBALL
BY C
MOUEMOUETTE
BY DORIAN
BOEING 747
BY DOM
X-WING
BY CATSCAN93
FROSTY
BY BIG A.C.
B2 SPIRIT
BY BOEING777

Planes created by users of the Red Bull Flugtag Flight Lab website.

180 Amsterdam

BMW: Unstoppable GPS Drawing

'Advertising's always been about using entertainment to push a product and nowadays there are so many more channels to engage with people.'

Andy Fackrell, executive creative director, 180 Amsterdam

Unstoppable was created by 180 Amsterdam to advertise BMW Motorrad motorcycles. The campaign emphasized the GPS device on the bikes by encouraging riders to use it to create 'drawings' via the Google Maps website. Instructions for taking part were given on a website, which explained how users could begin by mapping out their drawings on the site. Coordinates were then supplied, which, when transferred to the bike's GPS device, would instruct participants where to drive in order to create their drawing on the map. The website also offered a section where users could upload their journeys, photographs and films to share with others.

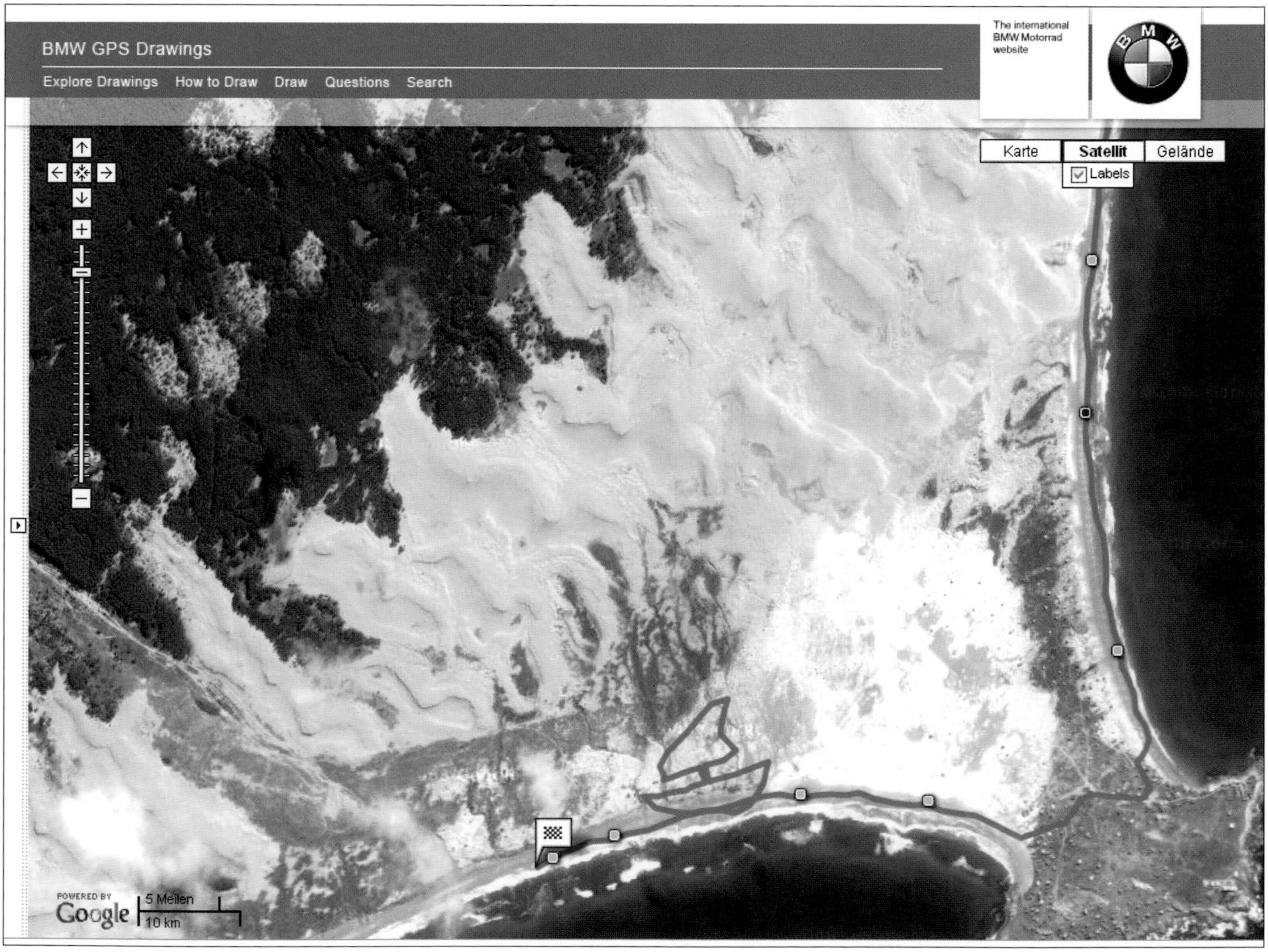
BMW GPS Drawings
Explore Drawings
How to Draw
Draw
Questions
Search
The international BMW Motorrad website
BMW
Karte
Satellit
Gelände
Labels
POWERED BY Google
5 Meilen
10 km

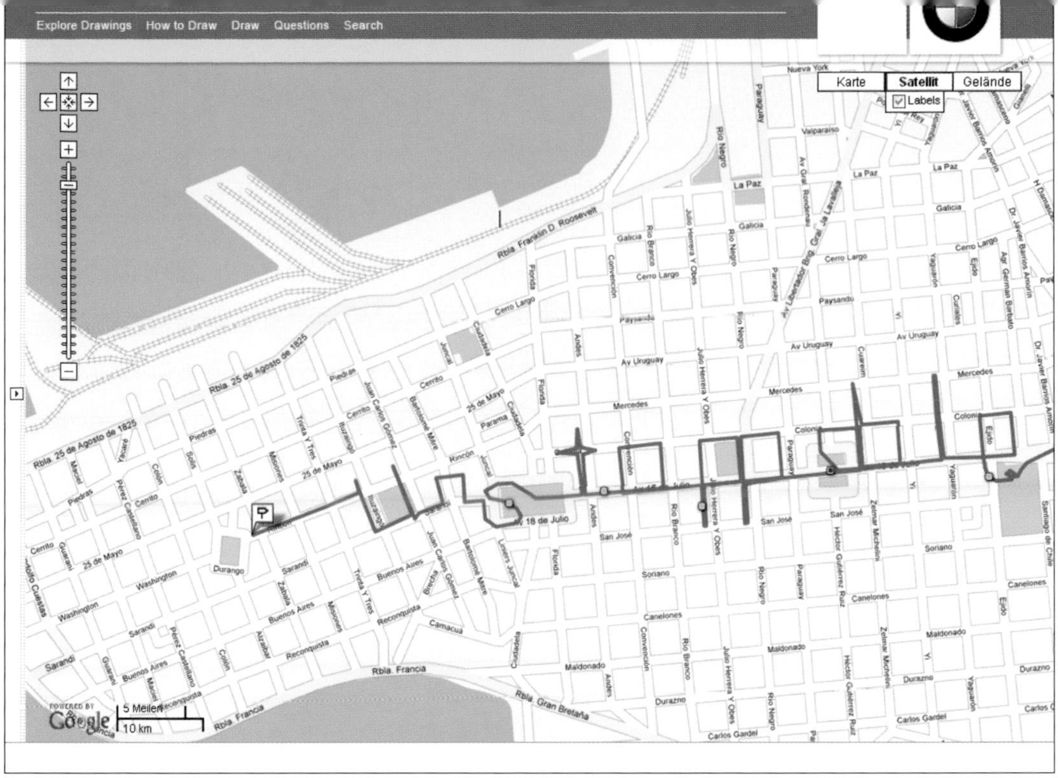

Explore Drawings
How to Draw
Draw
Questions
Search
Karte
Satellit
Gelände
Labels
Rbla. Franklin D. Roosevelt
Rbla. 25 de Agosto de 1825
Rbla. Francia
Rbla. Gran Bretaña
Av 18 de Julio
5 Meilen
10 km
POWERED BY
Google

BMW GPS Drawings
Explore Drawings
How to Draw
Draw
Questions
Search
The international BMW Motorrad website
BMW
Karte
Satellit
Gelände
Labels

Far left, left and below: GPS drawings shown on Google Maps. **Bottom:** Stills from film made to accompany the Unstoppable GPS Drawing campaign.

StrawberryFrog, New York

Scion: Scion Speak

StrawberryFrog advertising agency created www.scionspeak.com for US car brand Scion, which draws on the tradition of customization of the cars by fans. StrawberryFrog worked with graffiti artist Tristan Eaton to create a visual language for Scion enthusiasts that could be used to create individual coats of arms online. Designs could then be downloaded from the website for personal use. The designs were created after discussions with Scion fans in LA and New York. 'Scion has a very strong sense of community and culture,' explains StrawberryFrog creative director Chaz Mee. 'They are a highly expressive and creative group of individuals brought together by a common bond and that is Scion. It was very important for us to go into the culture and not just talk to them but to immerse ourselves in and collaborate with that culture to really get a sense of who these people were. We had an idea of what we wanted to do but kept it fairly open so there was room to incorporate them into the process and into the final outcome.'

SCION SPEAK
Make | Look | Watch
Scion Speak
your own crest and show the world what you're made of.
Download, print, or post it to the
the exclusive 'making of' video with designer Tristan Eaton.

SCION SPEAK
Make | Look | Watch

SAN FRANCISCO
tC

DETROIT
xA

NEW YORK
xA

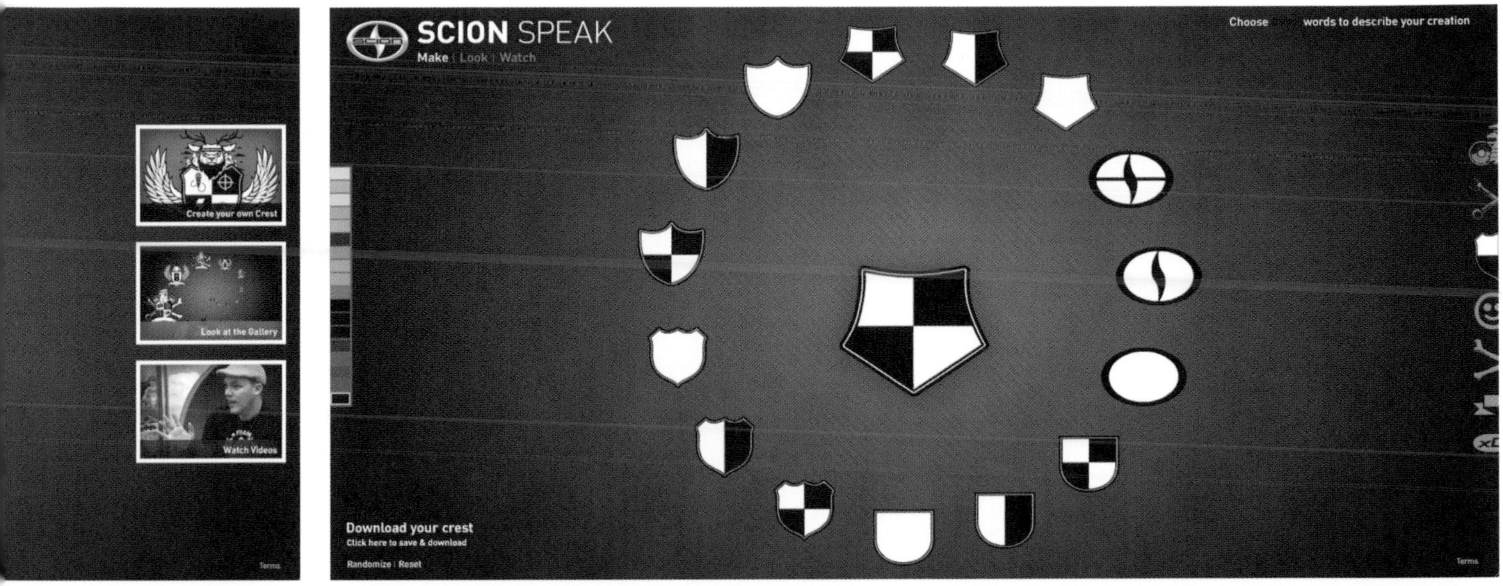
Create your own Crest
Look at the Gallery
Watch Videos
Terms
SCION SPEAK
Make | Look | Watch
Choose words to describe your creation
Download your crest
Click here to save & download
Randomize | Reset
Terms

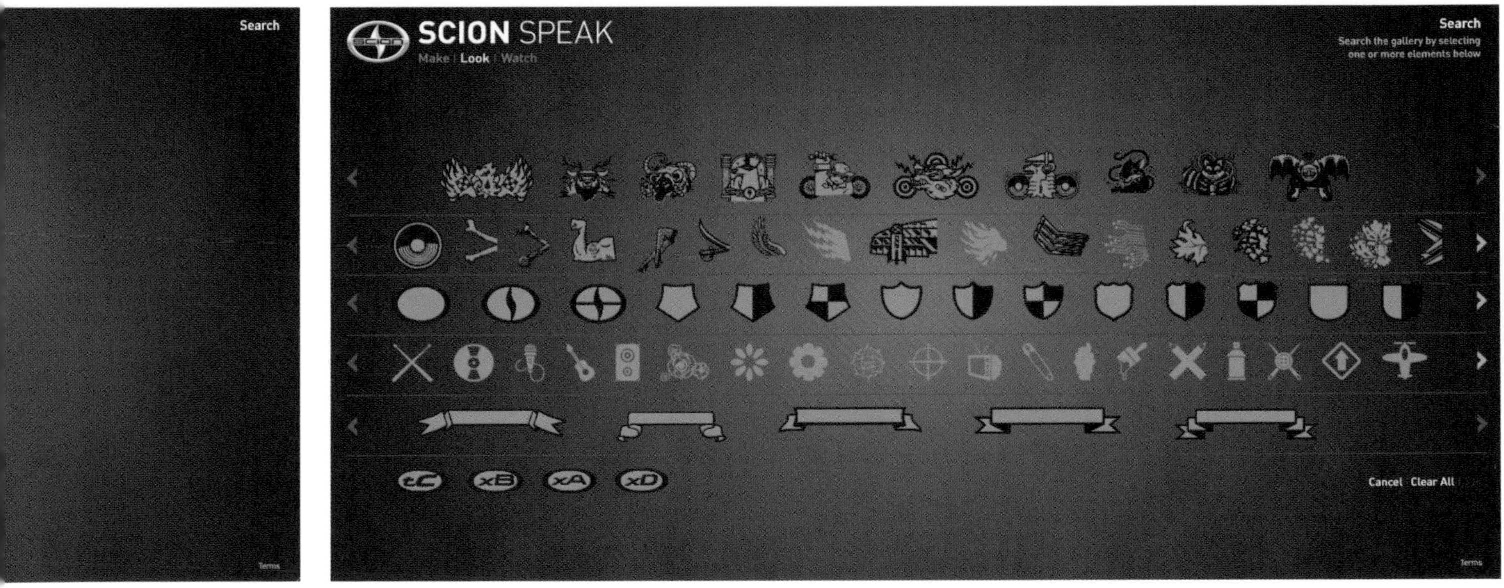
Search
Terms
SCION SPEAK
Make | Look | Watch
Search
Search the gallery by selecting one or more elements below
Cancel Clear All
Terms

Above: Stills from the Scion Speak website. **Left:** Examples of Scion crests.

LOS ANGELES
xD

Interview:
Will McGinness

Will McGinness is interactive creative director at San Francisco-based advertising agency Goodby, Silverstein & Partners, which has created innovative digital campaigns for clients that include HP, Adobe and Specialized Bikes, and the award-winning Get the Glass online game for the California Milk Board (page 46).

EW: **How would you describe the kind of advertising that you create?**

WM: Well, I'd like to think that we treat the consumer with respect. With new technology, people have been empowered to opt in or out of your work, which has amplified the need for good work. Let's be honest, for the most part nobody likes advertising. This new-found power to veto advertising has honed the consumer's ad-speak radar, so it's important to communicate with them as real people, not as demographics. This seems really obvious, but now, more than ever, it's crucial that you create work that people can appreciate.

EW: **Would you agree that advertising is going through a period of change? What do you feel is causing these changes?**

WM: Advertising is definitely going through a period of change. I think new technology has served to redefine the playbook for a lot of agencies. Television, print and outdoor were the media of choice for most agencies for a very long time. I think the internet and new technology really helped broaden the scope of how you could reach the consumer. It was a seismic jolt to a system that had become complacent with a formula that was in dire need of restructuring. It was a shift that not only introduced a new venue but helped people rethink the way that they speak to consumers. The internet can be a pretty non-linear, experiential place. People can come in and move around your ad, speak to it, pass it around and leave at any time. I believe that this fundamental change has helped lead to the media innovations you see coming out of good agencies today. It's helped us all to realize that there are endless ways to reach the consumer and we've only begun to tap into them.

EW: **Do you think it is important now for advertising companies to offer a variety of skills across all media? What do you see as the pitfalls of this level of diversifying?**

WM: As the media landscape continues to expand, the need for a central agency that has the experience and expertise to work in these spaces will become more and more important. I know there are people who think the exact opposite but I feel that we're in a weird state of transition where most traditional agencies haven't been able to adapt. This has created a market for a whole host of speciality companies. Clients are hiring 'idea' companies that tout their strategic ability to offer non-traditional ideas; there are digital specialists, branded content, viral and alternate reality gaming experts etc. The fear that clients have about their brands being left behind is real, and is justified in most cases. A lot of traditional agencies are too rooted in an old school approach to advertising to change. Either they'll learn to adapt or die a slow death as a new crop of agencies take the lead and allow clients to entrust an agency of record with the reins of their brand again. That doesn't mean an agency has to be an expert in everything – there are obvious dangers in spreading out too thinly. I think the agency of the future will be largely comprised of a new breed of creative and strategic thinkers who are comfortable at the helm of a pretty erratic and unpredictable ship. They'll also be dialled into the industry enough to know how and when to collaborate with various production partners that bring specialized skillsets to the table.

EW: **Has the office set-up/style of working within agencies changed too, in your experience?**

WM: Well, I think it's probably got more collaborative. There can be so many arms to a campaign these days that it becomes hard for one team to work on everything. In my experience, creatives are now less guarded and proprietorial with their work. You need to be willing to open up and work with other people in developing ideas that can extend beyond the reach of one medium.

EW: **Which areas do you think will develop the most – branded content, digital etc.?**

WM: Well, I'm sure that we're on the verge of a mobile tidal wave of sorts here in the US. As mobile technology evolves, user habits will change and soon there'll be a viable new venue for reaching people in a rich and engaging way. Behavioural marketing will continue to evolve as well. The privacy debates and paranoia will continue but the industry will generally get more and more savvy in how they target consumers online. It'll be like Big Brother department stores, following, watching and selling you things based on your ever-growing internet profile. We'll all have our own creepy little digital biographies out there in cyberspace and that will undoubtedly continue to grow.

EW: **Do you feel that the relationship with your clients has evolved due to the changes in the industry? Are you now brought into the creative process earlier? Have you had more of an influence over the products that are being made by a client?**

WM: I think our client relationships have generally become stronger and more involved. There are so many different pieces to the puzzle these days that you simply need to work more with the client in developing the work.

I think it's really important to work with clients from a pure strategic place to figure out what it is that they need to communicate before the media is purchased and doled out. There are so many ways to reach the consumer that it's easy to get caught up in crazy media buys before the idea has been fully realized. Working closely with the client in developing that media strategy as the work unfolds is key.

I think good agencies continue to get more intimately involved in their client's business practices as well, which is smart. A client's brand is expressed from the ground up and every aspect of a company whether it's internal communication, the products themselves, packaging, point of sale etc. should be considered. We spend a lot of time thinking about all of the different ways we can help shape a cohesive brand for our clients.

ADACHI HOME
360 DEGREE
EXPLORE
BOARD
GET THE GLASS
PLAY
THE GAME

GET THE
GLASS
NEW GAME LEADER BOARD MAP
POINTS
00000
EXPLORE INSTRUCTIONS CRIME FILES

GET THE
GLASS
NEW GAME LEADER BOARD MAP
got milk?
POINTS
00500
TIME
EXPLORE INSTRUCTIONS CRIME FILES
VIEW SPOTS MUSIC OFF DOWNLOADS

GET THE
GLASS
NEW GAME LEADER BOARD MAP
BUSTED
PROCEED DIRECTLY TO
MILKATRAZ
POINTS
00350
EXPLORE INSTRUCTIONS CRIME FILES

Goodby, Silverstein & Partners, San Francisco

California Milk Board: Get the Glass

To move the hugely successful California Milk Board 'Got Milk?' campaign online, Goodby, Silverstein & Partners created Get the Glass (www.gettheglass.com), a beautifully designed online game starring the milk-deprived Adachi family. The game is presented as an old-fashioned board game, where players roll a dice to move around the board. The mission of the game is to help the Adachi family survive the five regions of the board and then break into Fort Fridge. Throughout, players must watch out for Fridge Security, who are looking to whisk the Adachis off to Milkatraz, and they must also cope with the various ailments caused by the family's lack of milk. If the Adachis make it to Fort Fridge they will get the glass, which will offer them an unlimited supply of milk and their health will be restored. This is a fun game that also underlines the brand's message that milk is good for you.

GET THE
GLASS
NEW GAME LEADER BOARD MAP
got milk?
FORTUNE
The basketball coach gives Tad a backpack on wheels to carry his books because Tad doesn't have milk to help his muscles rebuild after practice. Move ahead one space.
1
SPACE
CONTINUE
LIFE
EXPLORE INSTRUCTIONS CRIME FILES
VIEW SPOTS MUSIC ON

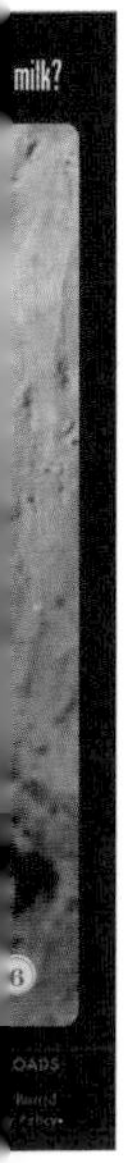

GET THE
GLASS
NEW GAME LEADER BOARD MAP
got milk?
SERVE YOUR
SENTENCE
DO YOUR TIME AND LOSE A LIFE
RISK
ESCAPE
FATE MAY BE KIND OR ESPECIALLY CRUEL
LIFE
POINTS
TIME
EXPLORE INSTRUCTIONS CRIME FILES
VIEW SPOTS MUSIC OFF DOWNLOADS

Big Spaceship, New York

Sony Pictures: 30 Days of Night

To promote Sony Pictures' blockbuster vampire movie *30 Days of Night*, Big Spaceship created this online multiplayer game (www.30daysofnight.com/game). The movie and game are set in the Alaskan town of Barrow, where for one month a year the sun never rises. While this is good news for the town's plentiful vampire population, it's not so good for the humans living among them. The game pits the vampires against the humans. Players must complete 30 days of missions to win, and, depending on where their allegiance lies, can play the game either as humans or as vampires.

KEEP YOUR TEAM ALIVE FOR 30 DAYS OF GAMEPLAY.
PLAY SIX MISSIONS TO PROCEED TO THE NEXT LEVEL

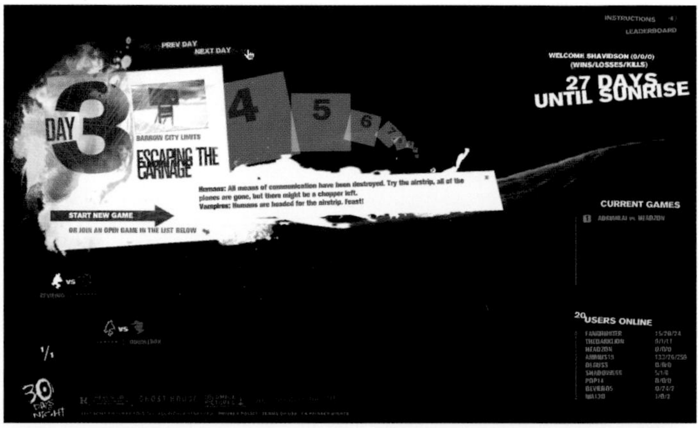
PREV DAY
NEXT DAY
DAY 3
ESCAPING THE CARNAGE
START NEW GAME
27 DAYS UNTIL SUNRISE
CURRENT GAMES
USERS ONLINE

DAY 3
BLOCK THE CHOPPER
BEVIEB05 VS SHAVIDSON
INSTRUCTIONS
LEADERBOARD
BACK TO LOBBY
CHAT
SHAVIDSON: OMG
BEVIEB05: what
SHAVIDSON: super ruffle time!
BEVIEB05: i'm really bad
LEXA [SHAVIDSON]
OLEG [SHAVIDSON]
DRAGOS [SHAVIDSON]

DAY 3
INSTRUCTIONS
LEADERBOARD
BACK TO LOBBY
BLOCK THE CHOPPER
CHAT
SHAVIDSON: OMG

DAY 3
BLOCK THE CHOPPER
INSTRUCTIONS
LEADERBOARD

DAY 3
GAME OVER
INSTRUCTIONS
LEADERBOARD
CHAT
SHAVIDSON: OMG
BEVIEB05: what
SHAVIDSON: super raffle time!
BEVIEB05: i'm really bad
BEVIEB05: so where am i
DIMITRI [SHAVIDSON]
LEXA [SHAVIDSON]
OLEG [SHAVIDSON]
DRAGOS [SHAVIDSON]
GHOST HOUSE
COLUMBIA PICTURES
PRIVACY POLICY | TERMS OF USE | CA PRIVACY RIGHTS

Herraiz & Soto, Barcelona

Hewlett Packard and Fútbol Club Barcelona: Showtime

From top, left to right: Close-up of the fans holding sheets for the club mosaic; The FCB Showtime website; The crowd holds up the FCB mosaic of the club shield; Merchandise sold through the FCB Showtime website.

The FCB Showtime website was created for Barcelona's premier football club, Fútbol Club Barcelona (FCB), and Hewlett Packard (HP). The site offers the chance for fans of the football team to upload personal photos of themselves at matches or dressed in FCB strip, and then mix them with professional shots of the players and create their own customized photo albums, calendars, posters and greeting cards. All the printing on the site is done through HP. To launch the site, advertising agency Herraiz & Soto decided to focus on the most important match of the year, when FCB play the 'El Clásico' derby match against arch rivals Real Madrid. One of the key moments of this match is when FCB spectators hold up a giant mosaic of the club shield. Herriaz & Soto requested that fans participate actively in the mosaic by uploading their pictures to the FCB Showtime website, thereby connecting personal images to an important FCB symbol. Over 100,000 fans took part, with HP providing the printing for the 26,000 sheets of the mosaic. Each sheet contained 72 photographs of fans, with a Pantone wash across them so that the photos would form part of the club shield when viewed from a distance.

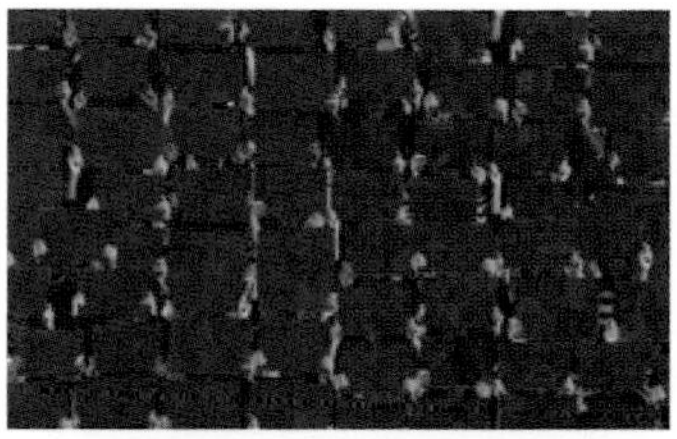

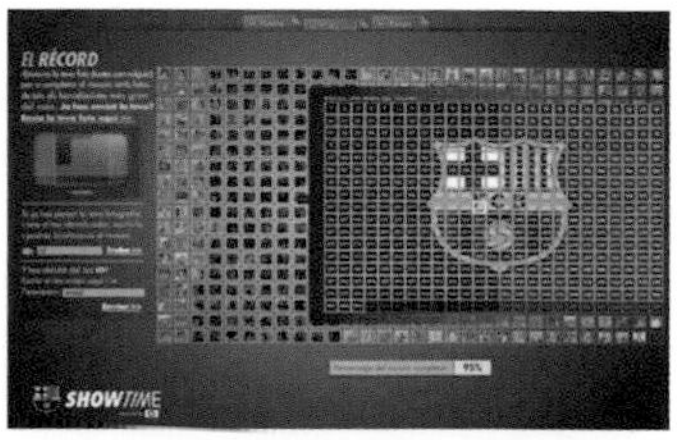
SHOWTIME

> **'I think advertising needs to be reinvented. All the content and entertainment is going to be on demand and the only opportunity for brands is to be part of the demand.'**
>
> **Rafael Soto, creative director, Herraiz & Soto**

FCBARCELONA

Big Spaceship, New York

NBC Universal: The Ultimate Search for Bourne with Google

The Ultimate Search for Bourne with Google was a website created to promote the final instalment of the Bourne movie trilogy, *The Bourne Ultimatum*. It set players a 15-day challenge to scour the internet using Google in search of rogue agent Jason Bourne. Agents logged in daily to a hub site where they were given all the tools a special agent would need, including decryption, instant messaging with a spy network, a media archive and surveillance. Clues could be found via fake websites specifically created to hide them, with many of the clues requiring further analysis using the hub site. Exclusive content was also released via iGoogle, and clues were distributed via YouTube. Along the way prizes such as an iPhone, a VW Touareg 2 car or a holiday to all the destinations featured in the film could be won. The final mission took players to a cryptic site and rewarded them with exclusive clips from the movie. Over 750,000 players joined in the game.

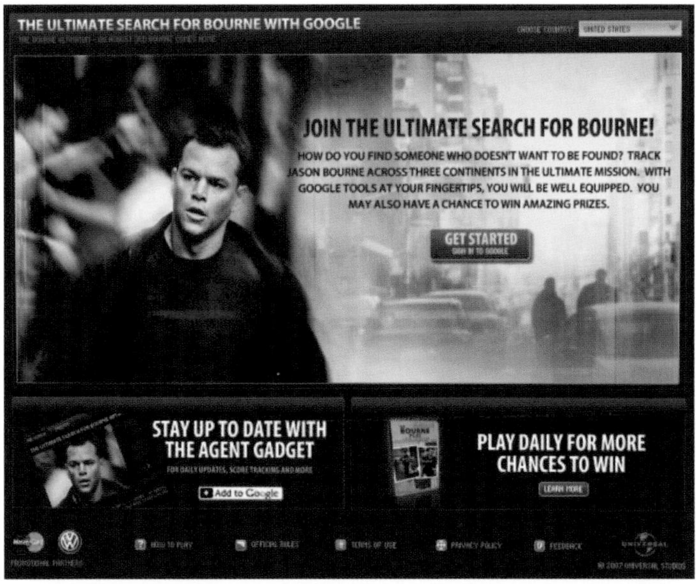
THE ULTIMATE SEARCH FOR BOURNE WITH GOOGLE
JOIN THE ULTIMATE SEARCH FOR BOURNE!
HOW DO YOU FIND SOMEONE WHO DOESN'T WANT TO BE FOUND? TRACK JASON BOURNE ACROSS THREE CONTINENTS IN THE ULTIMATE MISSION. WITH GOOGLE TOOLS AT YOUR FINGERTIPS, YOU WILL BE WELL EQUIPPED. YOU MAY ALSO HAVE A CHANCE TO WIN AMAZING PRIZES.
GET STARTED
STAY UP TO DATE WITH THE AGENT GADGET
Add to Google
PLAY DAILY FOR MORE CHANCES TO WIN

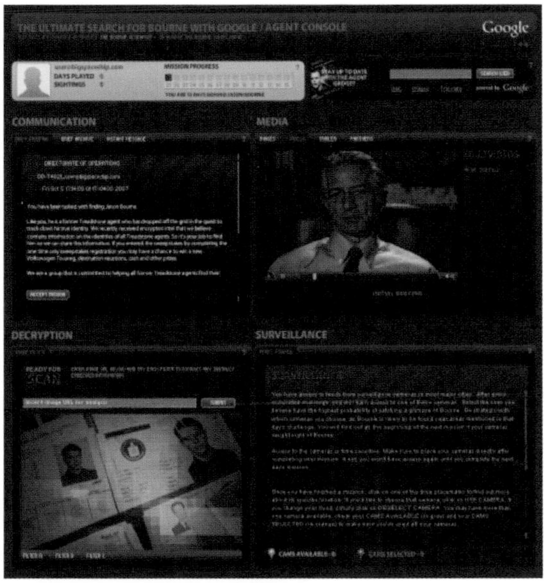
Google
COMMUNICATION
MEDIA
DECRYPTION
SURVEILLANCE

SURVEILLANCE
LONDON, ENGLAND
MAP
SATELLITE
HYBRID
Marylebone
London
CAMS AVAILABLE - 1
CAMS SELECTED - 0

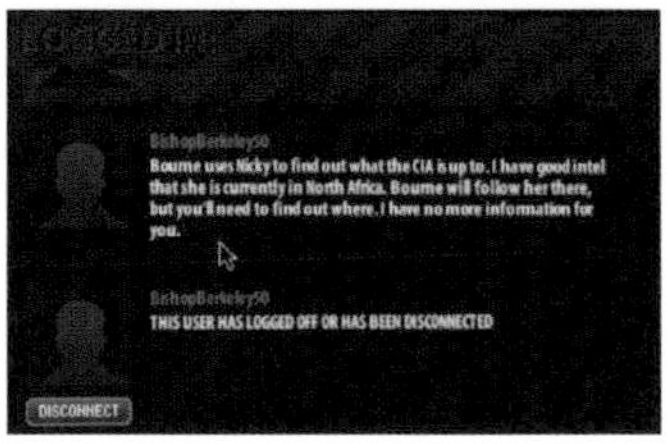
BishopBerkeley50
Bourne uses Nicky to find out what the CIA is up to. I have good intel that she is currently in North Africa. Bourne will follow her there, but you'll need to find out where. I have no more information for you.
BishopBerkeley50
THIS USER HAS LOGGED OFF OR HAS BEEN DISCONNECTED
DISCONNECT

DATER

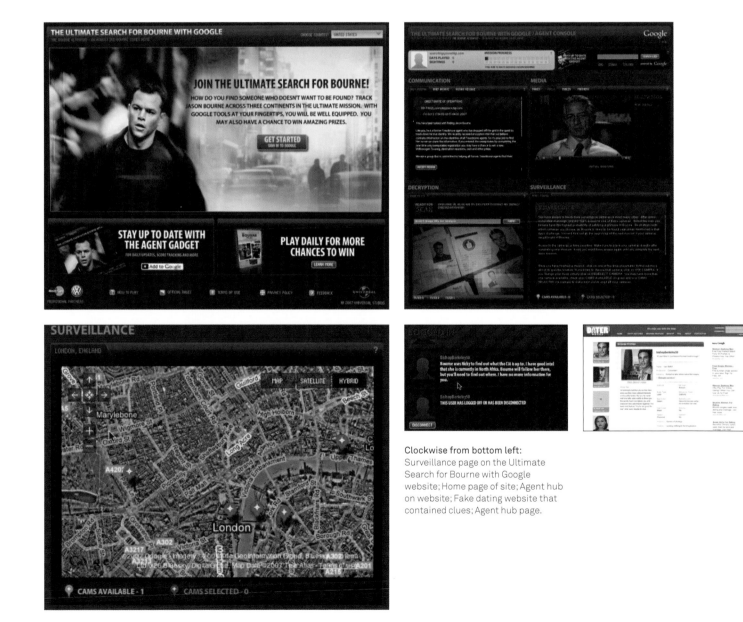

Clockwise from bottom left:
Surveillance page on the Ultimate Search for Bourne with Google website; Home page of site; Agent hub on website; Fake dating website that contained clues; Agent hub page.

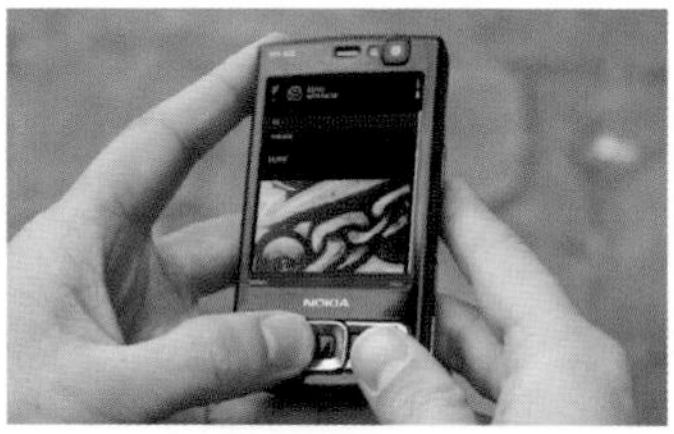

AKQA, London

Nike: PHOTOiD

Nike PHOTOiD gives Nike fans the chance to create personalized footwear inspired by colours in the world around them. The campaign encourages users to seek out interesting colourways in their environment, photograph the colours and then send them to the PHOTOiD mobile site. The two most dominant colours are taken from the photograph, matched to the NikeiD palette and then transferred to a pair of Nike Dunks shoes. If the users like the look of their colour combination, they can purchase the shoes. Nike PHOTOiD forms part of the NikeiD scheme, which has allowed consumers to customize their own shoes, bags and apparel since 1999, via a rotating selection of colours and materials on nikeid.nike.com.

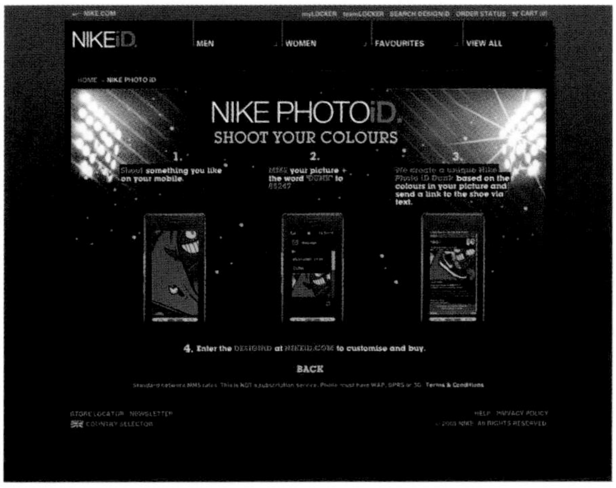
NIKE.COM
myLOCKER teamLOCKER SEARCH DESIGNiD ORDER STATUS CART (0)
NIKEiD.
MEN
WOMEN
FAVOURITES
VIEW ALL
HOME › NIKE PHOTO iD
NIKE PHOTOiD.
SHOOT YOUR COLOURS
1. Shoot something you like on your mobile.
2. MMS your picture + the word "DUNK" to 85247
3. We create a unique Nike Photo iD Dunk based on the colours in your picture and send a link to the shoe via text.
4. Enter the DESIGNID at NIKEID.COM to customise and buy.
BACK
STORE LOCATOR NEWSLETTER
COUNTRY SELECTOR
HELP PRIVACY POLICY

NIKE.COM
myLOCKER teamLOCKER SEARCH DESIGNiD ORDER STATUS CART (0)
NIKEiD.
MEN
WOMEN
FAVOURITES
VIEW ALL
HOME › NIKE PHOTO iD
NIKE PHOTOiD.
SHOOT YOUR COLOURS
NIKEiD
BACK
STORE LOCATOR NEWSLETTER
COUNTRY SELECTOR
HELP PRIVACY POLICY

Netthink, Madrid

adidas: Impossible is Nothing

Netthink created this banner ad as part of the adidas Impossible is Nothing campaign, which featured famous athletes sharing, and drawing, their stories of overcoming adversity in their sporting careers. Users could engage with the ad by clicking on the pen and 'drawing' a line across the screen. Urban scenes would appear automatically on the line and a runner would be seen moving along it. The ads would then lead through to the adidas Impossible is Nothing microsite, where users could upload their own drawings illustrating their personal experiences. The only stipulation was that there should be a line running from left to right in each drawing so that the drawings could be placed side by side and appear to run into one another, forming a continuous picture. Users could then vote for their favourite drawings and see their rankings. Over 5,600 drawings were uploaded to the site, which created a chain drawing over 3.2 kilometres (1.9 miles) long.

ya.com
Actualidad
Ocio
Chats
Correo
Servicios de Telecomunicaciones
MÁXIMA VELOCIDAD
20 Mb
LLAMADAS 24H
LLAMADAS A MÓVILES
Compras online
VANS
Publicidad
Impossible is Nothing
adidas

ya.com
Actualidad
Ocio
Chats
Correo
Servicios de Telecomunicaciones
MÁXIMA VELOCIDAD
20 Mb
LLAMADAS 24H
LLAMADAS A MÓVILES
Compras online
VANS
Publicidad
Impossible is Nothing
adidas

ya.com
X Cerrar
Impossible is Nothing adidas

ya.com
X Cerrar
nubes
Impossible is Nothing adidas

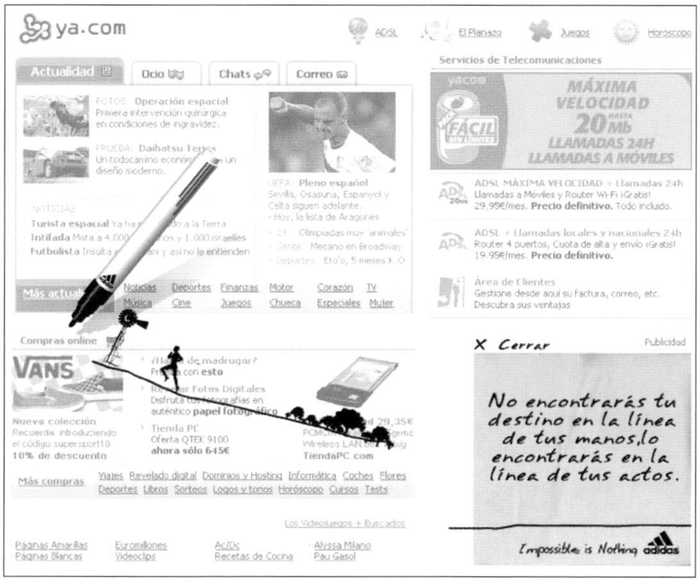
ya.com
X Cerrar
No encontrarás tu destino en la línea de tus manos, lo encontrarás en la línea de tus actos.
Impossible is Nothing adidas

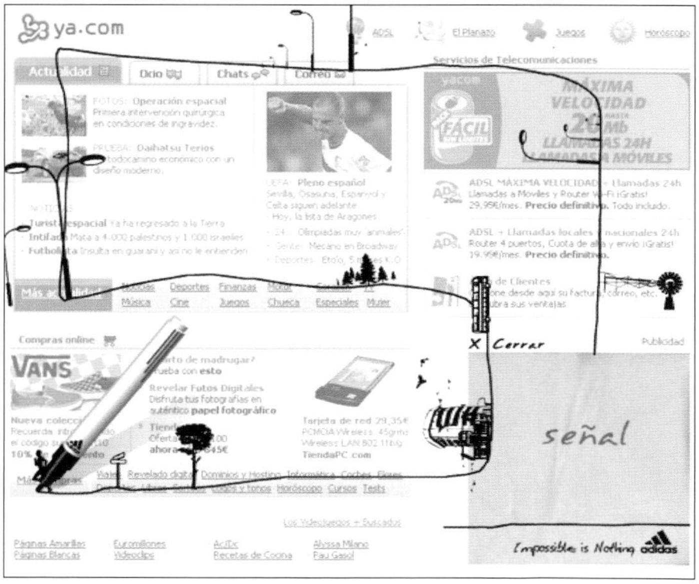
ya.com
X Cerrar
señal
Impossible is Nothing adidas

Videos have been used to sell music for decades now, but 2007 saw a new development in the field, with the arrival of the interactive music video, which acknowledged the fact that most videos were now being watched online rather than on TV. Vincent Morisset created www.beonlineb.com for the track *Neon Bible* by Arcade Fire. The elegant and simple site is centred around users interacting with lead singer Win Butler, whose head and hands loom out of a black backdrop. By clicking on Butler, preferably in time to the music, effects are unleashed. 'The project is created from a multitude of micro video clips looped, positioned and triggered with Actionscript,' explains Morisset. 'Every traditional music video ends up as a 400-pixel crunchy clip on a video portal. Since it would finish anyway as an online file, I thought it would be interesting to take advantage of the interactive potential of a project seen on a computer and create something new and different.' Following the success of the website, several other bands have begun taking an interactive, online approach to promoting their new releases.

Vincent Morisset, Montreal

Arcade Fire: *Neon Bible*

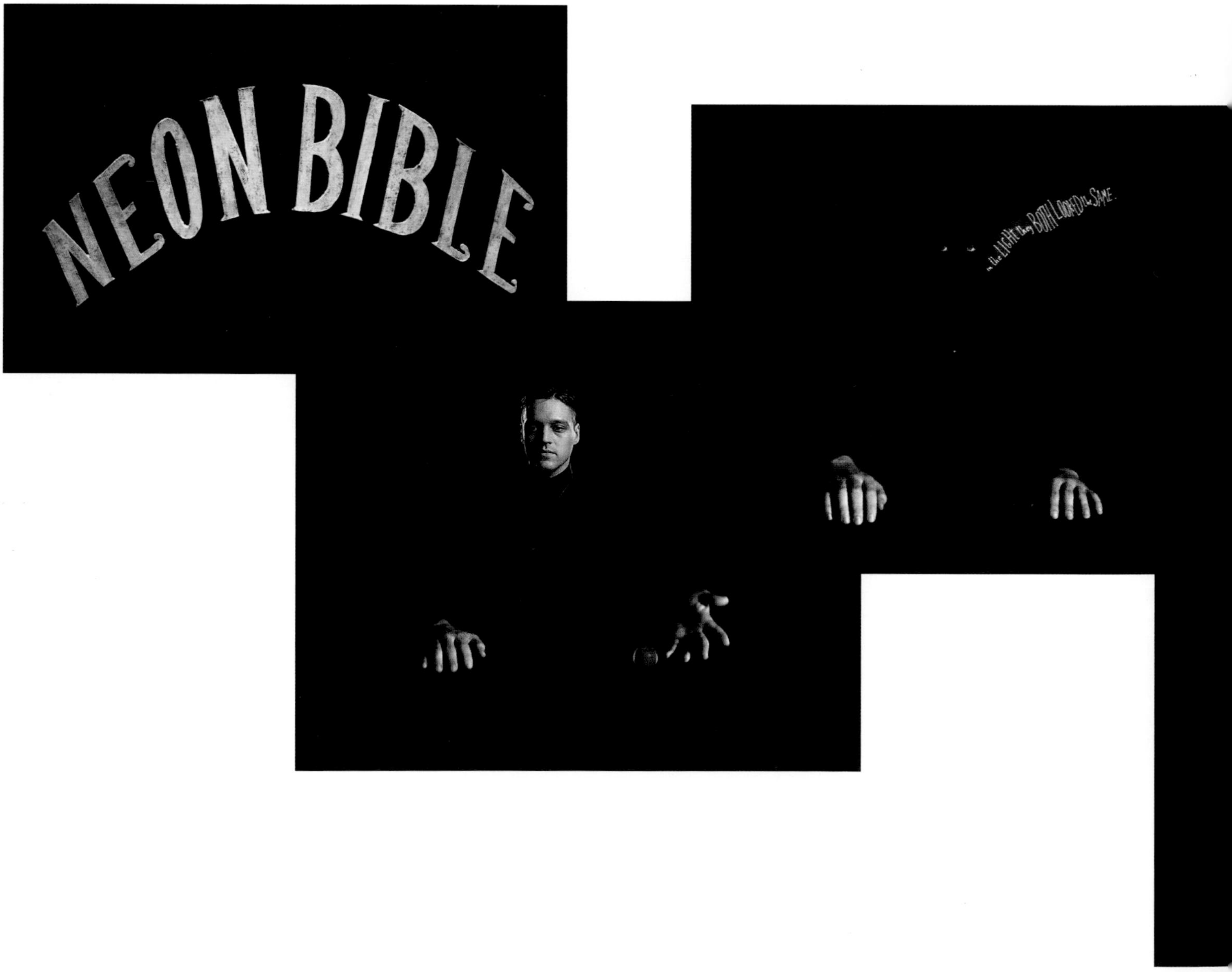
NEON BIBLE
the LIGHT they BOTH LOOKED the SAME.

'The advertisement has become an end unto itself, it's not just something that is inserted between two different things – like being inserted into a TV programme – but the advertisement has its own, independent, ultimate purpose.'

Koichiro Tanaka, co-founder and creative director, Projector

Chapter Two: Branded

Branded content has been around for decades – soap operas could be said to be one of the first examples – but the expression has come into its own in recent years, with brands realizing that one of the ways to get an audience to engage with them is to give them something they want to watch or experience. While branded content has multiple definitions, here it is used to describe some of the recent books, films or entertaining clips released by agencies to promote brands. The films are mostly distributed online, usually virally, with viewers sharing them with friends simply because they like them so much.

72andSunny, Los Angeles

Microsoft: Zune Arts

Advertising agency 72andSunny collaborated with a number of artists to create the Zune Arts series of animated films, which promote the Microsoft Zune digital media player. The films come in a multitude of forms and narratives but all contain ideas of friendship and sharing. Over 30 artists and animators from all over the world have contributed to the Zune Arts project so far; all the films in the series can be watched online at www.zune-arts.net.

Clockwise from top left: Stills from *Endless Cookie*, directed by SSSR; *Intergalactic Swap Meet*, directed by againstallodds; *Le Cadeau Du Temps*, directed by Cory Godbey; *Tickle Party*, directed by Sam Borkson and Arturo Sandoval III; *Masks*, directed by Jonathan Garin and Naomi Nishimura; *Mother Like No Other*, directed by Yves Geleyn.

Dare, London

Sony Ericsson Xperia: *Who Is Johnny X?*

To launch the new Sony Ericsson high-end handset range Xperia, Dare created the online episodic thriller, *Who Is Johnny X?* The series shows our hero using his new Xperia X1 phone to help piece together his life when he loses his memory after being kidnapped by an organized crime gang. The film, which was written and produced by Dare, was shot in Bangkok and deftly shows off the phone's complex functionality while also being an entertaining story. The nine episodes of the story were released online over a three-week period, with the final instalment appearing on www.whoisjohnny-x.com just before the launch of the new phone.

VANTED
$50M REWARD
$50M REWARD
WANTED
Rondel Rawlins called "Fineman"

JWT Paris

Kit Kat: Ultimate Break

This charming viral animation was created for Kit Kat by JWT Paris. The three-minute film sees a hapless office worker struggling to concentrate at work due to the distractions of an overbearing boss and a series of irritating co-workers. Salvation comes in the form of a Kit Kat, the eating of which, in a somewhat unlikely twist, transforms the office building into a rocket that hurtles into space, giving our hero the 'ultimate break'. Viewers are directed to a website where they can suggest ideas for their own ultimate break and also upload films.

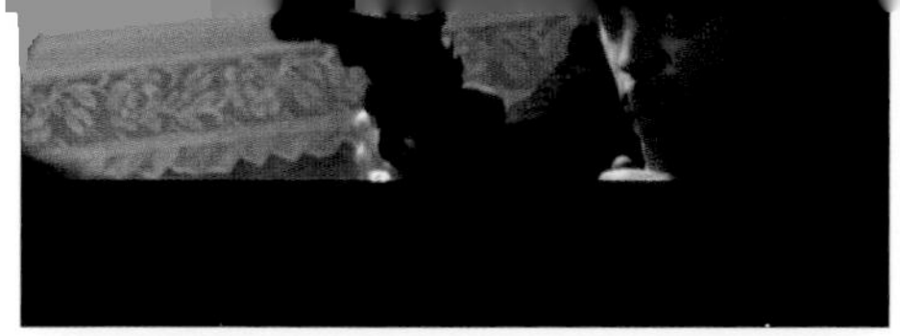

'We live in a saturated society populated by media savvy consumers. Which means we needed something out of the norm, askance, different. So it's brilliant having a client advanced enough to allow us to stretch and invent something fresh, distinctive and a little devious.'

Nick Worthington, executive creative director, Publicis Mojo

Publicis Mojo, Auckland

Schweppes: Schweppes Short Film Festival

In a bid to redefine Schweppes, a brand often associated with children's soft drinks, as a drink for an adult audience, New Zealand agency Publicis Mojo worked with production company The Sweet Shop to create the Schweppes Short Film Festival. Entitled *Schhh...*, the films were aimed at adult audiences only and thus could only play out online. All the films contained a section that was used as a TV ad initially, before directing viewers online to www.schhh.eu/shortfilms/ to see the rest of the film. Each TV ad ended at a pivotal moment, with a character holding a finger to their lips and saying 'Schhh'. Aside from this 'Schhh Moment', the directors were given an entirely open creative brief. Sweet Shop directors Noah Marshall, Melanie Bridge, Kezia Barnett and James Pilkington created films for the campaign, which included stories of hitmen, bank robbers and the perfect penis.

Idealogue, New York

adidas: adicolor

The adicolor podcast is a series of seven short films created for adidas to celebrate 'colour, customization and personal expression'. The films were created to be specifically viewed on iPods, PSPs and online, which was still a fairly revolutionary proposition back in 2006 when the films were made. A team of excellent directors was put together, with Neill Blomkamp, Psyop, Happy, Tronic, Roman Coppola and Andy Bruntel, Saimon Chow and Charlie White each given an entirely open brief to create a film based on their emotional response to a particular colour. The podcasts related to the adicolor global digital campaign for which adidas had asked 20 artists to design a shoe based on their response to a colour. The films feature such surreal scenes as an orgiastic dinner party involving green paintball splashes and a pink-loving teenager's transformation into a bejewelled figurine. With an original goal of achieving one million views globally, the campaign actually achieved over 25 million views in just seven weeks.

Stills from Saiman Chow's film for the colour black. The film is a surreal tale about a lonely, crazed panda.

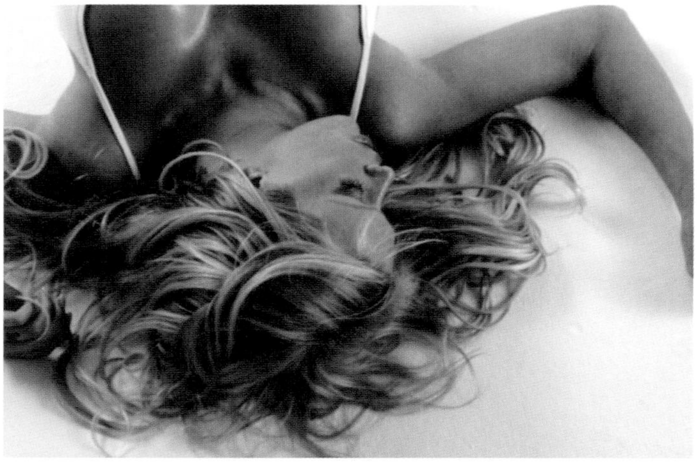

adicolor white was directed by Tronic and sees Jenna Jameson enthusiastically playing a funfair game.

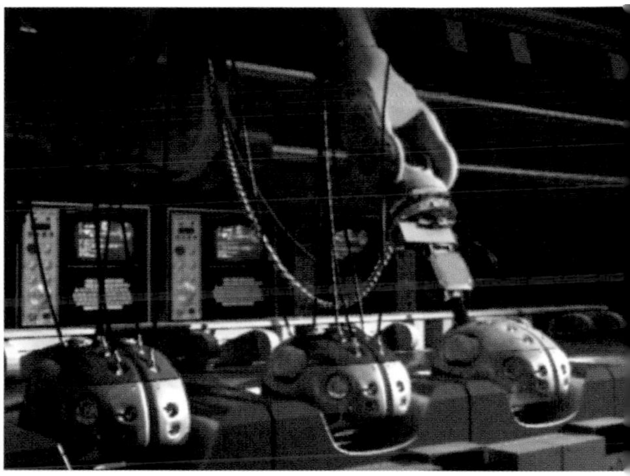

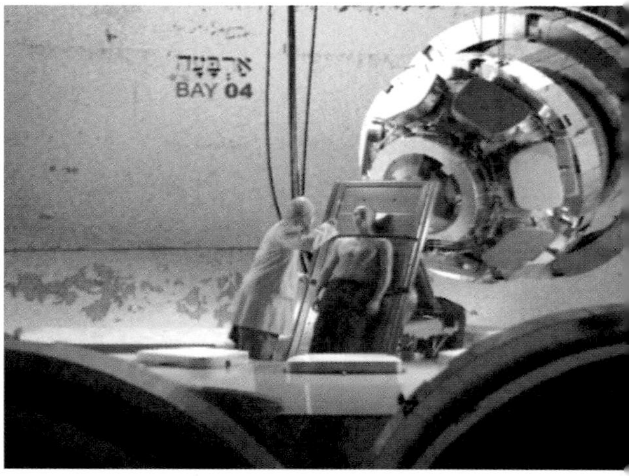
BAY 04

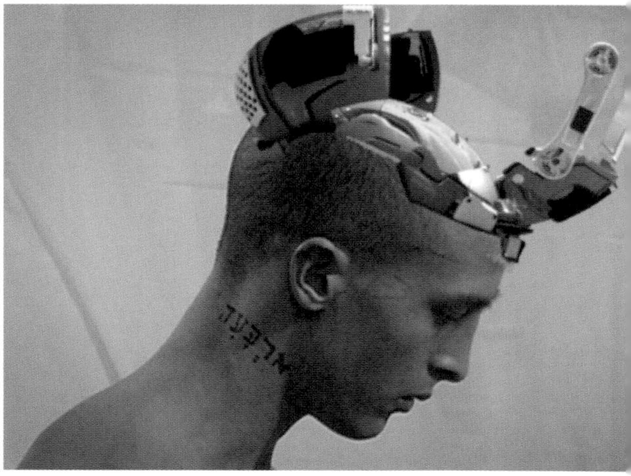

Neill Blomkamp directed the adicolor yellow film, a gripping tale about robots and artificial life.

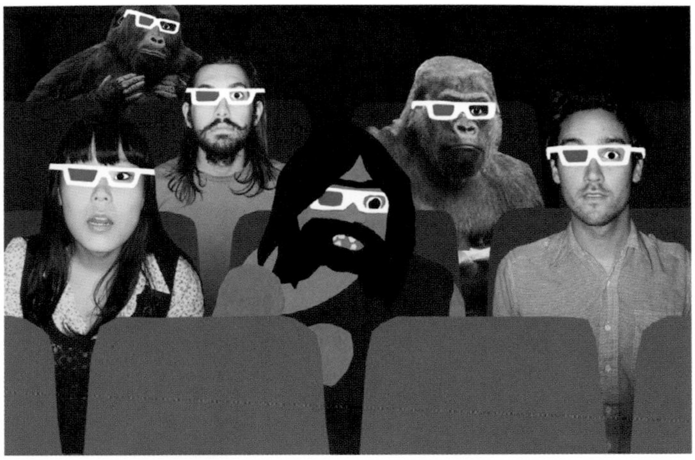

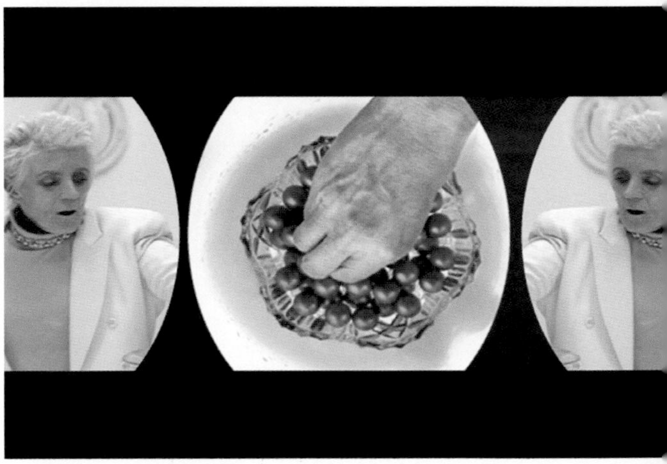

Roman Coppola and Andy Bruntel created this animated history of the colour red for the adicolor red film.

Adicolor green by Happy shows a space-age dinner party where everything gets a little out of hand after some green treats are consumed.

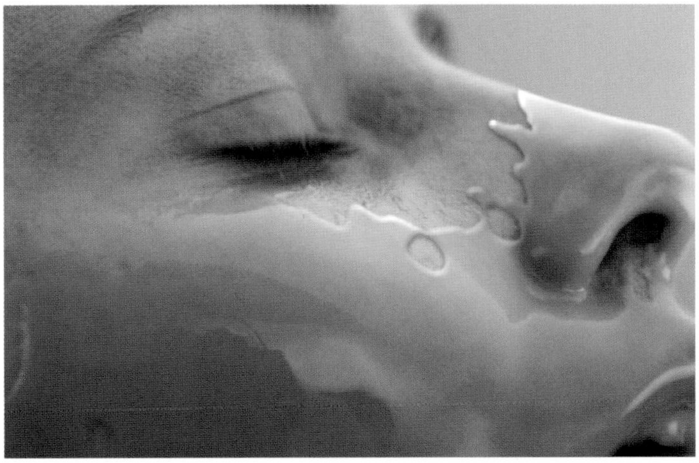

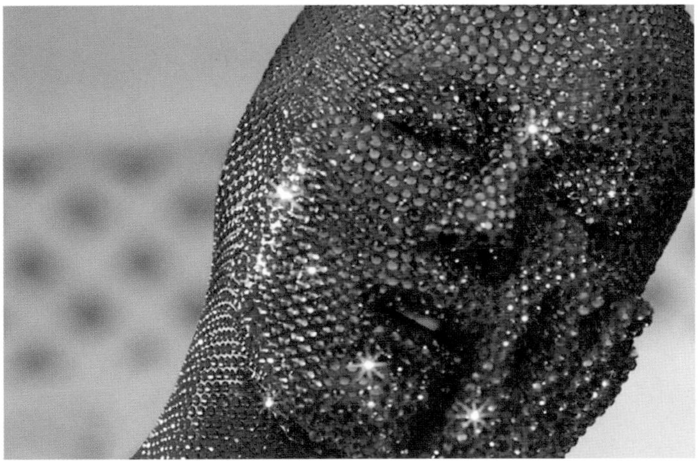

Charlie White directed the adicolor pink film, which sees a teenager turn into a bewelled figurine while her pink teddy looks on helplessly.

VISCO

mazda
NEW YORK
CYE-5553
EMPIRE STATE

Psyop is behind the adicolor blue film, where New York City is turned black and white, apart from the odd splashes of blue.

95
495
SOUTH
Richmond Va
Andrews AFB

UNITED STATES

Droga5, New York

eckō Unltd: Still Free

Droga5 and clothing brand eckō Unltd caused a media storm when a viral film, appearing to show someone tagging graffiti on Air Force One, appeared online. eckō Unltd was founded by designer and graffiti artist Mark Ecko, and the brief for Droga5 was to reinforce eckō Unltd's graffiti heritage, as well as emphasizing his position as an 'urban icon'. The aim was for eckō to 'tag the impossible'. Despite its authentic look, the whole film was, of course, a hoax, but when it was dropped anonymously on 20 websites it caused a storm across the internet and TV, and even led the Pentagon to deny the authenticity of the video three times. The tag that appears in the film references www.stillfree.com, a website that shows how it was all done. Despite no media spend by eckō, reports of the hoax film appeared in over 17,000 separate news outlets, according to the Associated Press, and a documentary of the whole story was also shot by director Henry-Alex Rubin. The estimated audience for the campaign was over 115 million.

Fallon, London

Cadbury Dairy Milk: Gorilla

Fallon's Gorilla advertisement for Cadbury Dairy Milk began life as a traditional television commercial, yet it really made its breakthrough online, where it has received over 10 million views (and counting) on YouTube and garnered over 70 fan groups on Facebook. Its premise was an unusual one from the beginning. Used to launch a new series of ads for the chocolate brand, under the banner of A Glass and a Half Full Productions (which refers to the amount of milk included in each bar of chocolate), there was no mention of chocolate in the ad, which featured a man in a gorilla outfit drumming along ecstatically to the Phil Collins track *In The Air Tonight*. By subtly emphasizing the simple pleasures of eating chocolate and watching something amusing, Fallon's ad led to sales of Cadbury Dairy Milk rising by seven per cent and Collins's hit returned to the charts. The ad also spawned numerous remixes on YouTube, with the Gorilla ad set to various soundtracks. One of these, Bonnie Tyler's *Total Eclipse of the Heart*, was then used as a new 'official' soundtrack when the ad played out on TV again a year after its original release.

Wieden + Kennedy London/
4 Creative, London

Honda: Jump

In May 2008, in the first ad break of innocuous reality TV show *Come Dine With Me*, Britain's first live TV commercial took place. Nineteen skydivers launched themselves from an aeroplane in Spain before coming together to spell out the word 'HONDA' in an ad for the car brand. The ad formed part of a wider campaign entitled 'Difficult is worth doing'. 'We chose skydiving formations because of their delicate precision moves in the air,' says Wieden + Kennedy London's creative director Tony Davidson. 'Human engineering. A metaphor for the Honda engineers' work on the ground. We wanted to attempt to make shapes of parts of the car using real skydivers as it was a challenge – quite literally a leap of faith. The "Difficult is worth doing" blog and teaser spots introduced you to some of the jump team and the difficulties that they faced. This built conversations online.

'Channel 4 came to us with media space for a live three-minute spot. We took them through the strategy and our idea of skydivers creating formations. They took our original concept and had the idea of building the Honda logo live in freefall. We produced the main TV spot while they were producing the live jump. This is a great example of collaboration with new media opportunities. Releasing the live event just before the spot broke caused even more noise.' The live jump was successfully completed well within the narrow window of time available.

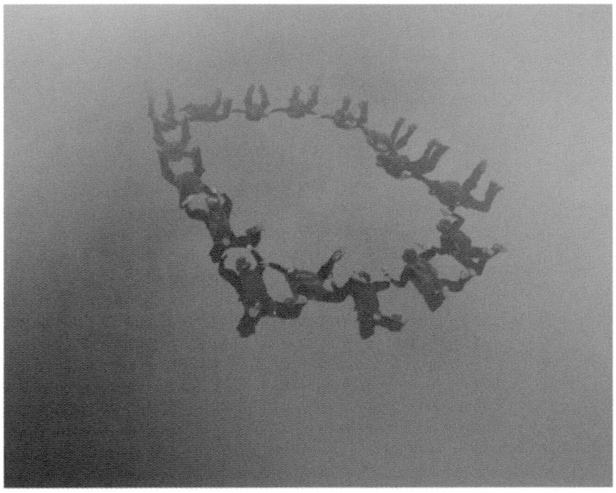

The skydivers launch themselves from the aeroplane in Spain before forming the word 'HONDA' in the UK's first live TV ad.

Interview: *Andy Fackrell*

Andy Fackrell is executive creative director at 180 Amsterdam, where he has worked on advertising projects as diverse as creating a book and a series of short films for adidas (page 80), and an interactive website that brought together BMW and Google Maps (page 40).

EW: **Would you agree that advertising is changing?**

AF: If you think about it, there were probably decades where TV commercials were the be all and end all. TV and radio was all anyone ever used to talk about. You don't even realize how traditional the advertising system was, how locked into these formulas. You used to come to work every morning knowing exactly what you'd do for what format. It was really cloistered. You have the perception that the most creative people in the world were just locked into these formulas. So it has opened up for any kind of thinking, any kind of creativity. There's a lot of people that say it's not as creative as it used to be because we can't make the big blockbuster commercials, and I think that's rubbish, there's so many more things people can do.

EW: **I think it's more creative now.**

AF: Sure. I don't think anyone knows quite how to define it. Non-traditional advertising works especially well with clients that don't have the money to spend. Nike spends much of their money on TV, so for adidas it was always 'How do we attack Nike in a different way, outside of spending a huge lot of money and making it look as if we're just aping their big TV commercial?' I think that's the problem though – you create another way of thinking and everybody else follows that way of thinking. You see it now, where everybody runs out and does a YouTube clip. Soon that gets boring and people want to move on to something else pretty quickly. It's interesting because there are new media things and, just like in TV commercials, there are techniques that people steal and then they replicate them and it gets tired. Those leaps happen every five to ten years, where someone does something significantly different to change people's opinions. But I don't know that the industry has changed that much. People pretend that it has, but we're still doing the same basic human interactions.

I still believe that people know what they're getting with a TV commercial, however. They accept it – there's a TV break and they like it, because they know there's no sneakiness involved with an ad break. That's the biggest thing for me – whether people will begin to think advertising is a bit insidious, whereas now they accept it for what it is. It's a weird psychological space that's there ... but if it's any good it goes beyond that, anyway.

EW: **Do you feel there's a freedom now to make more unusual work?**

AF: Yeah. The big question, though, is still how to reach a lot of people, or are you being selective? You have to ask that fundamental question before you start doing any project. Are you trying to blanket coverage and bring people in who aren't necessarily interested in what you've got to say, and get them through to liking you, changing their opinion? Or do you get people who've already been converted? I think that's the thing, people don't quite know. People have to decide what their intention is, in terms of a macro audience or a micro audience. So you're always going to have that debate – that a big 60-second TV ad is going to be seen by 60 million people, and you're going to convert an awful lot of those people, or you have a YouTube clip that you can get to 600,000 people, that you can target more precisely. There's a big debate and a lot of people are saying one's better than the other. The digital revolution has meant that people are saying 'That's the way to do it, target marketing', but then you have what you might call the old school people saying 'Wait a minute, the idea is to get it talked about on a mass scale', so I think that's the debate going on right now.

EW: **What do you see as the answer to that – a bit of both maybe?**

AF: A bit of both, because both have their values. Obviously if you could target every single person interested in your product and get 100 per cent returns off that and not spend the money on getting to them, well, it's just direct marketing isn't it? I think digital is just a more emotional way of saying direct marketing, bringing that element in from the mainstream into a direct marketing concept.

EW: **How about advertising agencies making products for clients? What do you think about that?**

AF: That's opened up completely now. You have to find other ways of making an income. When you work with a client so long, you become part of their fabric too, so you start doing other things for them.

It's more collaborative now with the client. The secret is to diversify the people we have in the agency now – that's the big difference as well, the spread of creatives you have. For instance, out of 20 or 30 people there are multi-specialists inside there. It's an advantage when different projects call on different resources, but it's a disadvantage when you have one brief that you want lots of different opinions on. Say with a big TV commercial – in the past you could put ten different teams on it and see who comes up with the big one. Now it's more like four of the teams are digital designers and, yeah, they can come up with a TV spot but their skillset is something else. So the traditional model of lots of teams working on the one big commercial of the year is a thing of the past – you can't afford that anymore. You have to diversify your staff to work on separate projects. The mix is much more interesting now, though – at the end of the year you might look and you've got a book, a short film, a play and a documentary.

EW: **Do you feel clients are getting this, or does it vary completely from client to client?**

AF: Oh, for sure. It's just the old adage that the client's got to be smarter than you are for you to get to the next stage with them, because if they're not prepared to stick their necks out one iota.... Concept research still dominates the business. Luckily we don't do that but you can still see the stuff that is, because it's all just watered down, pandered to, and trying to cut out all the potential mistakes in there, which are the things that make things good.

EW: **How about blogs – have they affected things?**

AF: If no one's writing about something then you obviously know that something is wrong. You can figure out if the campaign is working in a day or two, as opposed to getting groups together and finding out the results in two months' time – you can just see it right before your eyes. That's pretty cool too because you can react straight away to something. It's much more immediate – you get responses immediately, and because you don't have to buy media, you can post stuff, you can get stuff out as quick as you like, as quick as anyone can make it. That's the exciting bit – being faster at getting stuff done, not having these long lead times of media bookings.

You have a chance to influence everything – you can be your own PR if you want. You can create a story about your campaign yourself – you don't have to rely on everyone else. I think that's what advertising people are more skilled at now, probably self-promotion has let them get that way! But now they understand how they can work promotion around what they've just done and get it talked about.

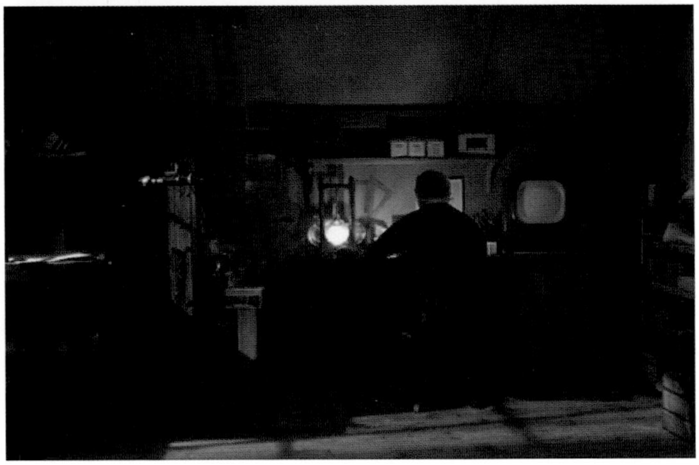

Stills from the stop motion animation documenting the story of the inventor of the adidas shoe, Adi Dassler.

180 Amsterdam/180 LA

adidas Originals: Celebrate Originality

To launch the adidas Originals collection, 180 Amsterdam and 180 LA created the Celebrate Originality campaign, which began with a charming stop motion animation documenting the story of shoemaker Adi Dassler. Dassler created the adidas brand in Germany in 1936, when he created a pair of running shoes for Jesse Owens for the Olympics that year. The film was made available to view on the adidas website, alongside an interactive section allowing visitors to explore Dassler's workshop online.

This was followed by further short films from 180 Amsterdam, which showed the achingly hip everyday lives of young creative talents (and adidas fans), including US DJ and producer Theo Parrish and Amélie, a Frenchwoman living in Berlin. Continuing in this vein, the agency then made *The Superstar*, a film in which two groups of artists from the East and West Coasts of America are pitted against one another. Each group was challenged to customize a giant-size pair of adidas Superstar trainers – the right shoe went to the East Coast contenders and the left to the West. They were given only three days to complete their work before both shoes were sent to Venice Beach, LA, by truck, where they were reunited. The entire artistic venture was made into a three-minute short film, which was then shown online.

adidas

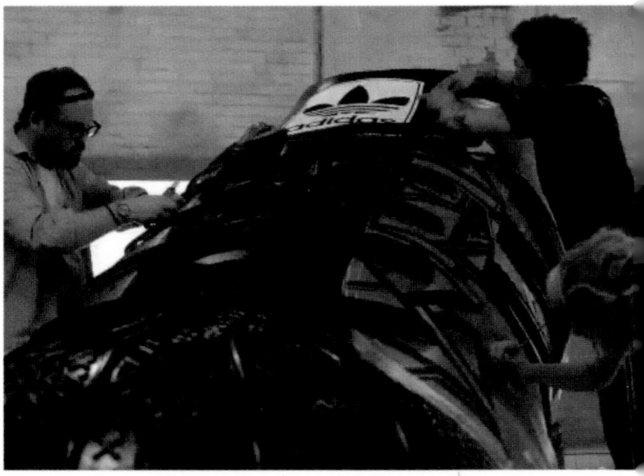
adidas

Stills from *The Superstar*, a film that saw two groups of artists challenged to customize a giant-size pair of adidas Superstar trainers.

Wieden + Kennedy China

Nike: *Dare*

Wieden + Kennedy China created the *Dare* documentary for Nike as part of the brand's marketing campaign for the 2008 Beijing Olympic Games. *Dare*, which is 30 minutes long, tackles an unusual subject for a sports brand: failure. It tells the story of the 1984 Olympic Games, when China sent a national team to the games for the first time, and the world record holder in the high jump, Zhu Jianhua, was faced with the difficult decision of whether to sacrifice the silver medal in order to attempt to win the gold. He came away with bronze. Fear of failure is a large problem for participation in sport in China, making a documentary where athletes talk openly about defeat particularly unusual. Ultimately the film salutes Zhu Jianhua's bravery in taking risks in the pursuit of glory. The *Dare* documentary premiered at an event in Beijing and was then screened on CCTV (China's main TV station) and seven other Chinese channels.

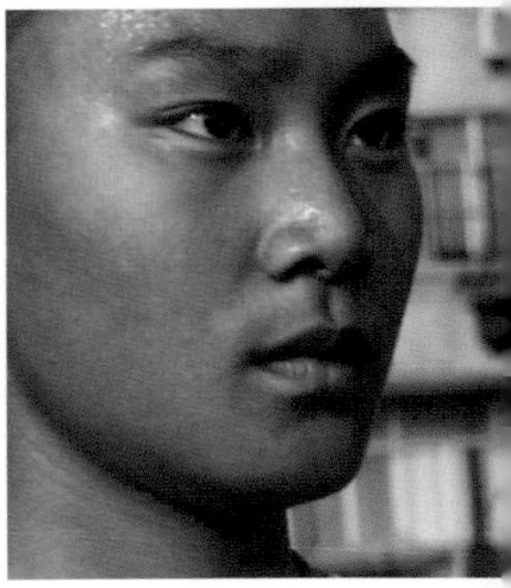

'Consumers aren't walking around talking about great branded content. They're talking about TV shows, or music videos or video games or websites or uploaded videos.'

Kevin Proudfoot, co-creative director, Wieden + Kennedy New York

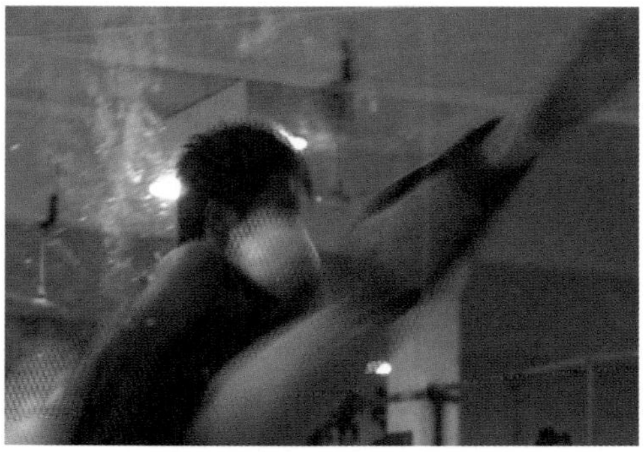

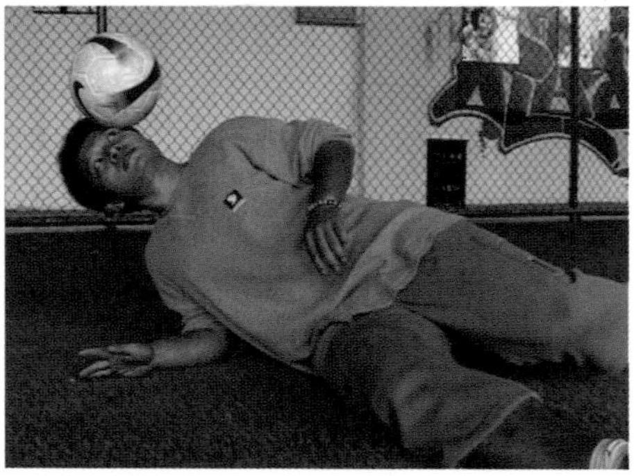

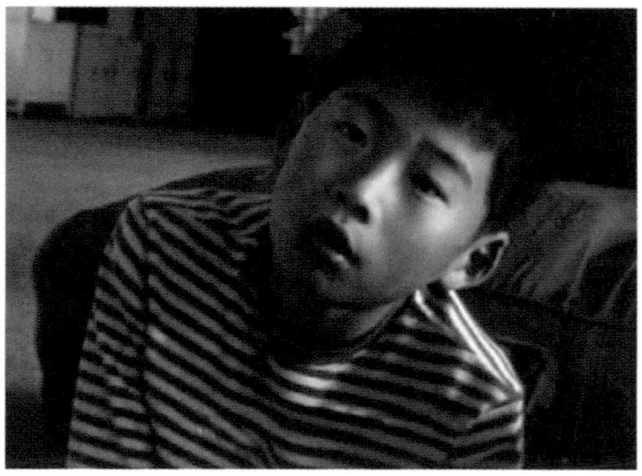

Ogilvy & Mather, Toronto

Dove: *Evolution*

The Dove *Evolution* film uses time-lapse footage to show how an averagely pretty model is turned into a billboard pin-up by the use of hair and make-up and later by retouching in Photoshop. The final photograph of the girl looks significantly different from the original, and the film ends with the tagline 'No wonder our perception of beauty is distorted'. Viewers are then directed to take part in the Dove Real Beauty Workshops for Girls via www.campaignforrealbeauty.ca.

The film was created to be viewed online, and had a low budget. 'I wanted the girl to look as bad as possible in the beginning, so shooting on video with ambient sound and poor lighting was conceptualized to not only fit within our budget, but to enhance the video,' says Tim Piper, writer and co-director of the film. 'Time-lapse footage is always interesting. So are before and after images of people. This concept was an excuse to merge the two and create not only a positive message, but a piece of eye candy that resembles art more than advertising.'

Jeh United, Bangkok

Smooth E: *Love Story*

Love Story, a four-part tongue-in-cheek romantic drama based around facial cleaning product Smooth E, was screened in serial form every two weeks on two of Thailand's most popular TV channels. Each new episode was supported by poster, newspaper and radio ads. The series depicts a tale of unrequited love. Its heroine, Joom, is a tomboy, who tries to attract the attention of the local hunk, Ake. Helping her on her quest is the local pharmacist, who, in a sequence interspersed with some deliberately comical product placement shots, is shown giving Joom a makeover with the help of Smooth E cream. Joom wins Ake's heart before realizing that her true love is actually Yae, her best friend whom she had previously overlooked. Love blossoms after Yae defends her from a gang of attackers and the campaign ends with the two falling in love.

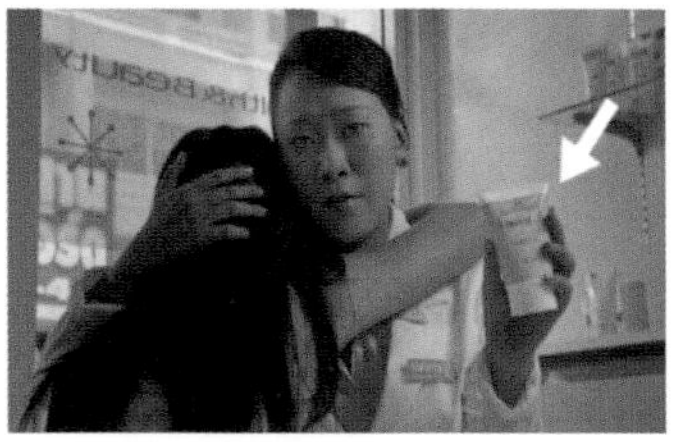

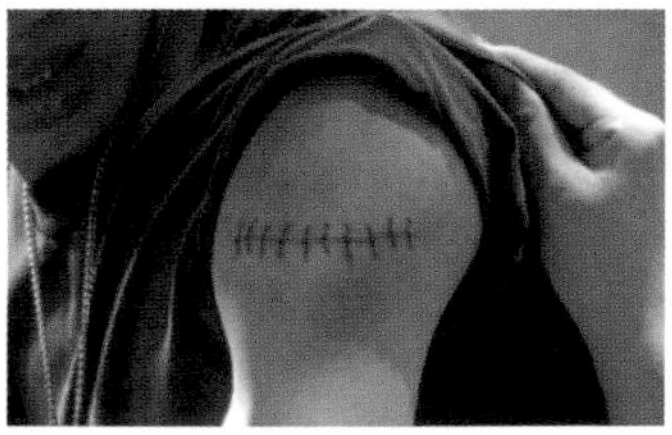

Crispin Porter + Bogusky, USA

Burger King: Whopper Freakout

Crispin Porter + Bogusky deftly demonstrated Burger King fans' brand loyalty in this eight-minute viral, which can be viewed at www.whopperfreakout.com. The film shows customers at an outlet of the fast food restaurant attempting to order a Whopper sandwich, only to be told that the Whopper was no longer available and had been discontinued forever. This leads to the 'freakout' of the campaign's title, all of which is captured on hidden cameras. The film features various amusing corporate moments, such as one customer being told that the burger was 'too popular, the sandwich got too big for the menu', and another being offered a hand-signed photo of Burger King character 'The King' as compensation. It also sees several customers explaining how much the Whopper means in their lives, alongside a lot of angrier responses to the sandwich's removal. Later in the film, customers were given burgers from competitors instead of Whopper sandwiches and the mayhem continued. Finally though, the film ends with 'The King' appearing in the restaurant and placating irate customers by giving them their beloved Whopper sandwich.

BURGER KING
[LAS VEGAS, NV - 11/02/07]

[ACTUAL CUSTOMERS ON HIDDEN CAMERA]

[ACTUAL CUSTOMERS ON HIDDEN CAMERA]

WHOPPERFREAKOUT.COM

WHOPPERFREAKOUT.COM

PERFECTION!
DOUBLE WHOPPER WITH CHEESE
[ACTUAL CUSTOMERS ON HIDDEN CAMERA]

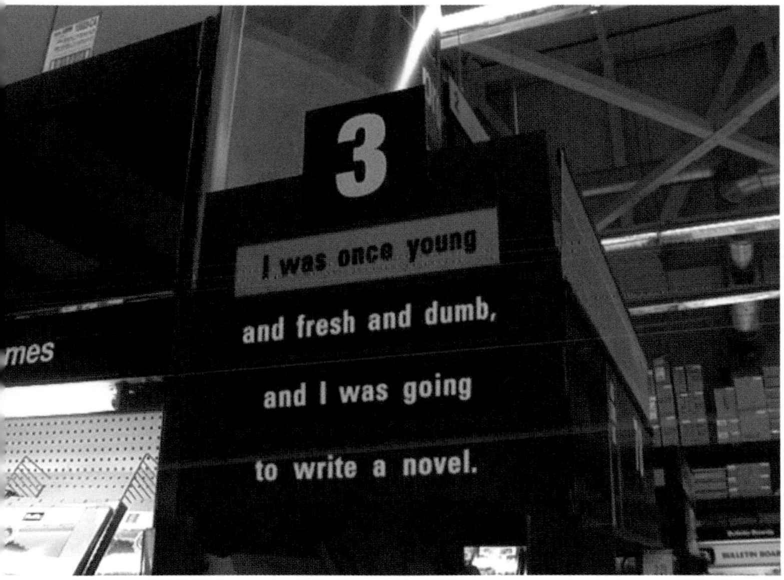
3
I was once young
and fresh and dumb,
and I was going
to write a novel.

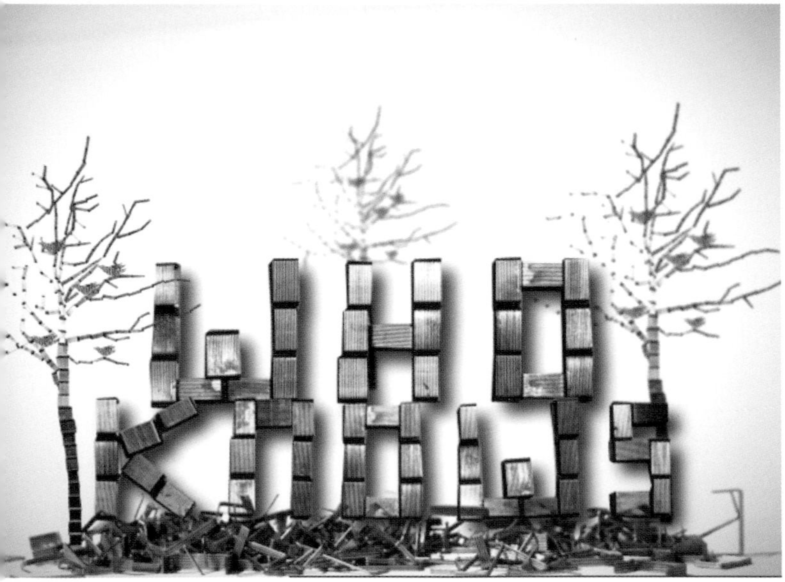

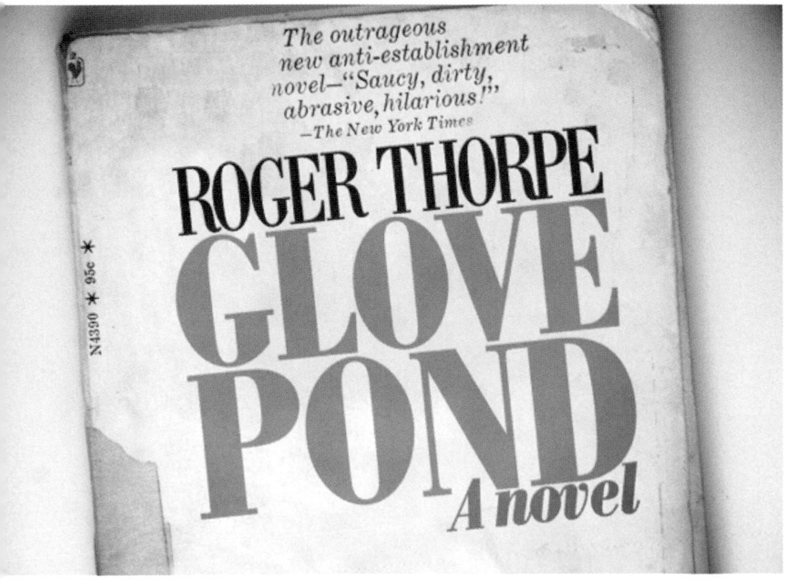
The outrageous
new anti-establishment
novel—"Saucy, dirty,
abrasive, hilarious!"
—The New York Times
ROGER THORPE
GLOVE
POND
A novel
N4390 ★ 95c ★

Crush, Toronto

Random House Canada: *The Gum Thief*

Short film is rarely used to promote a new book release but this is the approach taken by Random House Canada for the launch of Douglas Coupland's novel, *The Gum Thief*, described by the publisher as 'a story of love and looming apocalypse set in the aisles of an office supply superstore'. Toronto-based production company Crush created nine short clips to bring sections of the novel to life. The films were all released on the internet (www.crushinc.com/gumthief/) and feature narration by Douglas Coupland himself. 'We felt that the nature of the narrative lent itself to a less traditional form, and thought Doug's readers would be visually sophisticated and net savvy enough to appreciate this approach,' explains Crush's managing director/ creative director Gary Thomas. 'The narrative is basically divided into the journal entries of Roger, a 40-ish stationery store employee, the correspondence of Bethany, his 20-something co-worker, and *Glove Pond*, the novel-within-a-novel that Roger is writing. We wanted to do a series of short pieces focusing on the text of the novel. No attempt at a cheesy dramatization, no author interview, just the text and Doug's deadpan narration. We also felt that each stream should feel like it had been done by the characters themselves.'

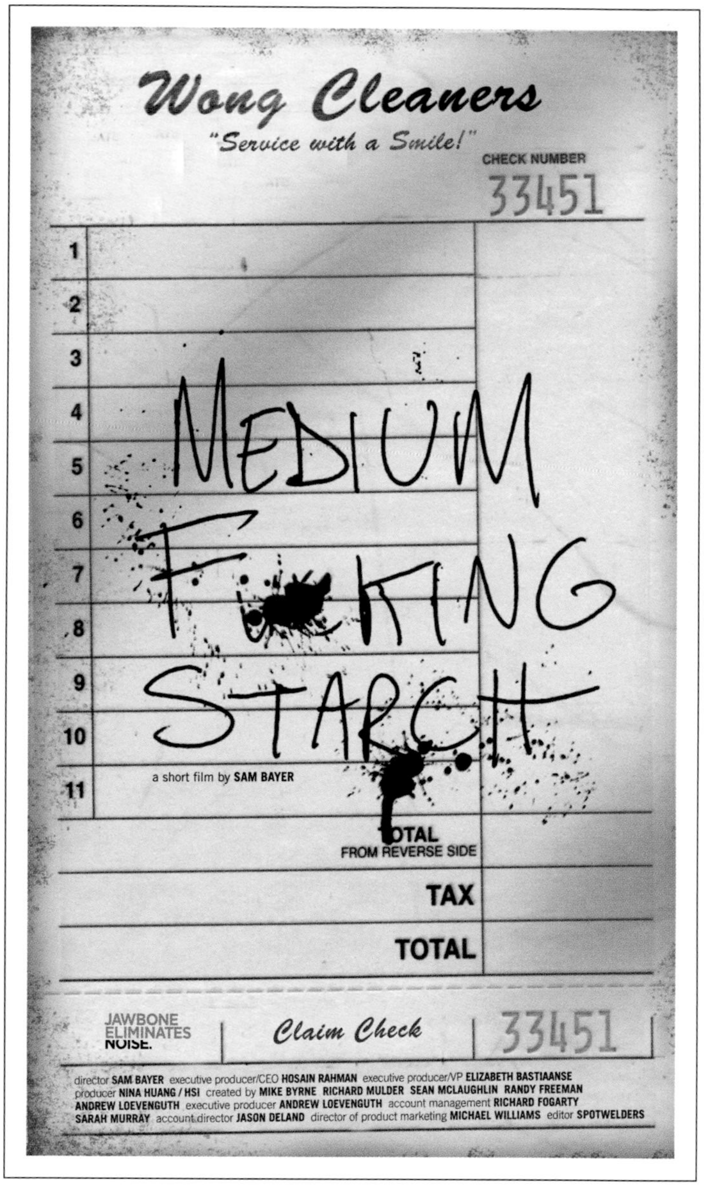

Wong Cleaners
"Service with a Smile!"
CHECK NUMBER
33451
1
2
3
4
5
6
7
8
9
10
11
MEDIUM
F KING
STARCH
a short film by SAM BAYER
TOTAL
FROM REVERSE SIDE
TAX
TOTAL
JAWBONE ELIMINATES NOISE.
Claim Check
33451
director SAM BAYER executive producer/CEO HOSAIN RAHMAN executive producer/VP ELIZABETH BASTIAANSE
producer NINA HUANG / HSI created by MIKE BYRNE RICHARD MULDER SEAN MCLAUGHLIN RANDY FREEMAN
ANDREW LOEVENGUTH executive producer ANDREW LOEVENGUTH account management RICHARD FOGARTY
SARAH MURRAY account director JASON DELAND director of product marketing MICHAEL WILLIAMS editor SPOTWELDERS

Anomaly, New York

Aliph: Jawbone

Mobile phone headsets have never been particularly cool. Anomaly intended to reverse this image with the Jawbone headset, in terms of both the product itself and the way that it was advertised. The company worked with acclaimed designer Yves Béhar to create a sleek Bluetooth headset for Aliph, which would be genuinely desirable to own. It then promoted it in an innovative way by creating several witty short films, which were released online. The shorts emphasize, in amusing and risqué fashion (thereby making them impossible to screen as TV ads), the way in which the Jawbone eliminates noise. The films have received millions of hits via YouTube.

JAWBONE PRESENTS
A SHORT FILM BY SAM BAYER
SOUP DU JOUR
JAWBONE
ELIMINATES

JAWBONE PRESENTS
BOO
BOO
A SHORT FILM BY SAM BAYER
JAWBONE
ELIMINATES
NOISE.

Above: Posters advertising the Jawbone short films. **Below:** Images from the website hosting the Jawbone short films.

JAWBONE
EARWEAR
ELIMINATES
BOO
BOO

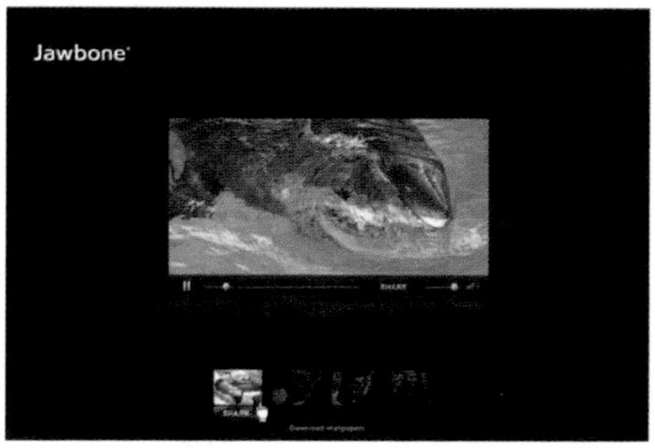
Jawbone

Mother, London

Eurostar: *Somers Town*

Somers Town is a feature length film directed by acclaimed UK director Shane Meadows. A gritty tale of urban life and friendship set on the streets near King's Cross in London, it fits well into Meadows's oeuvre, which includes films such as *This Is England* (2006) and *Dead Man's Shoes* (2004). What sets *Somers Town* apart, however, is the way in which it was developed and funded. The film was the first release from Mother advertising agency's film and entertainment division, Mother Vision, and was funded by Eurostar as part of the promotion for the launch of the UK's first high speed rail service. The service runs from St Pancras station, which reopened at the time of the launch.

What is most surprising is that the film has no overt Eurostar branding, although the train service from London to Paris plays a central role in the story-line, and the film is set near St Pancras, with the station making regular appearances. Yet, unusually, the word 'Eurostar' is not mentioned once and there are no logos to be seen. Eurostar and Mother also gave Meadows free reign to make the film that he wanted. 'They were interested in marking the occasion [of the launch of the rail service] with a piece of communication that had more longevity than perhaps a traditional ad campaign, something that could be enjoyed long after the station opened,' says Robert Saville, co-founding partner and creative director, Mother.

TERRY HENRY
14

RAZOR
WIRE

'Instead of filling the gaps in between the entertainment that people watch, brands have the opportunity to create the entertainment itself. If we can tell genuinely entertaining stories that are authentic to the brand's core values, then it's good news for everyone – brands find an audience, and that audience is entertained.'

Robert Saville, co-founding partner and creative director, Mother

Interview: Chris Kyle

Chris Kyle is vice president of Global Brand Communications at adidas. He worked on the Impossible is Nothing campaign, which incorporated TV and print advertising, and on a series of short films and a book, *Power Within* (page 96).

EW: **Do you feel that advertising is changing – is it important now to approach consumers on a number of different platforms?**

CK: Advertising isn't really the thing that's changing. The communication mix you need to be successful is what's evolving and getting more complex. We're a long way removed from when a broadcast and print campaign, combined with a retail effort, was all you needed. There are many more opportunities to consider, especially in the digital world, and they offer a much more personalized, one-to-one opportunity than the media of old. So, yes, a range of platforms is needed, but it's about finding the right balance. On the one hand, you need a plan that drives awareness through the broad and mass media, but you also need to get close to your consumers where you can talk to them personally and your product can be a meaningful part of the conversation.

EW: **Has your relationship with advertising agencies changed with these developments? Has it affected which agencies you choose to work with?**

CK: Yes, our relationship with 'advertising agencies' has certainly changed. Simply put, we don't need an advertising-focused agency anymore. We need a marketing agency that can think strategically and creatively, and deliver ideas that work across all channels. That's a much bigger challenge than making an ad campaign. It comes with a higher level of partnership and brand understanding and reliance on the agency to deliver great ideas. All things then spring from this starting point.

EW: **How important is it for adidas to create a dialogue with consumers, and to encourage them to interact directly with the brand?**

CK: Consumer interaction is extremely important, especially for a brand that wants to have a strong, ongoing relationship with its consumers. Consumer interaction, whether it's at retail level, online, at events or anywhere else, pulls people closer to the brand. It gives the brand a face and personality and helps consumers understand what makes it different and special. If brand building 20 years ago was about getting the name out there and giving a sense of the brand attitude through advertising, it's now about letting people in, getting them involved and asking them to come closer than ever before.

EW: **How do you understand the term 'branded content'?**

CK: Here's my understanding of 'good' branded content. It should have three factors. First, it should be something unique, something that only one brand has the ability to deliver (either through access, assets or knowledge). Second, it needs to create a meaningful role for the product or brand. And third, it needs to be good content. Everyone is creating something, so it needs to meet all the usual criteria of being entertaining and relevant and able to drive maximum interest. In other words, it needs to be of value to the audience, not just to the brand.

EW: **Do you think adidas is likely to increase its multi-platform advertising, or is TV/print still seen as the most important way of reaching consumers?**

CK: adidas will continue to increase its multi-platform communication as long as new media presents new and meaningful consumer connections. It's not about expanding for the sake of it; it's about evolving our plans as consumer habits and media opportunities change. For the time being, television and print continue to have important roles. Film is still massively successful in delivering an emotional, engaging message. Film content can now be in more places than ever before (broadcast, digital, retail, events etc.) but broadcast still delivers the widest and most immediate effect. Print has advantages and disadvantages but still offers impact in a specific environment against a fairly broad audience. The bottom line is that neither broadcast or print is disappearing, they are just taking on more specific roles in a broader communication mix.

'In an increasingly high-speed and disposable world we felt that we should make a tangible object from this campaign. Something that could be kept and revisited at your own pace over time. After word and mouth, books are the oldest way of saving ideas, thoughts and stories – perhaps still the most valued and in this case certainly the most relevant.'

Julian Wade, design director, 180 Amsterdam

Circle of Life
Jonah Lomu

180 Amsterdam

adidas: *Power Within*

180 Amsterdam published the *Power Within* book as part of an ad campaign for adidas in which various athletes, including Jonah Lomu and David Beckham, 'visualize their own personal journeys from nothing to the impossible' through paintings. The ads had an intimate feel and this extended to the book, which contains images and transcripts from the campaign, as well as photographs of the finished artworks. With good art direction and design, and fulfilling content, the book was an unusual record of the ads, as well as a product in its own right (it wasn't sold, but was used as a promotional tool by 180 Amsterdam).

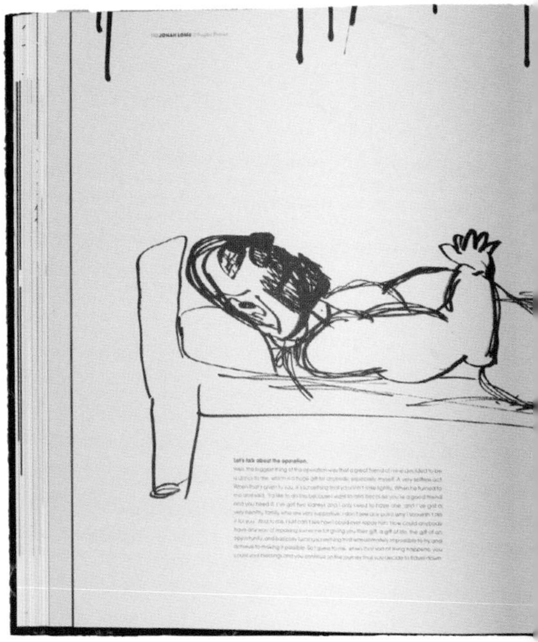

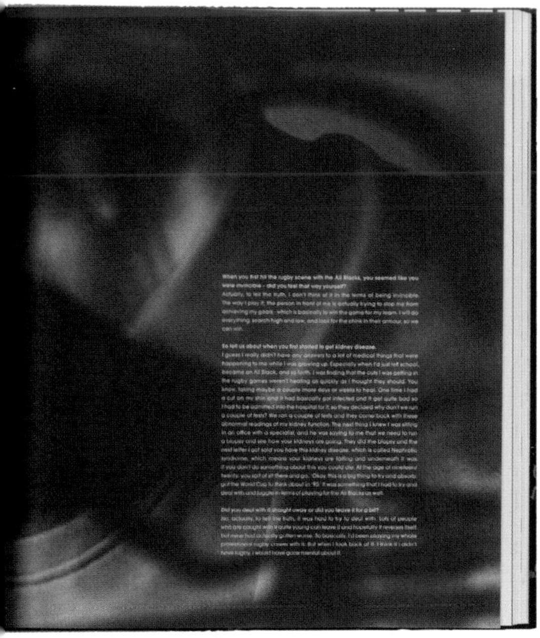

Belief
David Beckham
Footballer – National Team Captain 2000 – 2006
England

If man can step on the moon,
I can step on a rugby field again."
06 Nov 2006

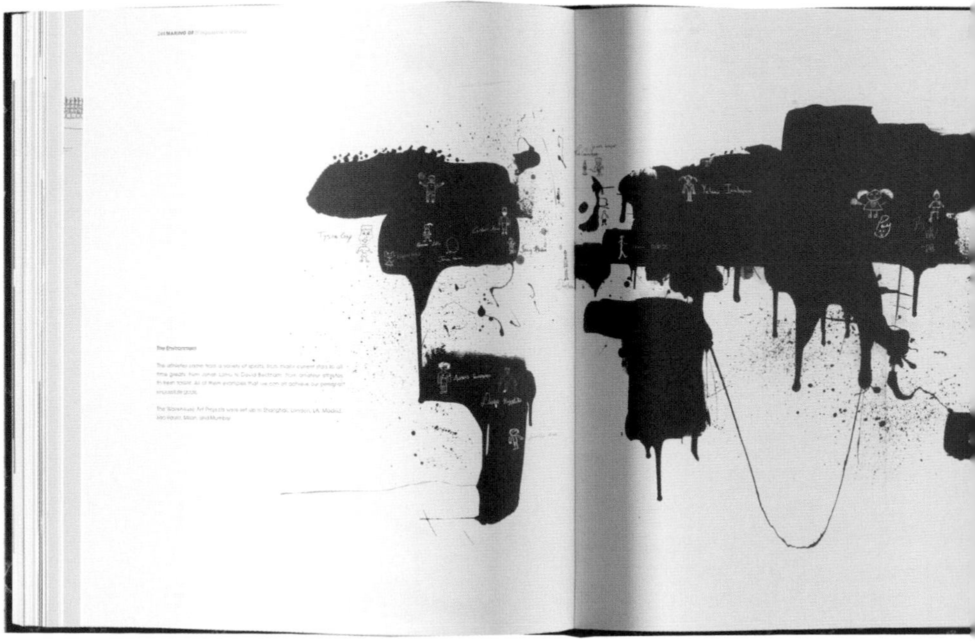

KesselsKramer, Amsterdam

Hans Brinker: Budget Hotel Collection

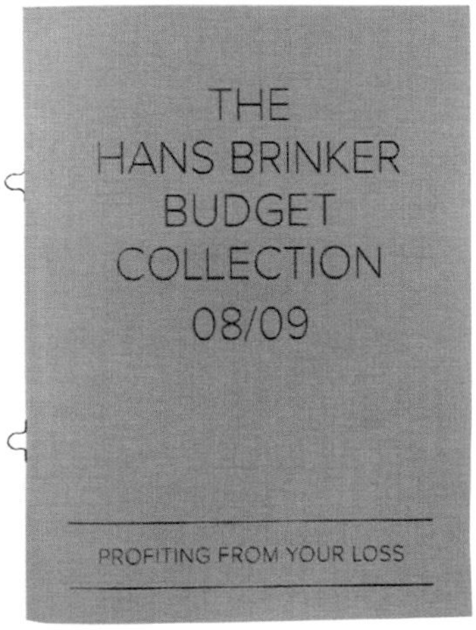
THE
HANS BRINKER
BUDGET
COLLECTION
08/09
PROFITING FROM YOUR LOSS

In its previous advertising for the Hans Brinker Budget Hotel in Amsterdam, KesselsKramer had established a satirical tone with a series of ads that emphasized the 'budget' nature of the hotel and all that this could entail. This humorous style is continued in the Hans Brinker Budget Hotel Collection. The Collection is drawn from the lost and found office of the hotel, where numerous abandoned items, including teddy bears, sleeping bags and T-shirts, are placed. Instead of attempting to trace the owners of these sad items, KesselsKramer has turned them into a set of designer objects – The Hans Brinker Budget Hotel Collection. Thus a teddy bear becomes a stylish winter hat, the ragged old sleeping bag becomes a seat, and so on. Before-and-after shots of the items are all illustrated in a book of the Collection.

LOST
A gang of lonely stuffed animals
Forgotten under beds, first and third floors

FOUND
A warm and attractive faux fur hat
Includes matching scarf for added protection against the elements

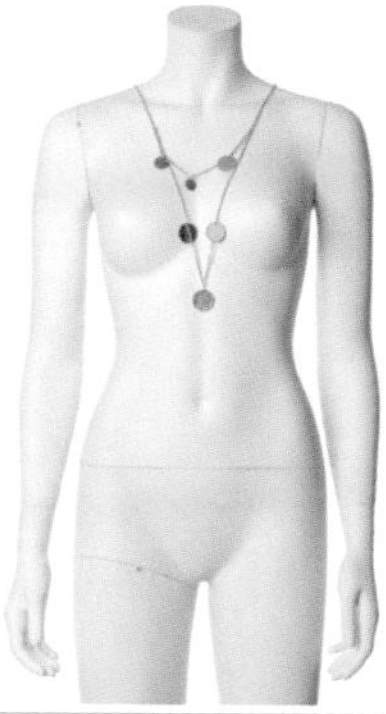

LOST
Various buttons and pieces of currency, totaling roughly 1,37 €
Scattered in multiple nooks and crannies, all floors

FOUND
A lushly detailed, multi-stranded necklace
Can be doubled or worn long depending on occasion and preference

Wu Tang

Killer Bees

LOST
Stretched and faded T-shirts
Stuffed next to toilets, behind doors, in sinks, all floors

FOUND
Lightweight drawstring backpacks
Each bag features decorative bottom corner brass grommets for reinforcement

LOST
A dank and dingy sleeping bag
Rolled up in the back of a locker, second floor

FOUND
A one-of-a-kind fabric foot stool
Durable foam interior makes for a sturdy, yet mobile piece of furniture

LOST
Twenty-five individual socks
Dropped in hallways, all floors

FOUND
A multi-colored, multi-layered scarf
Made from 40% Cotton, 39% Polyester, 18% Nylon, 2% Spandex, 1% Viscose

KesselsKramer, Amsterdam

Amsterdam Partners: I Amsterdam

I Amsterdam was a photography exhibition devised by the ad agency KesselsKramer (in conjunction with Amsterdam Partners) as a promotion for the city of Amsterdam. Twenty well-known photographers, who were either Amsterdammers or Amsterdam-based, were commissioned to capture the city from their own perspectives, resulting in a personal and diverse portrait of contemporary Amsterdam.

The exhibition opened initially at the FOAM photography museum in Amsterdam before travelling the world, proving a subtle promotion for the city as a place to live and work. A 308-page book of the exhibition was also published, and the motto 'I Amsterdam' has continued to be used in promotion of the city.

I amste

I amste

Iam®

I amsterdam®

Iam®

I amsterdam®

'For an advertiser and his agency, there are two ways of getting noticed: one is to jostle and shove, to be persistent, even unsubtle and invasive. The advertiser who takes this path will quickly be deemed tiresome, to be avoided at all costs. The other is to prove that there was every good reason for the advertising to bother you. Because it's interesting, because you enjoy it, because it makes you laugh. This is obviously the kind of advertising we stand for.'

Rémi Babinet, founder and chairman, BETC Euro RSCG

Chapter Three: Ambient

Ambient, or guerrilla, advertising is used to target a local audience in an imaginative, eye-catching way. Campaigns usually involve some interaction with the audience, or present an event that will get everybody (and usually the media) talking about them. While ambient advertising may have a small target audience, it can be one of the most effective marketing techniques, and is increasingly favoured by brands. Some of the best recent examples of this type of advertising are shown in this chapter.

Tiger
onitsukatiger.com
CELEBRATING 60 YEARS
Onitsuka
Tiger
MADE OF JAPAN

Amsterdam Worldwide

Onitsuka Tiger: Made of Japan

Amsterdam Worldwide created a series of sculptures as part of its advertising for Japanese footwear brand Onitsuka Tiger. All the sculptures feature huge versions of the brand's shoes, but constructed from unexpected materials that all reflect Japan, hence the 'Made of Japan' campaign title. The first, created in 2007, saw a Fabre 74 style of shoe turned into a 1.5-metre (5-foot) long sculpture constructed from various Japanese iconic items such as sushi, origami, urban vinyl toys, noodles and chopsticks, as well as koi carp. In 2008, Amsterdam Worldwide created a shoe sculpture inspired by Tokyo's cityscape, which included highways with cars, high-rise buildings and even a replica of Tokyo's Narita Airport in the tongue. In 2009, for Onitsuka Tiger's sixtieth birthday, the agency created a diorama based on the Asian legend of the Zodiac Race. The sculptures have all featured in print and TV campaigns for the brand, and have been exhibited at venues around the world.

onitsukatiger.com
MADE OF JAPAN
Onitsuka
Tiger

MADE OF JAPAN
Onitsuka
Tiger

Clockwise from far left: The Onitsuka Tiger sculptures as they appeared in press campaigns for the shoe brand in 2009, 2008 and 2007.

'We wanted the brand to be in people's minds, in videos, on YouTube, out in the street.'

Carlos Bayala, creative director and partner, Madre

Madre, Buenos Aires

Porta Hnos: 1882

To launch 1882, a new brand of the Italian alcoholic drink Fernet, in Argentina, Madre agency created a complex multimedia campaign, which included 12 cryptic TV spots and outdoor ads, plus a teaser campaign featuring a number of mysterious installations, including one of inflatable dolphins. 'The idea was to get people talking about the number 1882, without knowing what it represents,' says Madre creative director and partner Carlos Bayala about the dolphins, which were installed in the Argentinian province of Córdoba. 'The dolphins became the talk of the town, media, news shows and blogs. They were there for two and a half days, and then we gave away each dolphin to people who queued for hours to get them. After that we launched our outdoor and TV campaigns, but the kick-off had been made and 1882 was already out there.'

The Partners, London

The National Gallery, London: The Grand Tour

Design and brand consultancy The Partners created The Grand Tour to promote the permanent collection of the National Gallery, London. Framed reproductions of some of the gallery's best-loved masterpieces, including paintings by Caravaggio and Constable, were placed around the streets of London. A website (www.thegrandtour.org.uk) designed by Digit provided downloadable maps and audio guides so that users could tour the collection, viewing the 'paintings' in their unlikely new habitats. With some thoughtful placement of the reproductions in settings relevant to the scenes depicted in the paintings, the collection felt newly fresh and exciting in an urban context.

Clockwise from bottom far left:
Paintings by Gainsborough, Rubens, Holbein, Caravaggio, Bronzino, Van Gogh and Drouais as they appeared in The Grand Tour in London.

TANNING
WAXING
dermalogica
NAILS

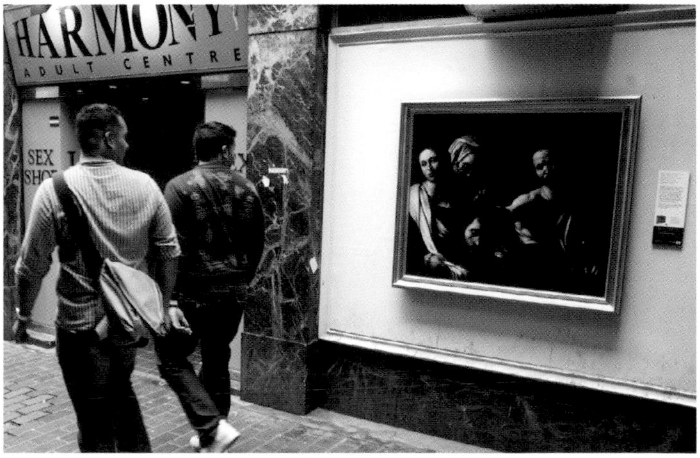
HARMONY
ADULT CENTRE
SEX

Clemenger BBDO, Wellington

The New Zealand Netherlands Foundation: World Press Photo

To promote the arrival of the World Press Photo exhibition (an exhibition of the most prestigious press photography in the world) at the New Zealand Netherlands Foundation, Clemenger BBDO took an unusual approach with the limited budget available. The agency wrote to 74 world leaders inviting them to attend the exhibition and ran a teaser press campaign explaining why. Replies came in, declining the invitation, and the agency placed the actual letters received within poster displays around Wellington, where they could be read by the public. The campaign became an exhibition in itself and the agency's follow-up calls were used as viral and radio spots. The letters received coverage in the national press and TV and led to record attendance at the show, making it the most successful World Press Photo exhibition ever held in New Zealand.

"MAJOR COMBAT OPERATIONS IN IRAQ HAVE ENDED"
GEORGE W. BUSH, MAY 2003
We're inviting him to see this.
WORLD PRESS PHOTO

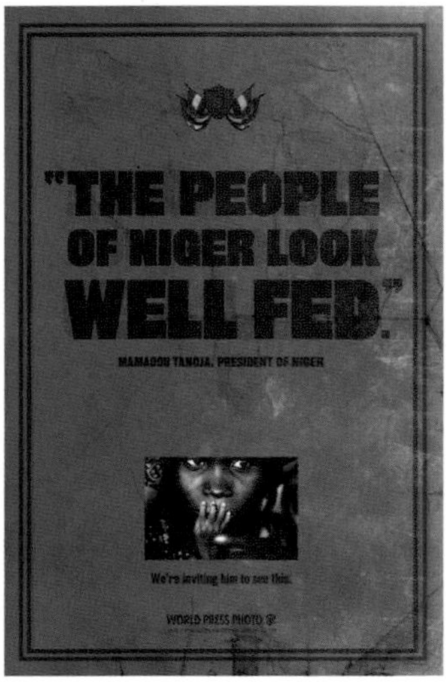
"THE PEOPLE OF NIGER LOOK WELL FED."
MAMADOU TANDJA, PRESIDENT OF NIGER
We're inviting him to see this.
WORLD PRESS PHOTO

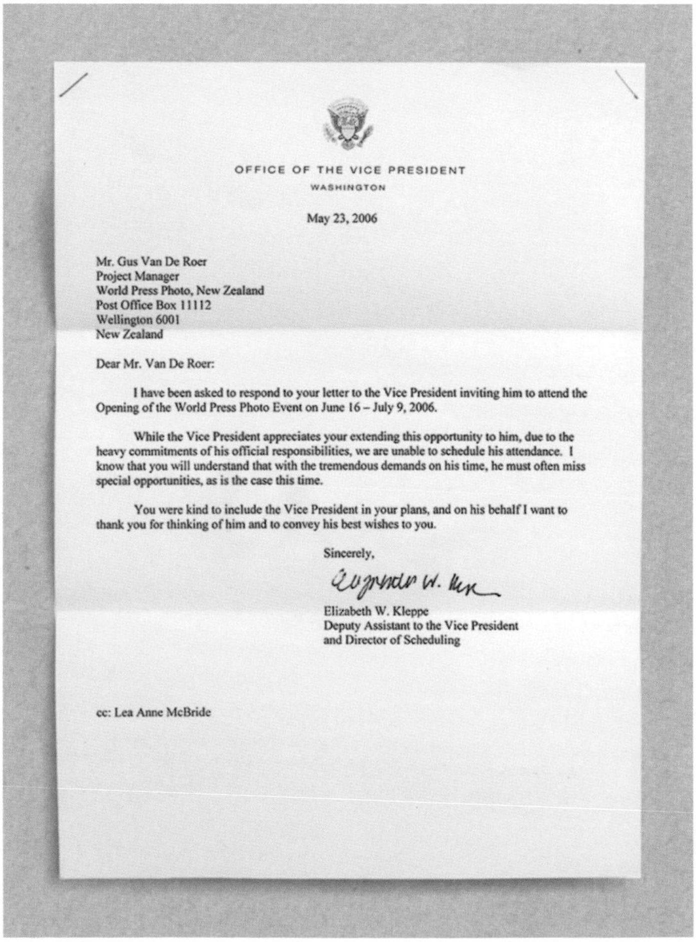

OFFICE OF THE VICE PRESIDENT
WASHINGTON

May 23, 2006

Mr. Gus Van De Roer
Project Manager
World Press Photo, New Zealand
Post Office Box 11112
Wellington 6001
New Zealand

Dear Mr. Van De Roer:

I have been asked to respond to your letter to the Vice President inviting him to attend the Opening of the World Press Photo Event on June 16 – July 9, 2006.

While the Vice President appreciates your extending this opportunity to him, due to the heavy commitments of his official responsibilities, we are unable to schedule his attendance. I know that you will understand that with the tremendous demands on his time, he must often miss special opportunities, as is the case this time.

You were kind to include the Vice President in your plans, and on his behalf I want to thank you for thinking of him and to convey his best wishes to you.

Sincerely,

Elizabeth W. Kleppe
Deputy Assistant to the Vice President
and Director of Scheduling

cc: Lea Anne McBride

We invited
Dick Cheney to
our exhibition.
Here's the response.
See the photos they should be seeing.
WORLD PRESS PHOTO
SHEL

From far left: Images from teaser press campaign; Letter received from Dick Cheney in response to the invitation to visit the exhibition; Dick Cheney letter in situ on poster display in Wellington; Tony Blair letter featured in poster display.

We invited
Tony Blair to our
exhibition.
This came back.
See the photos they should be seeing.

Interview: Robert Saville

Robert Saville is co-founding partner and creative director at Mother advertising agency in London. Mother has created advertising for Orange, Pimm's and Channel Five, amongst many others. It has a film/book arm, Mother Vision, which made *Somers Town*, backed by Eurostar (page 90), and a comics arm, Mother Comics, which has created a series of graphic novels (page 196).

EW: **How do you think things in advertising have changed since you started?**

RS: It's always a difficult question, isn't it ... has it changed? I suppose it has, and I suppose some quite significant structural and social changes are happening. I think if you analyse them, you'll be able to identify them in very specific terms, and I'm sure there are people within agencies all over the world who are doing exactly that. I've never seen it that way though, because I think that change is incremental.

People have started to question almost everything that they've always believed was true, which is ridiculous. There's such panic among clients and creative communications communities that they've started thinking that posters don't work, that a person can't be interested or beguiled or captured by something that's good on a poster site, that everyone's rushing headlong towards the digital revolution, and suddenly TV is rubbish and radio doesn't make any sense. Everything is very reactive and reactionary because the nature of the change is invidious, and therefore for large organizations it comes at them in a really uncomfortable way because they are structured to work against systems. Mother never did that; we've only ever made it up as we've gone along.

When we started the agency, it was really about a group of people, including clients and some design people and some PR people and some media specialists, sitting around a table seeing how you might get to change people's attitudes.... Our structure has always been about greeting each problem as it comes and trying to be conscious of what we may or may not do to solve the problem. So I don't really acknowledge or think about major tectonic shifts in how communication works. I think it's the same thing it always was, which is that people need to be persuaded, people don't want to give you their time willingly –

and never did. In the past they'd pick their nose and go and make a cup of tea, now they press the fast forward button. People don't do stuff they don't want to do – even in the digital environment. Just because its 'gone digital' and something happens in a digital framework, if it isn't any good, you don't do it; in fact you definitely don't do it because you don't have to. So that contract, which always existed, still exists, and I think people knew that contract years ago.

If you look at the classic advertising creative people, whether they're the Charles Saatchis or the John Websters or the David Abbotts, everything they did was about engagement, and capturing people's imagination and rewarding them. So I don't think in that sense the thing has changed, I just think it's come as a surprise to some structures, and they've done exactly the wrong thing, which is swing radically in a completely different direction.... We still do work that looks as if it was made 40 years ago. Where John Webster did the Cresta Bear or Smash Martians, we do Alan Monkey [for ITV Digital] or Harry Fitzgibbon-Simms [for Pimm's] ... as the supposed *enfant terribles* of British advertising we tend to do quite traditional stuff.

EW: **But you are also doing things like Mother Comics, Mother Vision and so on...**

RS: Again, I don't think that's necessarily different. The job of an advertising agency has to be the same as a brand, which is to encourage the right kind of people to want to be here, whether they be clients or whether they be creative people. So part of the encouragement of keeping and encouraging creativity in an organization has to be to find a framework where people can express their creativity. Salman Rushdie worked in advertising at one point, so did Ridley Scott, so did Alan Parker.... Our job really is to try and make sure that people are able to explore their creativity in different ways, sometimes on their own behalf, to pursue their dream of writing a book, or making a comic or creating an event, and sometimes in association with clients. And clients want to know that they've got access to those people, so they want to find a place which is sympathetic to making sure that there's the right environment for those people to come, because creativity has phenomenal value.

So, Mother Vision, which makes films and TV programmes and books, is sort of what we've always been doing. We've formalized it a bit because we want to put a bit of a rocket behind it, but I don't think it's different from CDP when Ridley Scott and Alan Parker were directing their stuff and then making movies. They just had to leave to go and do those things and I want to create an environment where they don't necessarily have to leave. The brand can stretch far enough.

EW: **That's quite a shift though, to do them without having to leave.**

RS: Yeah, I think so. It is a shift, but it isn't a shift in the creative psyche. Creatively oriented people like finding different places for their creativity and, as they get older, they like finding deeper and longer forms, and stuff that they have more control over. I believe if you can create an environment where they can do that and do other things as well, then everybody benefits, because ultimately commerce needs to find the best ways of engaging consumers in conversations with their brands. Yes, there are going to be new opportunities and new places where they can do those things, because there is a change in the media landscape, but, most importantly, it's going to be about where the right people are – that is what will help them to realize those things. That's what we're doing, but in quite a loose way. There are a lot of people who have big divisions doing branded content, I'm not quite sure what that means ... we call it entertainment, branded or otherwise. The idea that brands need to find entertainment to engage consumers, because they have an off button and can turn away, they have to work to make sure the consumer has got a reward out of it ... well, great, that's what we should have been doing in the first place. If advertising wasn't doing that, it wasn't doing its job.... You can't create a division to do it, you just have to do it. We didn't create a division to create *Somers Town*, we had an idea and we had a brilliant client who was really excited and interested in the idea and we made a feature film.

EW: **I agree with what you're saying in terms of how in some ways the developments in advertising aren't new, but I feel things had got lost along the way, in terms of what people were expecting from ad agencies, so this new era of creativity does feel quite exciting and new.**

RS: British advertising was at its absolute pinnacle probably in the 1970s and 1980s. Now I'm not sure whether there was better work out there at the time; the commercial breaks were probably filled with rubbish, but I don't care. The agencies on the worldwide stage that demonstrated the brilliance of British advertising were the agencies that were run by creative people. They were run by David Abbott, John Hegarty, Dave Trott, Tim Delaney, and before that by many, many other great creative people who built agencies around the ideal that creativity unlocks consumers and allows you to communicate messages to those consumers. And that has to be entertaining, it has to be beguiling, it has to be impactful and it has to be persuasive. It certainly wasn't invented here – there were many, many great exponents of it in other parts of the world, but there was this kind of hotbed of brilliant, brilliant creative thinkers here, hundreds of them, actually.

When I started, they ruled the roost, they were the people in charge, and you did not move in our business unless you were conscious that that art, that crafting, that spark was what we ultimately were there for. And I think that they made an awful lot of money, they floated or sold their companies, and set a very bad example to the creative communities that were going to follow, which was that the product is a means to an end, and the end is to sell out and make large amounts of money.

You can only serve one master – if quality, and the craft and the art is the master, that's what will come through. And I think for quite a while the master was scale, was globalizing, was selling out ... it's a different agenda. Of course no one's stupid enough to think that creativity doesn't play a part in that, and that you have to have good product and do good work and be forward thinking in order to achieve those things. But it's not the reason you get up in the morning, it's the deceit you use in order to achieve financial success.

When that contract changed, and it did change, I think our industry changed quite significantly. I think the losing its way has largely been about the emasculation of creativity within the culture of an agency. I see magazine articles where they talk about the succession – the new hot kids on the block – and it's all pictures of people who are businessmen, not necessarily creative people. And there's nothing wrong with that – that's someone else's model. But we shouldn't then be surprised when we don't necessarily, as an industry, believe and deliver. I think there are some people coming through, and there are some changes and there are some characters and some cultures that are fighting that trend again. I hope, I really hope. Clients aren't stupid – they're choosing them, so I'm hopeful that it will come back again.

EW: **Do you feel clients are seeing that having a broader view is working and has appeal?**

RS: I think the unassailable nature of the classic above-the-line advertising agency has been dented quite significantly because of the digital revolution. If it has paid anything back, it's the idea that you have to do some different stuff, you can't just fit within the formula, and clients absolutely woke up to that before agencies did.

There are a number of young, highly energetic, creative people within those communities who challenged the constructs of the very reductive thinking that was going on in advertising agencies – structured planning down to single-minded propositions, the same old supports, the same old tone of voice, the same old target audience segmentations, the same solutions continuously. The digital world just didn't think like that and I think that changed the primacy of the above-the-line agency. Now I don't believe that that was necessarily the answer either, and I do think there is a move towards an agency with very smart, structured creative thinking at the core, with digital being a manifestation or part of something bigger, rather than a breaking up of the whole thing into small bits. I think that's where the move will ultimately take us.... Clients are smart, generally. We only disagree with that fact when they don't agree with us!

EW: **Do you think clients are beginning to expect agencies to offer the full range of media now – events etc. as well as advertising?**

RS: I don't know whether they're coming to agencies with the express intention of asking them to do everything, I don't think that's true. I think there are specialists that do stuff that we would cock up. We do a lot, but there are a lot of things that we don't have specific expertise in and clients are smart enough to realize that that's the case. They are, however, asking agencies to think more broadly about where the solutions might lie. Agencies are becoming much more of a partner hub, a creative hub alongside clients to help orchestrate a whole group of different people doing different things. Because fragmenting it doesn't work any more, imposing some kind of broad identity over everything doesn't work any more – consumers are inured to that kind of stuff. So they are asking agencies to have a different open-mindedness about who they invite to the table and some agencies are better at that than others. Some are very quick to use it as an opportunity to sell a whole bunch of additional services to clients, which I think again is the wrong way of doing it.

The solution requires a different matched team, and [clients] do ask agencies to help them orchestrate that more at the centre. Agencies have to be more open to the fact that the answer may not be the things that they've historically been practitioners of. But I don't know if they [clients] necessarily want it all from one place. But this to-ing and fro-ing has gone on as many times as brands have gone global, then local, then back to global ... agencies have been full service back to fragmented specialisms, back to full service.... I don't think you can glean trends from those things.

EW: **Who do you look to hire?**

RS: Rumour has it that we were the first people to bring a lot of people from around the world to work in London – we have 16 nationalities here, half of our creative department's from overseas, half of the agency's from overseas. We were probably the first people to do that, and that was really to try to break the myopic nature of British advertising agencies.

It's largely people who've shown enthusiasm and want to be here – that's what a brand does, isn't it? It attracts people. Then you're looking at people who don't judge things by the same criteria. We're not looking for people with perfect work – I think good creative direction is about realizing people's potential and getting them to use the skills they have in ways that they hadn't necessarily thought possible. We do look more widely afield and we look for people who don't think in the same straight manner, but you get that anyway when you get different cultures coming in – people tend to spark each other.

EW: **From the beginning with Mother there was always a strong feeling of trying to do things differently within the actual company, with the way you worked, and not having the traditional department divisions. Was this something that that was very important to you?**

RS: I don't think it was planned. I think an awful lot of social engineering goes on in agencies and I was really nervous about that. We started a certain way, pragmatically, because we had the launch of Channel Five. We had four of us, and a client, and we had no time to do it. We had to get on with it. We had no offices, we had a kitchen table. I would cook and we would solve problems together, everybody around the same table. As directly as you possibly can – putting work on the wall, sharing things, being as open and collaborative as possible. Treating the client with respect and hopefully them treating us with respect for our ability to understand the problems we're trying to solve. And that openness just worked. So we said 'That worked, that will be the principle, that's how we'll work'.

The reason for not putting intermediaries as a job title in is because we never had that luxury in the first place so it seemed ridiculous to have some sort of intermediary process. It's not to do with some deep philosophical belief, that's what worked. Creative people who were smart enough to represent their own views, strategic people who wanted to be involved in the creative process – we just put them together around the table. The kitchen table became a bigger kitchen table, became a bigger kitchen table, became a monstrous concrete table, which now spreads across three continents, ridiculously.

Mother, London

Discovery Channel: *London Ink*

Mother created this ambient campaign to advertise a UK version of Discovery Channel's popular reality TV series set around tattoo parlours in the US. *London Ink* was promoted using two large sculptures of people bearing tattoos that were placed in busy London locations. One was a man found 'swimming' by the river at Tower Bridge, while the other sculpture, of a girl, was installed at Victoria Station. The tattoos on the models were all created by 'tattooist to the stars' Louis Molloy, who features in the *London Ink* programme and who also created a set of temporary tattoos for the campaign, which were distributed via the *Observer* newspaper. The tattoos on both giant sculptures referred to different aspects of London life, with images such as fish and chips and pigeons.

PHOTOS
PHOTOS

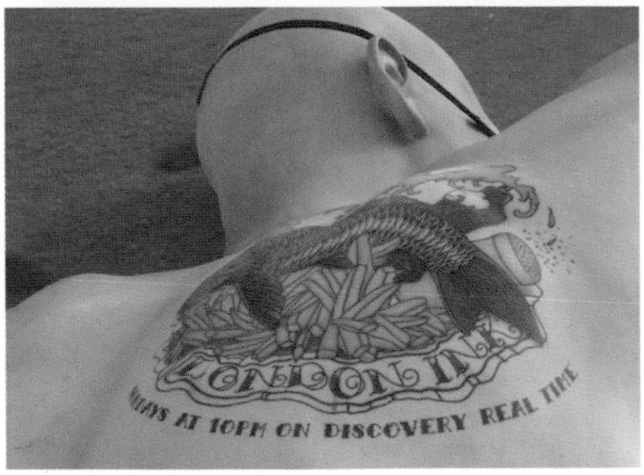
LONDON INK
AT 10PM ON DISCOVERY REAL TIME

‘The principles haven’t changed at all, you now just need different places to find those consumers – sometimes they’re in longer form pieces of film, sometimes they’re in digital spaces, sometimes they are on TV, sometimes they are in print, sometimes they’re on the street.’

Robert Saville, co-founding partner and creative director, Mother

Wieden + Kennedy London

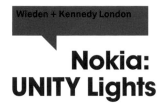

Nokia: UNITY Lights

For Christmas 2007, Nokia and Wieden + Kennedy London created an unusual piece of branded content for Nokia. To celebrate both Christmas and the imminent arrival of the Nokia Flagship Store on Regent Street in London (the store opened in January 2008), Nokia sponsored the Christmas lights on the street. Wieden + Kennedy brought together a team of specialists, including United Visual Artists, to create the unusual illuminations, which were titled UNITY. The display consisted of 14 3D light clusters, which responded to the people passing beneath them via motion cameras and changed formation depending on the density of pedestrians, as well as on environmental factors, including wind speed, weather and sunlight levels. The lights were also energy efficient, using a low energy LED core, and were 100 per cent recyclable. The interactive lights were striking yet subtle, and provided a welcome alternative to the cartoon-themed lights that usually line this part of London at Christmastime.

Carnaby
CARNABY STREET
FOUBERTS PLACE

Fallon, London

Anheuser-Busch: The Bud Booth

The Bud Booth is a section of the bar area in the Proud Gallery in Camden, London, which was given a Budweiser-themed makeover by Fallon. While the branding in the space was deliberately low key, Fallon gave the room a relaxed, Nashville theme that was in keeping with the agency's previous advertising for the beer brand.

Fallon was responsible for the overall design of the space, including the furniture, lighting and decoration, the highlight of which was a wall covered with a collage of Nashville-based band posters.

NEBULA
6-23-02
The End Nashville
EAR PROTECTION REQUIRED
Belleville Hotel
SON VOLT
7.31.05
EXIT IN NASHVILLE
FRUIT BATS
GWAR
CAT POWER
REV. HORTON HEAT
MAY 24
with LOS STRAITJACKETS & BIG LAZY
328 PERFORMANCE HALL
nashville tn.
12.1.05
MERCY LOUNGE
NASHVILLE
TED LEO + PHARMACISTS

Interview: Jonathan Kneebone

Jonathan Kneebone is co-founder of The Glue Society, with offices in Sydney and New York. The agency has no permanent clients, working instead with brands such as Virgin Mobile (page 174), Elle McPherson and Nike on a project-by-project basis. It also directs ads for other agencies and has created artworks for exhibitions in Australia and the US (page 208).

EW: **Would you agree that advertising is going through a period of change? How would you describe this change?**

JK: We are probably already undergoing a change. For years, it feels like advertising has been living out one life – and as a result slowly getting older and less and less relevant. It has taken a change in the way it is possible to communicate for advertising to wake up to the fact it can have many lives. So it does feel as if there is a rebirth of some sort going on. It is spawning new companies, new ways of doing things, new types of conversations and activities. It is very early days – but it does appear that some form of creative revolution is under way.

EW: **Do you think it is important now for advertising companies to offer a variety of skills across all media?**

JK: There is a strong financial desire from agency managements to want to have everything in one place. It makes for an easy argument to large corporations (we can solve everything here). But it is very difficult and expensive to have the best people from every discipline. By their very nature creative people who are good enough to stand on their own two feet want to be independent. Personally, I think there are two approaches. You can have moderately good people all under one roof, or change the model, such that a strong relationship-based, strategic agency accesses pioneers in every field on behalf of their clients.

EW: **What do you anticipate being the most significant trends to emerge in advertising over the next few years?**

JK: The distances between brands and audiences are getting smaller. The more technology allows for real time communication to happen, the more human that communication is likely to become. My personal opinion is that brands are destined to become more human in their language, behaviour and action. The type of relationship between customer and brand is going to be more like 'companionship'. You will turn to brands for entertainment, company, advice and new experiences.

EW: **Do you feel that the relationship with your clients has evolved due to the changes in the industry?**

JK: For the past ten years, we have decided to work on a project basis because it ensures we are always used for the right reasons. For me the project approach is one that allows for a higher degree of mutual respect and ultimately creative experimentation. Both sides share a mutual objective and this leads to a shared sense of ownership of any creative activity. For us the relationship hasn't changed then, but I suspect for others this short-term approach might become the norm. That said, it is very true to say that the type of project we are now working on is changing. We are being requested to create longer-form creative ideas, whether that be televisual or behavioural, work that explores or defines the personality of the brands we are working with.

EW: **Are you brought in earlier into the creative process now – have you had more of an influence over the products that are being made by a client?**

JK: Absolutely. We are being asked to contribute to defining the personality of our client's brands. And this is like creating a character in a book or movie. Unless you have defined the character, it is hard to know how to make it talk or behave. In brand terms, this means what it looks like, how it promotes itself, what types of products it should be making. The whole marketing process I believe is becoming far more organic and human. And, in a word, creative. That's why it is such an exciting time.

The Glue Society, Sydney

42Below: Because We Can

Below: The Glue Society wraps a street of cars in Sydney with Christmas paper for 42Below. Right: A UFO made out of milk crates is built in Queenstown, New Zealand.

For this unusual campaign for New Zealand vodka brand 42Below The Glue Society created a number of playful artistic acts that became the basis of a print campaign. The ads started life as pieces of art, which appeared unexpectedly at locations in Australia and New Zealand. These included an entire street of cars in Sydney wrapped in Christmas paper, a rainbow made of chairs displayed in Cardrona, New Zealand, 100 inflatable sex dolls laid on Bronte Beach, Sydney, and a milk crate UFO, which landed in Queenstown, New Zealand. The sculptures attracted a lot of free press coverage, and The Glue Society made films of their installation that were shown online. Finally, the photographed artworks ran as traditional print ads, alongside 42Below's tagline 'Because We Can'.

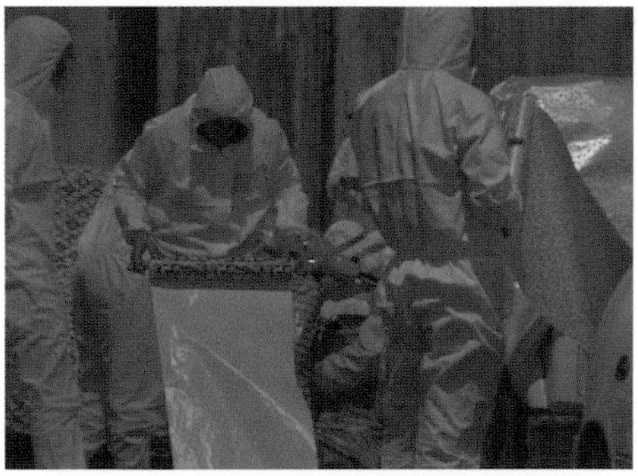

'This was born as a desire to create a really adventurous piece of work.... Our approach is all about bringing brands' personalities to life – but it is rare that we get to use our experience in the art world to create something for a commercial client.'

Jonathan Kneebone, co-founder, The Glue Society

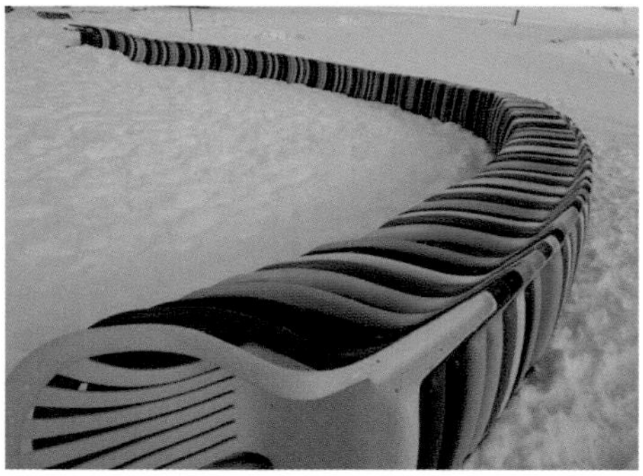

Left: A rainbow of chairs is built in Cardrona, New Zealand. **Below:** The rainbow as it appeared in the print campaign for 42Below.

BECAUSEWECANONLINE.COM
BECAUSE WE CAN

Jung von Matt, Hamburg

IKEA: Curtain

Jung von Matt created this interactive cinema commercial to promote IKEA's new fabrics and curtains to a specific local audience. Visitors to the cinema were presented with a particularly dreary, depressing scene, which showed the view through a window onto a grey, dull-looking courtyard. Suddenly the real screen curtain was shut across the dismal scene and text was projected onto the curtain, emphasizing how IKEA curtains can 'beautify your life, from just 2 euros'.

Schon ab 2.-
"From just 2.- Euros."

Vorhänge machen das Leben schöner.
"Curtains beautify your life."

Jung von Matt, Hamburg

UNICEF: Action Price Tag

In this ambient campaign for UNICEF, Jung von Matt wanted to target consumers of sports goods and clothes and highlight the problems of child labour. To do this they created a flipbook, which, on the surface, looked like an ordinary price tag. When flipped, however, the barcode on the tag transformed into the image of a young child in a sweatshop, then the final tagline, 'The Real Price Is Paid By Others. Stop Child Labour', appeared at the end of the book. Activist groups placed the message right at point of sale, by surreptitiously replacing the actual price tags in sports stores with the flipbooks. A film of the book being flipped was placed online, and the whole campaign attracted a lot of news coverage.

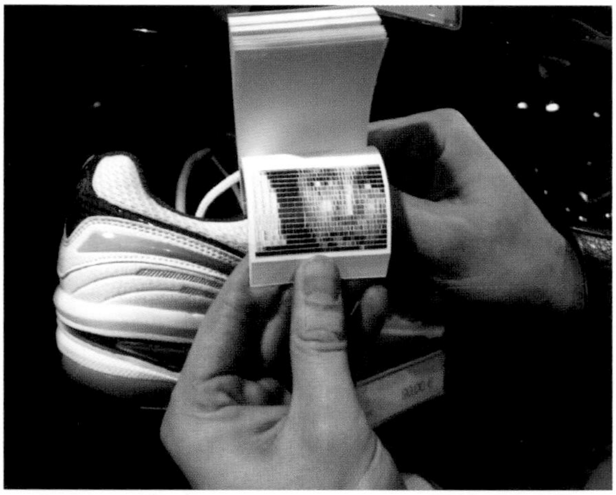

THE REAL PRICE
IS PAID BY OTHERS.

BBDO Argentina, Buenos Aires

Nike: Barrio Bonito

Barrio Bonito, which means 'Beautiful Neighbourhood', is the world's first football neighbourhood. Created in La Boca in Buenos Aires, a notoriously football-obsessed area of town that is also home to the Argentine team Boca Juniors, Barrio Bonito was inspired by Nike's global campaign, Jogo Bonito, and aimed to communicate its values – honour, joy, heart, skill and team spirit. La Boca is also known for its artistic community and BBDO Argentina called upon local artists to create artworks reflecting their love of the beautiful game. These included sculptures and murals of Nike football stars, including Carlos Tévez, a local idol, and Ronaldinho.

In the creation of Barrio Bonito, rundown buildings were renovated and repainted, and the new neighbourhood was opened by the city's mayor. While created initially for the World Cup in 2006, it remains a popular tourist attraction, although perhaps less of a draw to English tourists because of its inclusion of a football pitch containing statues of England players, where visitors are invited to recreate Maradona's goal against England in the 1986 World Cup quarter-final.

AGUERO
BY
AGUERO
SKILL

INSUA
FEDERICO INSUA . MIDFIELDER . BOCA JUNIORS

FORWARD

TEVEZ
BY
TEVEZ

RONALDINHO
BY
RONALDINHO

Clockwise from left: Football pitch at Barrio Bonito containing statues of England players in the 1986 World Cup quarter-final, where visitors can recreate Maradona's controversial goal; Murals of footballers Sergio Aguero and Emiliano Insua; Ballprint murals of Aguero, Carlos Tévez and Ronaldinho.

. MIDFIELDER . F.C.BARCELONA

The mural of Ronaldinho at Barrio Bonito in Buenos Aires.

RONALDINHO
JOY

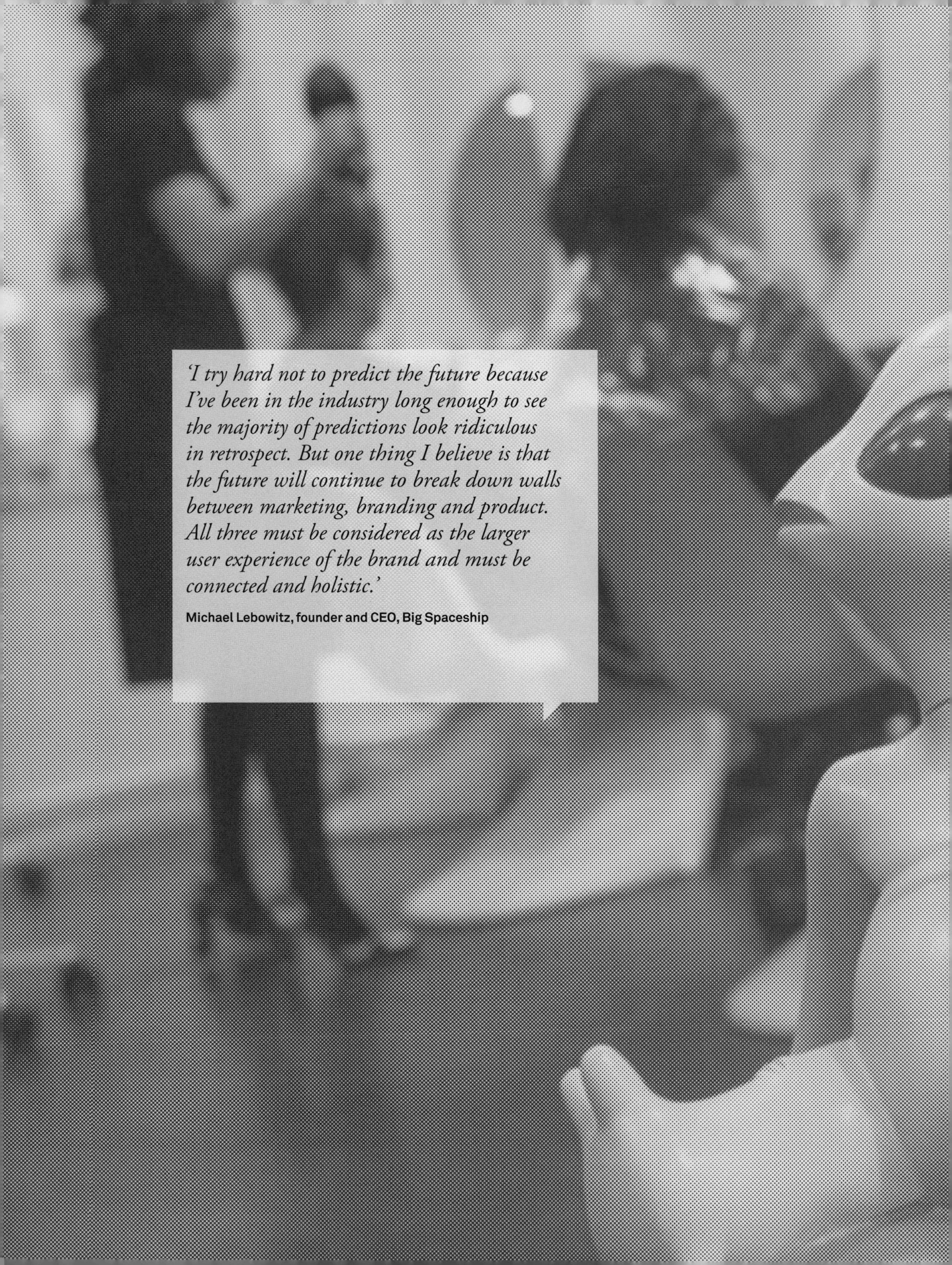

'I try hard not to predict the future because I've been in the industry long enough to see the majority of predictions look ridiculous in retrospect. But one thing I believe is that the future will continue to break down walls between marketing, branding and product. All three must be considered as the larger user experience of the brand and must be connected and holistic.'

Michael Lebowitz, founder and CEO, Big Spaceship

Chapter Four: Integrated

'Integrated' has become a catch-all term for any advertising campaign that spans several different media. Advertisers encourage audiences to seek out a campaign in lots of different places, making connections and forming a deeper relationship with a brand. Integrated advertising is probably the hardest type of advertising to pull off, but when it is successful, the rewards can be great. This chapter has examples of those campaigns that made the grade, becoming some of the most striking advertising initiatives of recent years.

Above: Chicago, the lead US city for Earth Hour 2008, plunges into semi-darkness for one hour. **Right:** Posters advertising the event in the city.

Leo Burnett Worldwide

WWF: Earth Hour

Earth Hour (www.earthhour.org) was first introduced to the world by Leo Burnett Sydney for its client WWF (the World Wildlife Fund). It requested that the inhabitants of Sydney turn off their lights at home and at work for one hour on 31 March 2007 in order to help prevent global warming. Over 2.5 million people participated. In 2008, Earth Hour went global, taking place in 35 countries and over 370 cities. Over 25,000 blogs covered the event, and Google had over 10,000 news items on it. Google itself also went 'dark' for Earth Hour, with a black landing page. Earth Hour continues to take place annually.

THOSE WHO
SEE
THE LIGHT
TURN
IT
OFF
PARK
HERE
109

IMPROVE YOUR VISION
TURN
OFF YOUR LIGHTS
CHICAGO

unicef
united states fund
AMERICAN EXPRESS
PROUD SUPPORTER OF THE TAP PROJECT
DURING WORLD WATER WEEK, MARCH 16-22, GO OUT TO EAT. DONATE A MINIMUM OF $1 FOR TAP WATER, AND A CHILD IN NEED WILL HAVE 40 DAYS OF CLEAN WATER.
TAP PROJECT
TO FIND A RESTAURANT OR DONATE NOW, TAPPROJECT.ORG

Droga5, New York

UNICEF: Tap Project

The Tap Project (www.tapproject.org) was launched on World Water Day in 2007 by UNICEF and Droga5. The campaign aimed to raise money for the over one billion people worldwide who have little or no access to safe water. All the major restaurants in New York participated in the scheme, which asked diners to donate $1 for tap water, which is usually free. For each dollar donated, a child in need received 40 days of clean drinking water. In 2008, the Tap Project went nationwide across the US, with other advertising agencies across the country volunteering to make work to help promote it. It went global in 2009 and has raised enough money to provide millions of children with clean water. Massive media coverage of the campaign has also raised awareness of the global water crisis significantly.

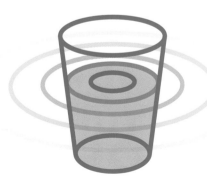

TAP PROJECT

News Corporation
Panasonic
YAHOO!
articipating resta

TAPPROJECT.ORG
unicef
U.S. Fund for UNICEF
NASDAQ
NO TURNS

Clockwise from below left:
Restaurant demonstrating its commitment to the scheme by putting a Tap Project sticker in its window; Tap Project logo; Press and outdoor advertising for the campaign.

TAP PROJECT
unicef
New review

'The principle of advertising is still essentially the same – technology has just opened up the options. There are now multiple canvases – as a creative person it's quite liberating.'

David Droga, founder and creative chairman, Droga5

Droga5, New York

NYC Department of Education: Million

After the New York City Department of Education approached Droga5 advertising agency and asked them to 'brand achievement', the agency came up with the Million, a new incentive-based phone/personal computer that will be provided free to the one million students in the New York City public education system. The Department of Education joined forces with Verizon to create the phone, which is automatically disabled during school time, but functions as a regular phone outside of school hours. The aim of the project is to connect the things that inspire kids out of school with learning and success in school. Improved attendance, participation, homework and grades are all awarded with airtime for phone calls, texts, music downloads and more. 'The public schools here are huge and have big issues,' says David Droga, founder and creative chairman of Droga5. 'We didn't want to just say "school is cool" and so on, so we said "why don't we talk to them in a way that uses technology?"'

The pilot programme for the Million was launched in February 2008 in seven schools in New York. After the four-month pilot was complete, over 75 per cent of parents noted that their child was either spending more time doing homework, getting excited about certain classes, studying more with friends, earning higher grades or receiving better progress reports, while 65 per cent of parents said their child had been doing better in school since the start of the Million programme. There is now interest in rolling out the Million elsewhere in the US.

SAMSUNG
million™
verizon

Goodby, Silverstein & Partners,
San Francisco

Specialized: Innovate Or Die

Goodby, Silverstein & Partners created the Innovate or Die Pedal-Powered Machine contest for bike brand Specialized (www.innovate-or-die.com). The competition was 'designed to inspire innovation and environmental change, one pedal stroke at a time', and challenged contestants to invent machines that harnessed the energy of pedal power for unusual and unexpected purposes. Contestants were asked to document their machines in action, with films of the entries put on a group page on YouTube. A total of 102 entries were received, with the Grand Innovate or Die Pedal-Powered Machine Award going to the Aquaduct Mobile Filtration Vehicle, a bike that filters water while being ridden. Its creators received $5,000 (£3,500) and five new Specialized Globe bikes.

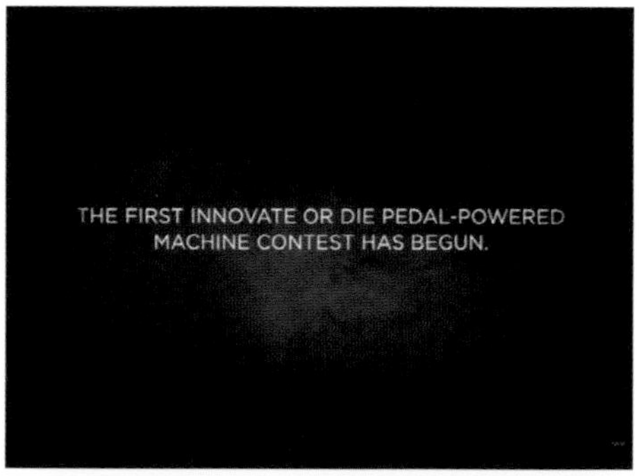
THE FIRST INNOVATE OR DIE PEDAL-POWERED
MACHINE CONTEST HAS BEGUN.

LET'S CRANK

INNOVATE OR DIE

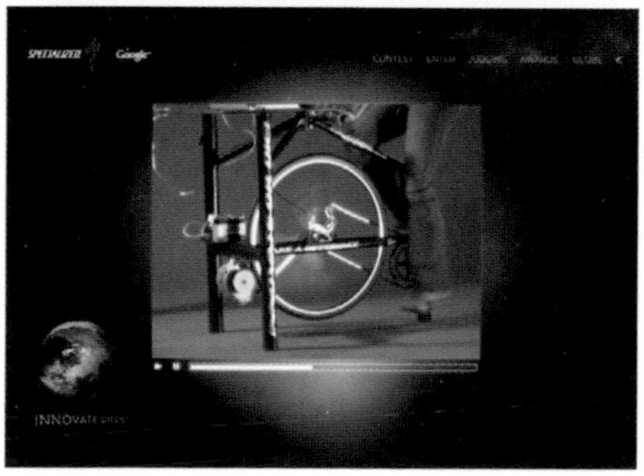

Below: Images from the Sony Vaio Online Script Project website. **Far right:** Stills from Laurie J. Proud's animated film, *Snow Angel*.

ONLINE SCRIPT PROJECT
STAY IN TOUCH
JOHN'S VAIO
Inspiration
SONY
be like.no.other
VAIO

ONLINE SCRIPT PROJECT
STAY IN TOUCH
Back
SONY
be like.no.other

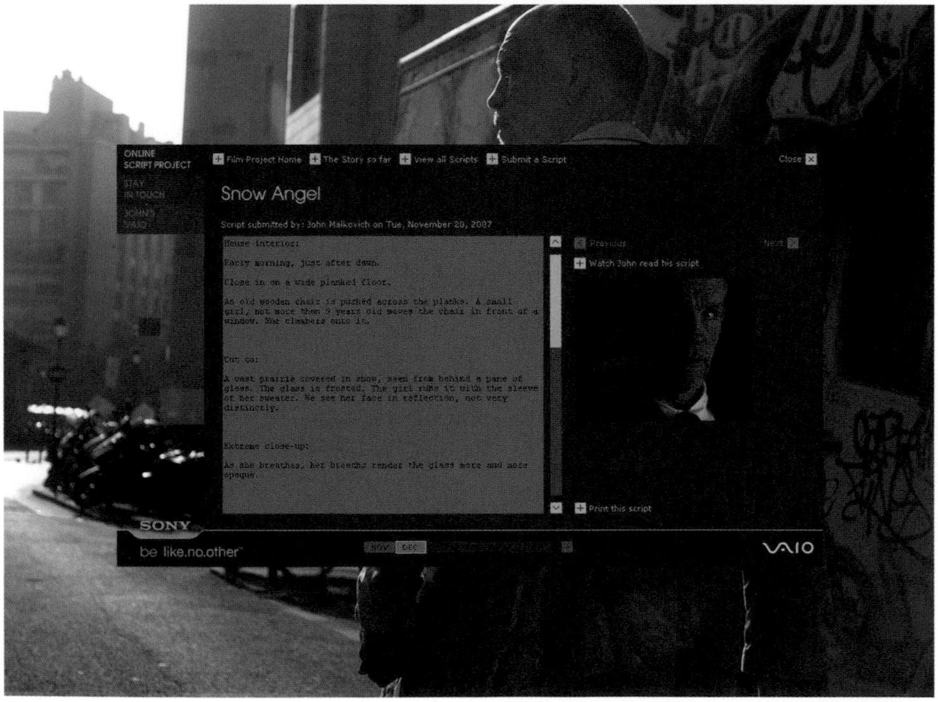

ONLINE SCRIPT PROJECT
STAY IN TOUCH
Film Project Home
The Story so far
View all Scripts
Submit a Script
Close
Snow Angel
Script submitted by: John Malkovich on Tue, November 20, 2007
House interior:
Early morning, just after dawn.
Close in on a wide planked floor.
An old wooden chair is pushed across the planks. A small girl, not more than 9 years old moves the chair in front of a window. She clambers onto it.
Cut to:
A vast prairie covered in snow, seen from behind a pane of glass. The glass is frosted. The girl rubs it with the sleeve of her sweater. We see her face in reflection, not very distinctly.
Extreme close-up:
As she breathes, her breaths render the glass more and more opaque.
Previous
Next
Watch John read his script
Print this script
SONY
be like.no.other
NOV
DEC
VAIO

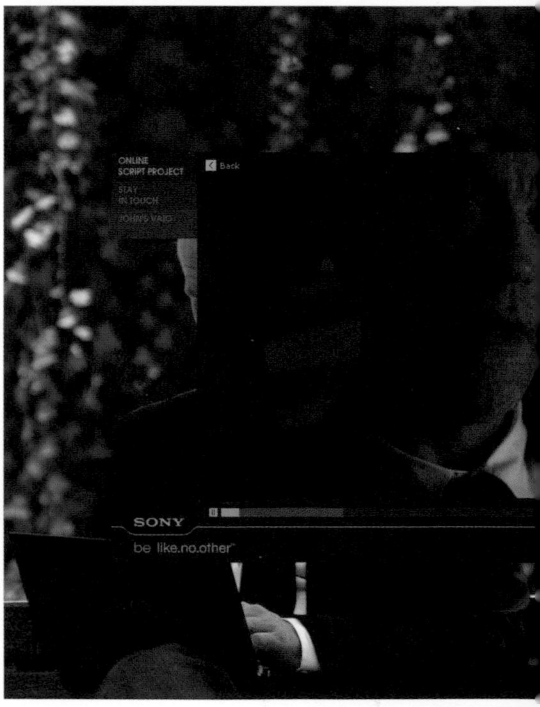

ONLINE SCRIPT PROJECT
STAY IN TOUCH
JOHN'S VAIO
Back
SONY
be like.no.other

Fallon/Dare, London

Sony: Vaio Online Script Project

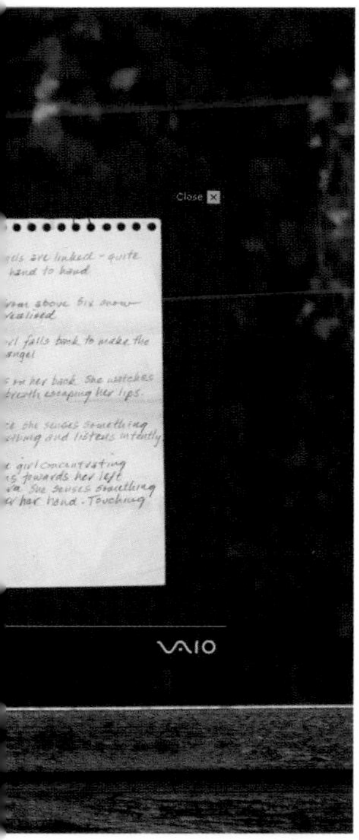
Close

The Sony Vaio Online Script Project appeared as part of a website (www.vaio-john.com) for Sony where actor John Malkovich introduced the audience to how he uses his personal computer. Malkovich kicked off the competition by writing the first scene of a short film, and then invited visitors to the website to continue the story. A film of Malkovich reading his first scene appeared on the site. It ends with him announcing, 'What happens next? It's up to you.' Each month a shortlist from the entered scripts was decided on by votes from other writers, then Malkovich chose the month's winning script, leaving feedback on the website explaining the reasons for his choice. This new part of the story then became the inspiration for the following month's entries. The competition lasted for three months, and when the script was complete, an animated film of the story *Snow Angel* was also made, directed by Laurie J. Proud.

Close

Below: Images of Absolut Quartet, designed by Dan Paluska and Jeff Lieberman. Absolut Quartet is an automated multi-instrumental orchestral machine, which includes components such as a series of wine glasses played by little robotic fingers.
Far right: Still from the Absolut Machines website, where users could interact with the machines online.

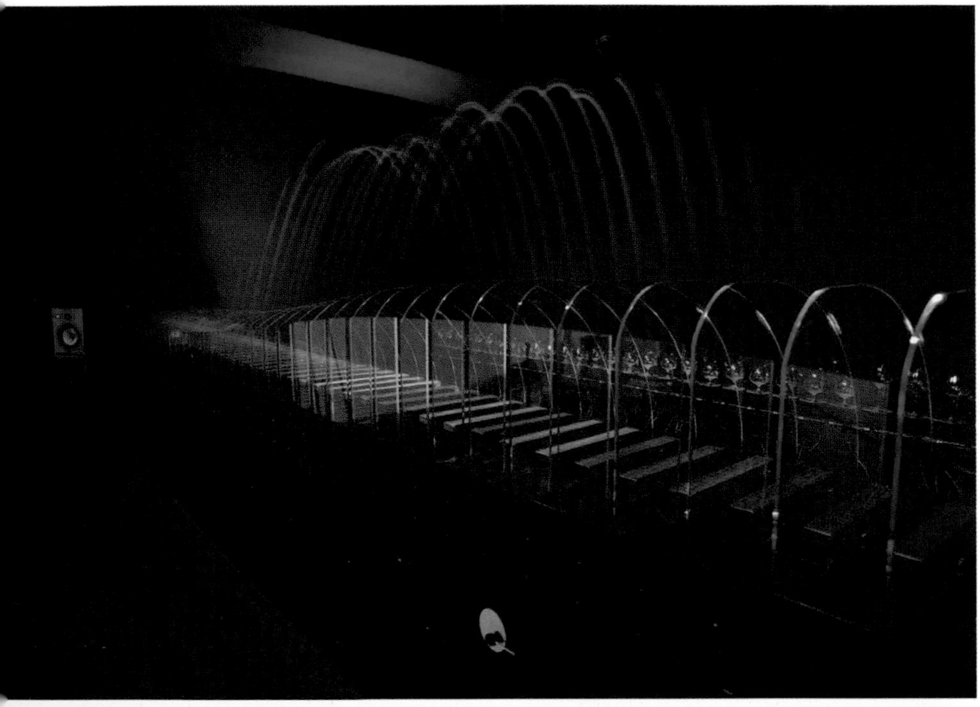

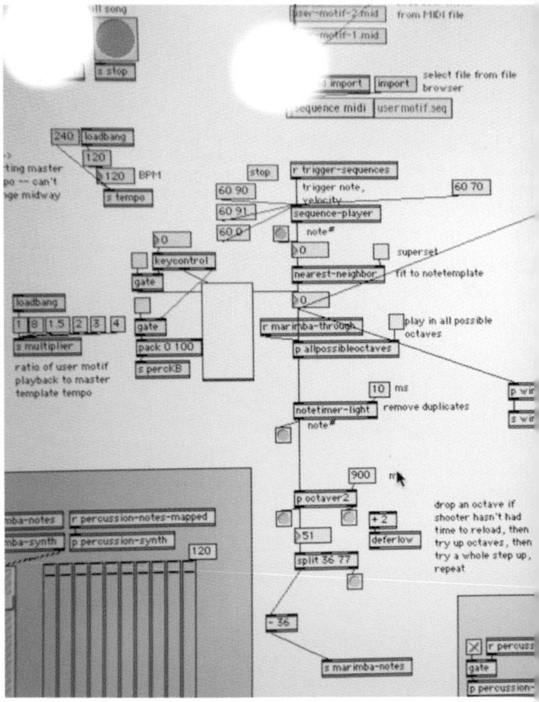

from MIDI file
s stop
import
select file from file browser
usermotif.seq
240
loadbang
120
120 BPM
s tempo
stop
r trigger-sequences
trigger note, velocity
60 90
60 91
60 70
sequence-player
note#
keycontrol
gate
superset
nearest-neighbor
fit to notetemplate
loadbang
1 8 1.5 2 3 4
s multiplier
ratio of user motif playback to master template tempo
pack 0 100
s percKB
r marimba-through
play in all possible octaves
p allpossibleoctaves
10 ms
notetimer-light
remove duplicates
900
p octaver2
+ 2
deferlow
51
split 36 77
drop an octave if shooter hasn't had time to reload, then try up octaves, then try a whole step up, repeat
r percussion-notes-mapped
p percussion-synth
120
- 36
s marimba-notes

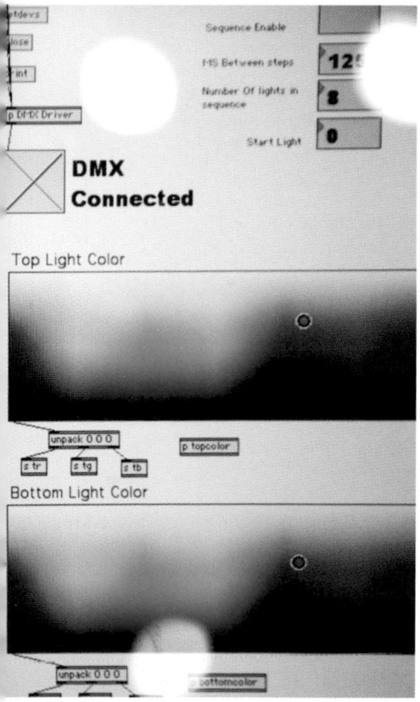
Sequence Enable
MS Between steps
Number Of lights in sequence
Start Light
p DMX Driver
DMX
Connected
Top Light Color
unpack 0 0 0
p topcolor
Bottom Light Color
unpack 0 0 0

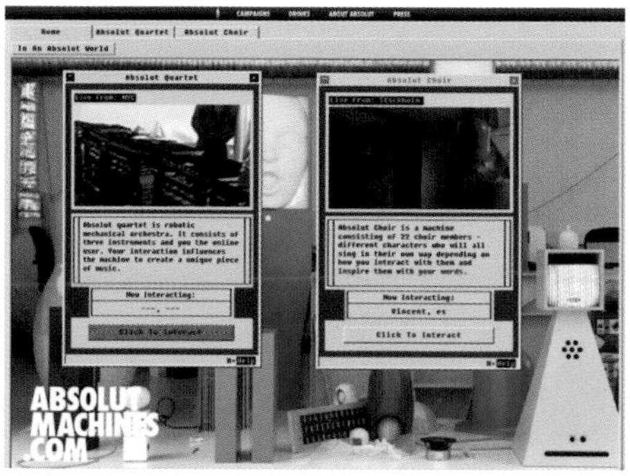
Absolut Quartet
Absolut Choir
Click To Interact
ABSOLUT
MACHINES
.COM

Absolut, Sweden

Absolut: Absolut Machines

Swedish vodka brand Absolut has a long-established association with the arts and creativity, with artists such as Keith Haring and Chris Ofili having created artworks based around the shape of the vodka bottle for its past poster campaigns. In 2008, Absolut moved this connection into the digital age, with a project that combines art and design with technology. Working with two teams of technical experts – Dan Paluska and Jeff Lieberman, who both have a background at MIT in Boston, and Teenage Engineering, a Swedish studio working with media – they created the Absolut Machines, two 'artificially creative' music-making machines with which audiences could interact via the internet. While highly technical, the machines were also works of art that have been shown in exhibitions in New York and Stockholm. Absolut Machines is a piece of creative content designed for audiences to interact and play with, and it built on the brand's creative integrity without once mentioning the word 'vodka'.

Image of Absolut Choir, designed by Teenage Engineering. Absolut Choir is a multi-channel robotic choir made up of ten singing characters of various shapes and sizes.

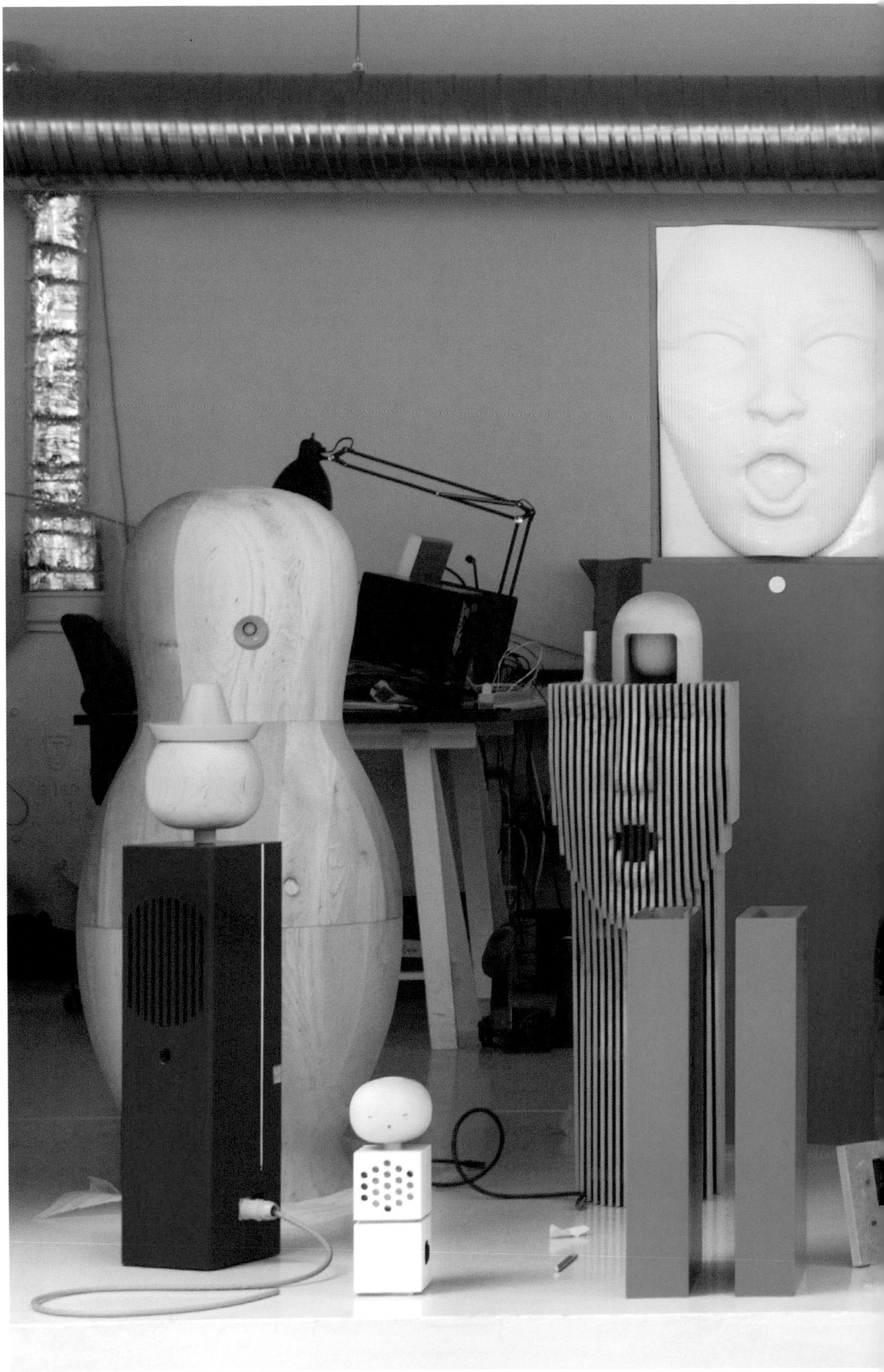

Interview: Richard Flintham

Richard Flintham is executive creative director and co-founder of Fallon, London, which has created some of the most exciting advertising in recent years, including films for Sony, a drumming gorilla for Cadbury's (page 72), and non-traditional work for Tate (page 150) and Budweiser (page 120).

EW: **Do you feel that people are accepting that advertising is changing?**

RF: I think more that people are open to where they might land their idea.... More and more people seem to be coming in and saying 'I've got this thing, what shall I do with it?', or 'I've got this issue, what shall I do with it?', not 'I've booked this thing and we need to be on air...' or 'We need to be in this magazine then', so you just do something shaped to fit that. Because I think they appreciate that they can get a wider conversation, and bigger ripples, when they put it in exactly the right place. Gorilla was put, not by us, onto a place where people go to feel happy and just goof around looking at stuff, and then that obviously exploded off the back of that.

EW: **Did you expect that to happen with Gorilla?**

RF: No, not really. You hope, don't you? The first time it happened was with the Sony Balls ad [where the agency threw thousands of coloured balls down a hill in San Francisco], which was a huge learning curve for us. It was terrifying, and ended up being brilliant. There was myself and Juan [Cabral, creative director and partner at Fallon] on the shoot in San Francisco, and people were taking pictures and posting them on Flickr, and then we got a message back from a friend in another country saying 'I've seen what you're doing'. And that was on the first morning of the shoot. So we immediately flicked into 'We're going to get fired, this is really bad, everyone knows what we're doing, they're going to nick it'. All that stuff. Which was crazy. It was 'How are we going to manage this?', and it just got bigger and bigger and bigger until we realized that people wanted to talk about it. So it was a massive learning curve – it was terrifying to start with.

EW: **And how did Sony react?**

RF: They were the same as us: 'How do we manage this?' 'What will the competition think?' 'What's this going to do?'....

And then we realized that the ad had started. There's a moment when we thought: 'We're supposed to be putting something out in a month's time but it's actually begun now.' And then it could have gone bad, but people liked it. Well, some people hated it ... which was a bit confusing as I'm not sure how you can hate bouncing balls. I suppose we set out with a traditional model for the Bravia – we were going to do this nice gift to the world. So I suppose we were trying to do something beyond that anyway, to get an experience beyond the TV commercial. But that started off as a very traditional piece, as did Gorilla.

EW: **So when you start a brief, do you not think about the medium particularly at the beginning?**

RF: No, it's the ambition of the brand or the size of the problem. It's very much about who it would be aimed towards. And then you start to feel tonally where it might live, and then off the back of that try and cultivate an idea. Rather than 'We've got this, where do we put it?', it's more that we try to understand it, and then look at which media channel would best support this tone and then what would the idea be after that. Which is probably the shift from: understand it, start to have an idea, have an idea and work out where you put it. Because the channel could be the idea.

EW: **Do you feel now as an agency that you have to offer in-house diversity to your clients? Do you think that's important for a modern advertising agency?**

RF: Yeah, I think so. We've, rightly or wrongly, been quite opportunity driven, I think because we've got faith in a diverse group of people around the table, deciding what the right idea would be. We've got faith in working out which way it should be, and obviously you've got to provide some sort of infrastructure. But I don't think you should be overburdened to provide the complete infrastructure. We've worked with good digital agencies – we've got digital capability here, but you find sometimes that you've got a client who's got a digital partner and you go: 'Great, well let's work together on this.' I think it's important to have a clash: what happens if a fashion photographer shoots a car or what happens if we go on this medium and we try and do something that's more intellectual than goofy, it's always that clash. I think it's always important to keep fresh perspectives available to you. We've got producers from Channel 4, we've got creative directors from record companies, we've got magazine editors, we've got a film thing downstairs ... we've got enough lookout towers.

EW: **Has that changed the industry, having people like that involved, say compared to ten years ago in advertising?**

RF: Yeah, it's great. I think it would be quite irresponsible if we said, 'We've got this creative director of a record company – here's a brief for chocolate, what do you think?' That wouldn't be the right use. But when you have those people in a very open forum, you notice that an awful lot of time has been saved by having them in the room. It's great to have those people floating around. I think if you try to advertising-ify them – if you try to make them what you are – I think it's wrong. But if they're guests and have a power of veto just as great as your own then life's really nice and interesting. If you say: 'Let's make something better than the both of us', it works really well, I think.

Apparently advertising's a dirty word though, isn't it? Maybe it limits your acceptance into wider organizations or different people. But the good people seem to be mucking about, and I don't think there's any risk in that at all, it's really healthy, and I haven't noticed it do anything but save us time and get to an answer quicker, which is essential isn't it? If there's someone who can look over your shoulder and say 'That should go that way, too', or 'I could make it this', great, go for it.

EW: **Are your clients finding this all attractive too? I imagine there's a lot of people coming to you now, after so much success in the last few years.**

RF: Yeah, and there are some really interesting people coming too. I've spent 18 years of my life trying to get permission to get to this point, so it's really exciting that people just come in and say 'I want this, I don't want you to pitch, I just want to do it with you because I like what you do'. It's really good. On the other side you might find some people who you work with don't want you to venture off into strange lands, because they want you to be a specialist in a particular medium. Which I think is a lesson to everybody that you need to keep people updated on the fact that you've comfortably grown into larger shoes or different shoes and it's all part of what you offer. Because some people do have an image of what they want you to be as well. Which I think will sort itself out, as long as you don't take your eye off the ball.

EW: **Are you also finding that clients want you to come in earlier and talk about products more now?**

RF: Yeah, but it's all different. You can't do it with everything. But if you really thought about it and you've got a great idea for somebody's product, why would anyone stop you from saying 'I think I've invented this thing that would be great'. It's obvious isn't it? But have a good idea first.

Tate Tracks was aimed at encouraging new audiences to visit the Tate Modern permanent collection. Fallon commissioned several UK musicians, including Graham Coxon, The Chemical Brothers, Roll Deep and Long Blondes, to create a new piece of music inspired by an artwork at the museum. During the course of the campaign one track was released each month and was placed on a listening post beside the relevant artwork, encouraging fans of the project to return to the museum regularly. The tracks were also made available online for a short period. Tate Tracks also included a competition for bands to create their own pieces of music inspired by works of art in the Tate Modern collection. More than 200 entries were posted onto MySpace, with a shortlist of 20 drawn up by a public vote before the final winner was chosen by a panel of judges. The winning track was then played in the gallery next to the artwork that had inspired it.

Fallon, London

Tate Modern: Tate Tracks

MODERN
TATE
Donald Judd, Untitled 1980 © Donald Judd Foundation/VAGA, New York and DACS, London 2006
From
01/12/06
Klaxons
vs.
Donald Judd
From
01/01/07
The Landscapers
vs.
Andy Warhol
From
01/02/07
Union of Knives
vs.
Cy Twombly
Only at Tate Modern
tatetracks.org.uk

MODERN
TATE
Roll Deep
vs.
Anish Kapoor
Only at Tate Modern from 01/10/06

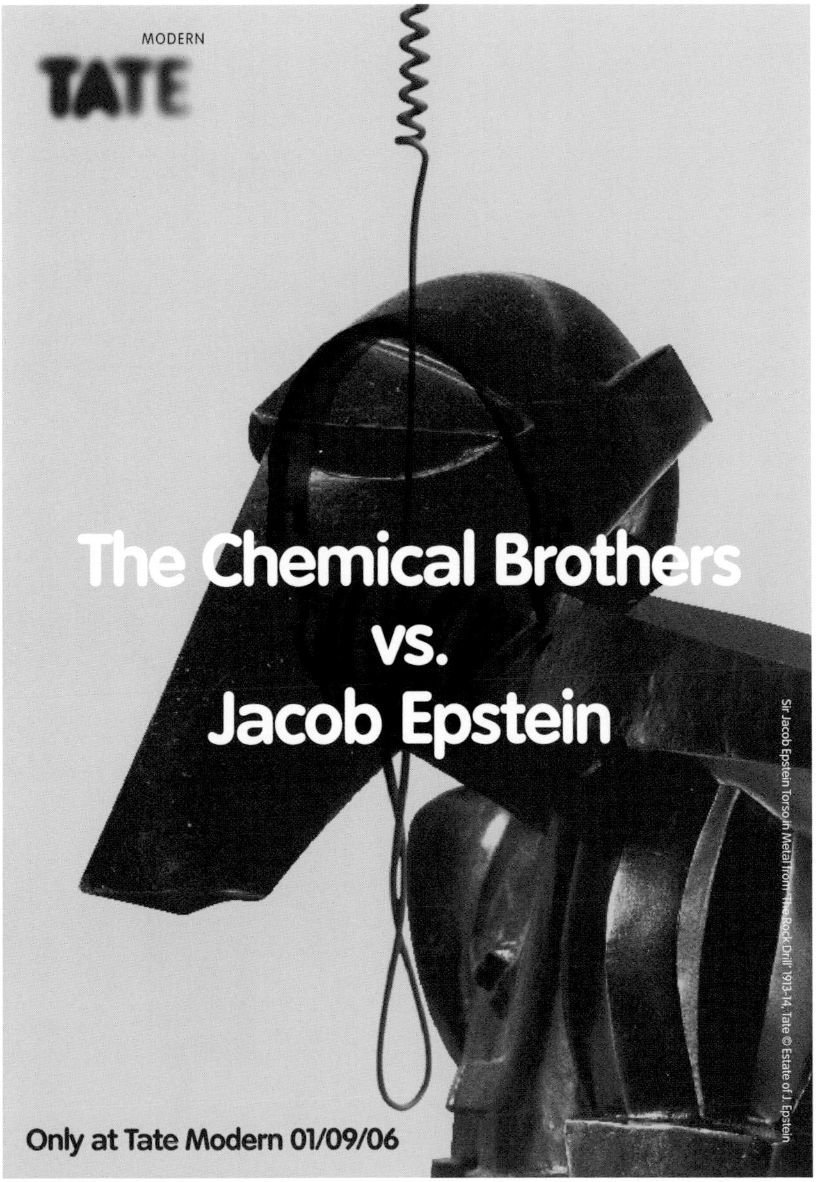
MODERN
TATE
The Chemical Brothers
vs.
Jacob Epstein
Sir Jacob Epstein Torso in Metal from 'The Rock Drill' 1913-14, Tate © Estate of J. Epstein
Only at Tate Modern 01/09/06

'There are more spaces to land your point of view now and more targeted places to put your idea. It's still about the idea and how do we speak to them in, hopefully, a mass way.'

Richard Flintham, executive creative director and co-founder, Fallon

KesselsKramer, Amsterdam

Absolut: Absolut Label

For Absolut Label, KesselsKramer asked a selection of designers to create their personal interpretation of the Absolut vodka brand in a basic garment. Each year the garment changed, with collections including items such as bags, T-shirts and underwear. The designers were also required to feature the word 'Absolut' within their designs. The garments were produced in a limited edition each year – these were sent to fashion insiders and also appeared within the editorial pages of fashion magazines, giving the brand far more press coverage than the original budget could possibly have afforded. In addition, KesselsKramer also produced books of the designs, with explanations from the designers on what had inspired their work.

'If you look at advertising agencies traditionally, there was a kind of mystery around them, with the production of commercials or the production of print, with photographers or illustrators ... but now it is so democratic, everybody is a graphic designer, everybody's a photographer, everybody's a filmmaker ... that's changed it a lot.'

Erik Kessels, co-founder and president, KesselsKramer

Famous
CONTENT

mirror-licker

1-off

MADAME
STUD

Far left bottom: From Absolut Label collection 2006. **Far left top:** Absolut Label box from 2005. **Above:** From Absolut Label collection 2005. **Left:** Absolut Label collection from 2004.

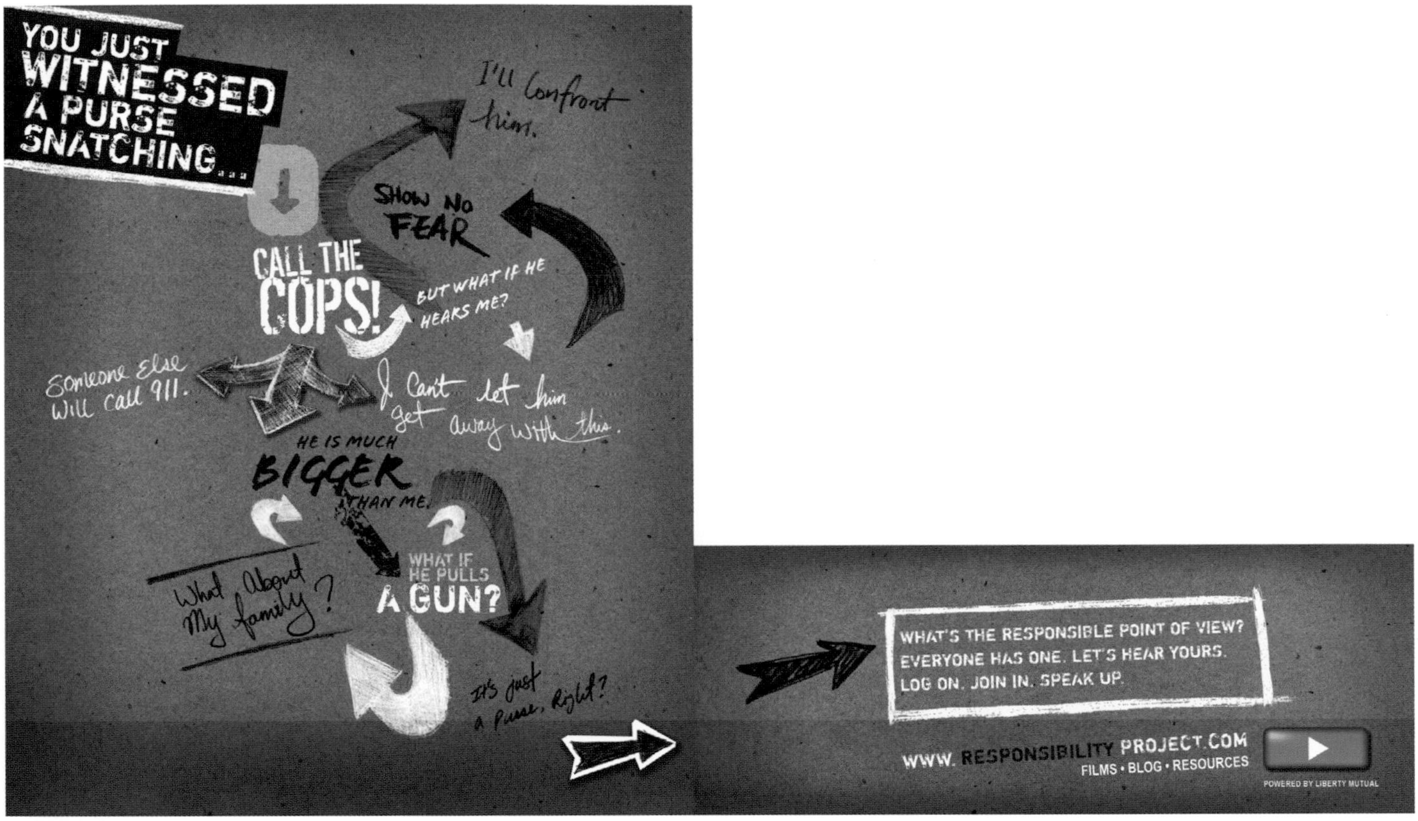
YOU JUST WITNESSED A PURSE SNATCHING...
I'll Confront him.
SHOW NO FEAR
CALL THE COPS!
BUT WHAT IF HE HEARS ME?
Someone Else Will call 911.
I Can't let him get away with this.
HE IS MUCH BIGGER THAN ME.
What about my family?
WHAT IF HE PULLS A GUN?
It's just a Purse, Right?
WHAT'S THE RESPONSIBLE POINT OF VIEW? EVERYONE HAS ONE. LET'S HEAR YOURS. LOG ON. JOIN IN. SPEAK UP.
WWW.RESPONSIBILITYPROJECT.COM
FILMS • BLOG • RESOURCES
POWERED BY LIBERTY MUTUAL

Hill Holliday, USA

Liberty Mutual: The Responsibility Project

Insurance is never an easy subject to make interesting, and advertising for insurance companies is rarely exciting. To break with this tradition, ad agency Hill Holliday created this complex campaign for Liberty Mutual, which incorporates film as well as online content and rarely mentions the word 'insurance'. The campaign evolved out of a conventional ad campaign for the brand, which featured the tagline 'Responsibility. What's your policy?' Following a positive result from consumers, Liberty Mutual launched the Responsibility Project, an online forum for discussing personal responsibility (www.responsibilityproject.com). Topical questions are posted regularly on the blog on the site, with users encouraged to join the debate. The issues range from our role in climate change, to motherhood, politics and sports. A series of independently produced short films in which the directors were invited to make a creative interpretation of the kind of decisions people make when they are trying to 'do the right thing' also appears on the website. The content of these films is varied, and the films take many forms, including dramatic narratives, animation and documentaries. The regularly updated content on the site encourages visitors to return frequently.

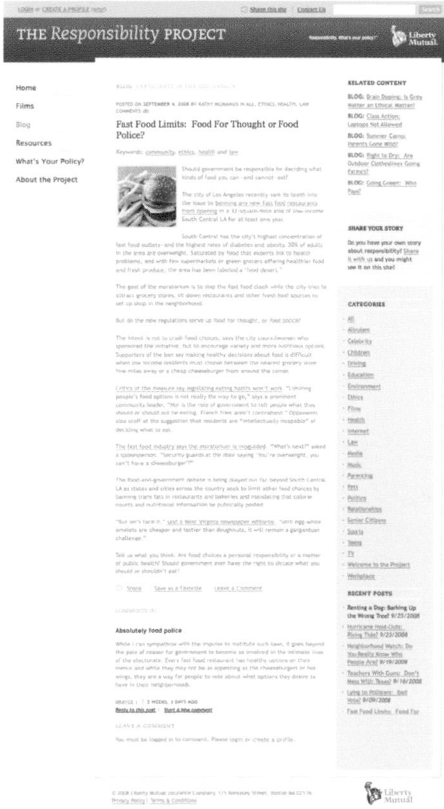
THE Responsibility PROJECT
Liberty Mutual.
Home
Films
Blog
Resources
What's Your Policy?
About the Project
Fast Food Limits: Food For Thought or Food Police?
RELATED CONTENT
SHARE YOUR STORY
CATEGORIES
RECENT POSTS
Absolutely food police

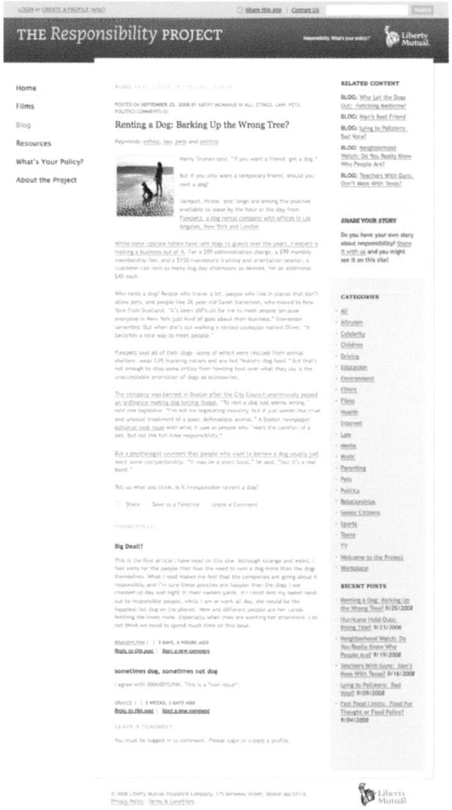
THE Responsibility PROJECT
Liberty Mutual.
Home
Films
Blog
Resources
What's Your Policy?
About the Project
Renting a Dog: Barking Up the Wrong Tree?
RELATED CONTENT
SHARE YOUR STORY
CATEGORIES
RECENT POSTS
Big Deal!?

Far left: Press ad for the Responsibility Project. **Above:** Still from *Lighthouse*, an animated film created for the website by director Charlie Short and Ming Hsiung. **Left:** Pages from the Responsibility Project blog.

BETC Euro RSCG, Paris

Sci Fi Channel: Adopt Sci Fi

BETC Euro RSCG created this integrated campaign, which incorporated ambient, radio, press, film and online elements, to raise awareness of the Sci Fi Channel in France. The campaign was based around ten alien 'children' toys that were placed in different locations across eight French cities. Fans were then encouraged to search for them by following clues found on a website and in radio ads. Posters were also displayed around towns to advertise the website.

The intention was to create an emotional link between the brand and people who were not already fans of science fiction. Each alien found earned its rescuer a reward of €500 (£460). When nine of the figures had been located it was revealed that the tenth had been placed in an 'orphanage', where it could be interacted with via a website and a page on Facebook. The treasure hunt aspect of the campaign appealed to fans of the Sci Fi Channel, while also attracting new viewers to the brand.

PERDU
ENFANT EXTRATERRESTRE DE TAILLE MOYENNE ET DE COULEUR CLAIRE
Si vous retrouvez cet extraterrestre une récompense de 500 EUROS vous sera remise. Renseignements sur:
www.findscifi.fr

PERDU
CRÉDIT AGRICOL
P
E-DE-FRANC

Far left: Lo-fi posters were placed around towns, promoting the website for the missing aliens. **Below, clockwise from top left:** Still from a film that formed part of the campaign; Image from the Sci Fi website; A winner with his alien toy; Image from the orphan alien's Facebook page.

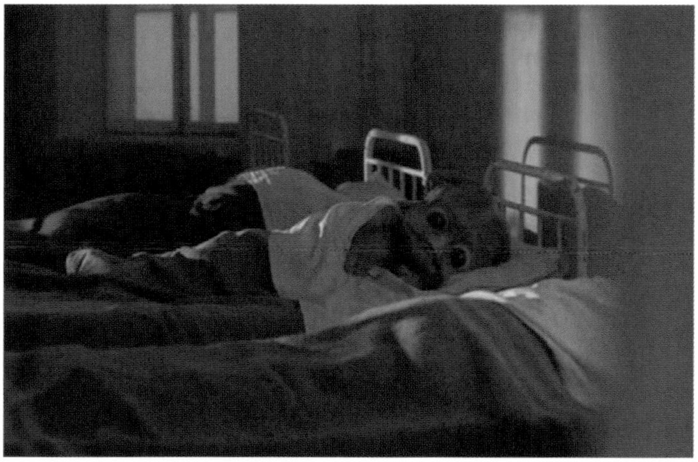

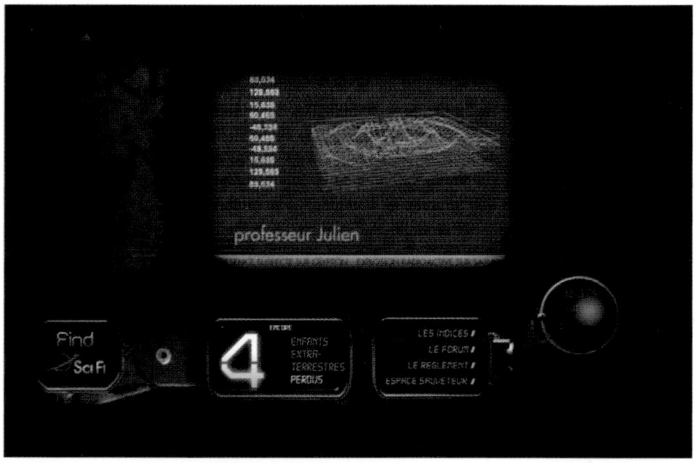
professeur Julien
Find
Sci Fi
4
ENFANTS
EXTRA-
TERRESTRES
PERDUS
LES INDICES
LE FORUM
LE REGLEMENT

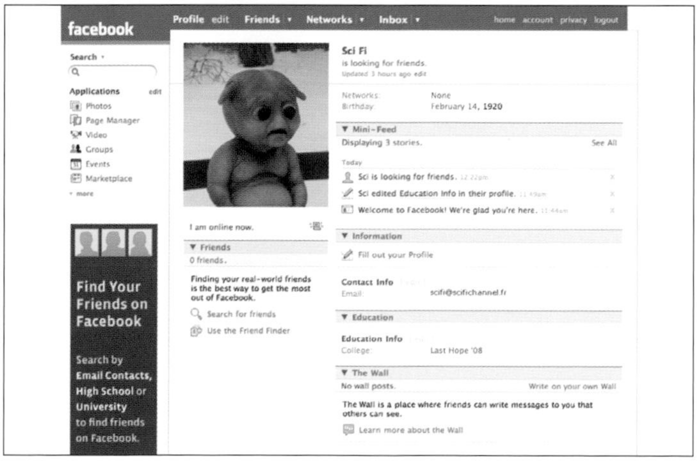
facebook
Profile edit Friends Networks Inbox
home account privacy logout
Search
Applications edit
Photos
Page Manager
Video
Groups
Events
Marketplace
Find Your Friends on Facebook
Search by Email Contacts, High School or University to find friends on Facebook.
Sci Fi
is looking for friends.
Networks: None
Birthday: February 14, 1920
Mini-Feed
Displaying 3 stories.
See All
Sci is looking for friends.
Sci edited Education Info in their profile.
Welcome to Facebook! We're glad you're here.
I am online now.
Friends
0 friends.
Finding your real-world friends is the best way to get the most out of Facebook.
Search for friends
Use the Friend Finder
Information
Fill out your Profile
Contact Info
Email: scifi@scifichannel.fr
Education
Education Info
College: Last Hope '08
The Wall
No wall posts.
Write on your own Wall
The Wall is a place where friends can write messages to you that others can see.
Learn more about the Wall

CLUB

One of the missing alien toys that when found earnt its rescuer €500 (£460).

THE CHASER'S WAR ON EVERYTHING
9PM WEDNESDAY MARCH 28 ABC TV

THE CHASER'S WAR ON EVERYTHING
9PM WEDNESDAY 28 MARCH ABC TV
12 11:26

The Glue Society, Sydney

ABC TV: *The Chaser's War on Everything*

Australian satirical comedy show *The Chaser's War on Everything* is known for lambasting everything, including advertising. So, when promoting a new time slot for the series, creatives at The Glue Society decided to take a satirical approach themselves, and advertised the show on the cheapest billboards in the world – in Iceland, India, Estonia, Kenya and Iraq. While the billboards were unlikely to be seen in situ by the required audience, The Glue Society posted images and viral films of the billboards online, generating a huge response and leading to enormous, free press coverage in Australia. They were able to achieve a far wider audience for the campaign than they would have via a billboard in Sydney, and ratings for the new series of the show doubled.

THE CHASER'S WAR ON EVERYTHING
9PM WEDNESDAY 28 MARCH ABC TV
countdowntothechaser.com.au
ABC
Television
مخزن
ثلج

THE CHASER'S WAR ON EVERYTHING
9PM WEDNESDAY 28 MARCH ABC TV
countdowntothechaser.com.au

Clockwise from far left: *The Chaser's War on Everything* posters as they appeared in Estonia, India, Iraq and Iceland.

Hi Steven,
Do I have your attention now?
I know all about her, you dirty, sneaky, immoral, unfaithful, poorly-endowed slimeball. Everything's caught on tape.
Your (soon-to-be-ex) Wife,
Emily
p.s. I paid for this billboard from OUR joint bank account.
city outdoor

Hi Steven,
Do I have your att
I know a
poorly-en
aithful,
pe.
p.s. I paid fo
board from OUR joint bank account.
our (soon-to-be-ex) Wife,
Emily
PARCO P.I.
NEW SEASON • TUESDAYS @ 10PM • PREMIERES AUGUST 15
city outdoor

Amalgamated, New York

Court TV: *Parco P. I.*

Court TV approached Amalgamated in New York to create a buzz around its second series of *Parco P. I.*, a show about a real-life detective, Vinnie Parco, who specializes in cases involving embezzlers and adulterers. Amalgamated's response was a poster, with no mention of the show, that appeared to be the work of a woman scorned – it consisted of an email that read: 'Hi Steven, Do I have your attention now? I know all about her, you dirty, sneaky, immoral, unfaithful, poorly-endowed slimeball. Everything's caught on tape. Your (soon-to-be-ex) Wife, Emily. P.S. I paid for this billboard from OUR joint bank account.' After appearing on billboards in both New York and Los Angeles, the poster captured the imagination of the media with news teams, blogs and websites across the US debating its origins. Amalgamated then followed up the poster with a blog by 'Emily' and a guerrilla stunt of having 'Steven's' car spray-painted and towed through the city. Stickers were eventually placed on the boards, revealing the connection to *Parco P. I.*, which led to yet more media coverage. For a tiny budget, Amalgamated was able to achieve nationwide exposure for the campaign.

HOPE SHE WAS WORTH IT
StevenIsACheatingDog.com
SYS·75B
PARCO P.I.
PAPITOS AUTO

Left: The poster containing 'Emily's' supposed revenge message before and after it was revealed that it was part of a promotion for *Parco P.I.* **Above:** In a continuation of the campaign,'Emily' scrawls graffiti over her 'husband's' car, which is then towed through the city with a *Parco P.I.* sticker on it.

eBay: You Are eBay

In this promotion for the auction website eBay, advertising agency BETC Euro RSCG auctioned off the website's TV advertising slots on the site. Over the week of the auction a bidding frenzy ensued before ten winners emerged. The winners worked with the ad agency to make a TV ad for an object that they were selling on eBay. The ads, which all starred the sellers and their objects, were written and produced by BETC in a TV studio, in near-live conditions, over just five days. The following week the ten ads were transmitted on all the main French TV channels, and the whole campaign got huge press coverage.

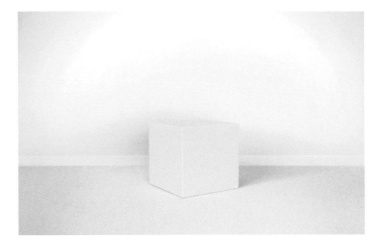

eBay met cet espace publicitaire
aux enchères.

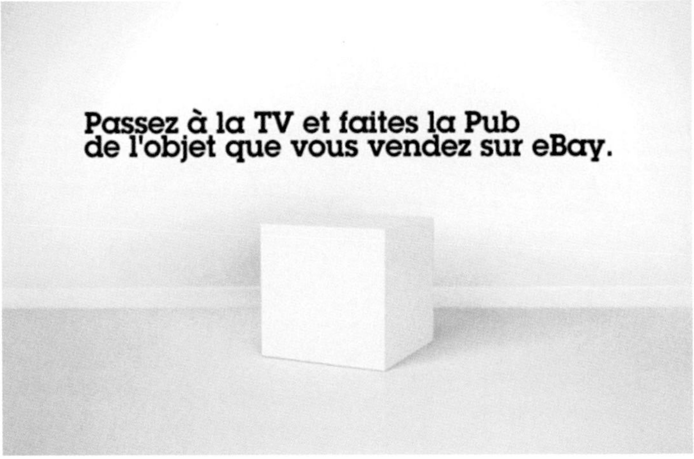
Passez à la TV et faites la Pub
de l'objet que vous vendez sur eBay.

Stills from the TV campaign promoting the opportunity for users to purchase eBay's TV advertising slots.

> 'The challenge for an agency is to find the time to construct an image and a meaning that is stable and interesting in the midst of general instability. Today, the world in which advertising agencies operate is a world that failed to foresee that the telephone of the future would be a computer and the camera of the future would be a telephone.'
>
> **Rémi Babinet, founder and chairman, BETC Euro RSCG**

soleil2121 (1) a remporté l'enchère
sur eBay. Voici sa pub.

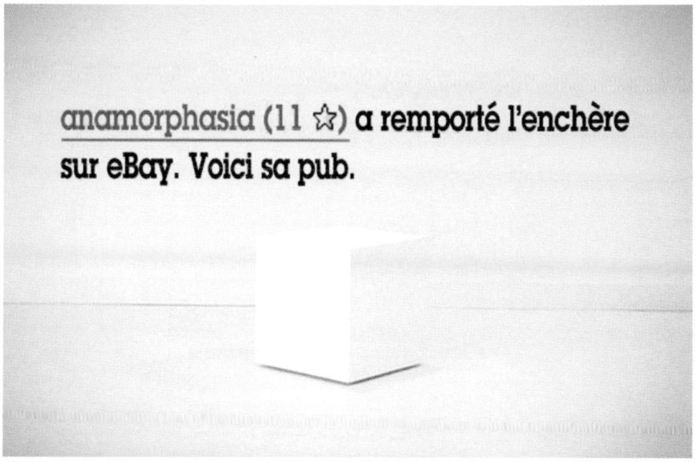
anamorphasia (11 ☆) a remporté l'enchère
sur eBay. Voici sa pub.

GAELLE
VEUX-TU
M'EPOUSER?

Stills from the resulting TV ads, created by BETC Euro RSCG, in conjunction with the winners.

IF YOU CAN'T TAKE
YOUR MATE
TO THE PUB
TAKE THE PUB TO YOUR MATE
It began with Tim, a good Kiwi lad in London missing his Speight's, and his mates. He told us about his problem. Something had to be done, he was a mate in need. So we set about sending him over a few dozen. But before it was sent, the question had to be asked: "How many Kiwis in London are also missing their Speight's?" It turned out there were plenty and a few dozen weren't going to do the job. Then, over a few cold Speight's, someone had the crazy idea of sending over an entire pub. "Can't be that hard, we've moved pubs before," someone added.
So it was decided to send a Speight's Pub over to London. James (Tim's best mate) said he'd go. Good on ya mate. We found a boat and all that was needed then was a crew. 2000 people applied for the vacant crew positions. Over a few Speight's, four keen lads were picked. Jamie, Tim C, Mark and Lindsay. The Great Beer Delivery could begin.
DUNEDIN
25/07/2007
SAMOA
04/08/2007
PANAMA
31/08/2007
BAHAMAS
NEW YORK
16/09/2007
LONDON
08/10/2007
SPEIGHT'S
FROM DUNEDIN TO LONDON
"FOR A MATE"
THE GREAT BEER DELIVERY
Pride of the South
THE PUB ARRIVES
IN LONDON
IT'S TIME FOR A BEER WE RECKON
Tim was waiting at the port. Finally his Speight's had arrived.
James poured him a cold one and they sat at the bar and exchanged a few yarns. What better way to end a journey to help a mate, than over a few cold Speight's.

Publicis Mojo, Auckland

Speight's: The Great Beer Delivery

This integrated campaign for New Zealand beer brand Speight's is based around the well-known Antipodean love of beer. The campaign claims to have been sparked by a plaintive letter to the beer company by a Kiwi living abroad in London who is missing home. 'It's not like at home, where a hard day's work would be a day of fencing, crutching or mustering on the farm,' wrote Speight's fan Tim Ellingham. 'But still a Speight's after a "pretend" London work day would really hit the spot and make me miss home just that wee bit less....' Speight's swung into action for poor Tim, and all other mates in the UK who were missing their Speight's, by launching The Great Beer Delivery, a boat trip that took a pub, literally, to London, via Samoa, Panama, the Bahamas and New York. Ads for crew were placed in New Zealand newspapers and after narrowing down the 2,000 hopeful volunteer sailors to five, the Speight's ship set sail from Dunedin with a hold full of beer and a fully working pub on deck. The crew's adventures along the way were made available to view online, and the boat arrived in London three months later.

POSITIONS VACANT:
ENGINEER WHO CAN ALSO FIX DINNER
We've got a pub on a boat heading to London, but only a couple of spots for the crew. So if you can rustle up a new transistor and a good steak you could be our man.
If you've got a mate in the UK missing their Speight's, join The Great Beer Delivery at speights.co.nz
Apply Now. Closes 11 May 2007.
SPEIGHT'S
FROM DUNEDIN TO LONDON
"FOR A MATE"
THE GREAT BEER DELIVERY
Pride of the South

CHEF WANTED
FOR A KITCHEN THAT'S GOING PLACES
Access to the freshest ingredients from around the world, mainly because you'll be around the world. But oddly enough never far from a Speight's pub.
If you've got a mate in the UK missing their Speight's, join The Great Beer Delivery at speights.co.nz
Apply Now. Closes 11 May 2007.
SPEIGHT'S
FROM DUNEDIN TO LONDON
"FOR A MATE"
THE GREAT BEER DELIVERY
Pride of the South

Dunedin
Samoa
Panama

SPEIGHT'S
FROM DUNEDIN TO LONDON
"FOR A MATE"
THE GREAT BEER DELIVERY
Pride of the South

WE'RE TAKING A PUB TO LONDON, YOU COMING?
BAHAMAS
NEW YORK
LONDON
SPEIGHT'S ALE HOUSE
DUNEDIN
SAMOA
PANAMA
JOIN THE GREAT BEER DELIVERY AT SPEIGHTS.CO.NZ
SPEIGHT'S
FROM DUNEDIN TO LONDON
"FOR A MATE"
THE GREAT BEER DELIVERY
Pride of the South

Far left: Ad explaining the Speight's Great Beer Delivery. **Above, clockwise from top left:** Ads for an engineer and a chef for the boat's crew; Still from a TV ad accompanying the campaign; Poster for the campaign showing the boat arriving in New York. **Left:** Billboard poster for the campaign.

AST
SPEIGHT'S ALE HOUSE

LIDA

The Speight's boat during its journey. The boat's fully working pub can be seen on the deck....

Anomaly, New York

Converse: Connectivity

To celebrate its hundredth anniversary, Converse shoes launched a new global advertising campaign entitled Connectivity. The campaign emphasized the brand's link with music, with a print and in-store campaign that featured black-and-white images of both emerging and iconic musicians shot against a simple white background. From there, things took a more unusual turn when Converse commissioned three musicians (Pharrell Williams, Santagold and Julian Casablancas, lead singer of The Strokes) to write and perform a new song for the brand. The resulting track, *My Drive Thru*, was made available for free download online at www.converse.com, and a music video, directed by Marie Hyon and Marco Spier of Psyop, was also released online. The video featured a similar aesthetic to the print work, with the three musicians appearing as animated paper dolls on a stark white background. The song was also distributed to radio stations and, despite being clearly attached to a brand, received favourable reviews from critics and fans alike.

CONVERSE
PED X G

东安市场
乐天银泰百货
INTIMESTYLE

CONVERSE
CONVERSE
The Original
GINO'S EAST
PIZZERIA
PIZZA PASTA
SALAD SANDWICHES
327-3737
DELIVERY CARRYOUT
DINE-IN PARTIES
327-3737

CONVERSE

14:07:08
CONVERSE

132
Cterio. FLORES
ONCE - RETIRO
NUEVOS RUMBOS
AXE

Vegaolmosponce, Buenos Aires

Unilever: Axe 3

The concept behind the Axe 3 campaign is that two bottles of Axe deodorant, which work independently, can also be mixed to create a third fragrance: Axe 3. As well as emphasizing the mixable fragrances, the campaign reiterated the overall brand message that Axe is a highly seductive deodorant: previous campaigns depicted packs of women chasing after men who are wearing it. Vegaolmosponce came up with the slightly questionable concept of 'mixing women', with different types of women representing the two base fragrances, who could then be mixed into a new type of woman altogether. The campaign combined traditional advertising, such as TV and poster work, with events and more unusual approaches, including an interactive billboard where people could vote on their favourite combination of women via their phones and the Axe website. Women dressed as the most popular combinations visited radio shows and popular areas in the participating cities to encourage people to vote for them. The final winning combination was then displayed on the billboard.

Far left: The Axe 3 girls at an event promoting the deodorant. The girls were representing mixtures of different types of women as part of the Axe 3 campaign, where audiences were given the chance to vote for their favourite combination. **Above:** Stills from the Axe 3 TV campaign.

Virgin mobile
IMPORTANT ANNOUNCEMENT
It has been brought to the attention of Virgin Mobile that information regarding one of our higher profile customers has leaked on to the internet. We strongly urge people not to call or text TV's Jason Donovan on
0403 JASOND
5c TEXT AND 5c PER MIN* VIRGIN TO VIRGIN 24/7
ENJOY OUR RATES RESPONSIBLY

FOR SALE
0403 527 663

The Glue Society/
Host, Sydney

Virgin Mobile: Jason

In this campaign for Virgin Mobile, The Glue Society and Host pretended to post pop singer Jason Donovan's phone number on the internet. The number was advertised through spoof spots that show Donovan getting increasingly irate as he receives endless calls to his phone. The ads feature a serious voice-over, intoning that 'We do not encourage this activity or the abuse of our excessively low rates', before requesting that viewers do not call or text the number on the screen. But call and text they did, over a million times.

Campfire, New York/
McKinney, Durham

Audi:
Art of the Heist

For the launch of the new Audi A3, a premium compact (small family car), which in 2005 was a new category of car in the North American market and retailed at a higher than expected price, Campfire and McKinney created an elaborate narrative-based campaign that rolled out across all forms of media. Blurring the lines between reality and fiction, the immersive campaign invited the consumer to join in with the story, and play a role within it. Created in collaboration with Hollywood screenwriters, the plot included blackmail, murder and double-crossed lovers, with the public invited to speculate on the crimes and help solve them. At the heart of the narrative were six new A3s containing coded plans for the largest art heist in history. One car contained the key to decrypting the information hidden in all the others, and part of the story tells of the 'theft' of this car from Audi's Park Avenue headquarters in New York City. The mystery surrounding the 'heist' unfolded in real time over three months across the country with the final chapter of the story played out in front of a live audience at the Viceroy Hotel in Los Angeles, where the villain of the piece was finally revealed. The campaign received acres of news coverage and brought over two million unique users to www.audiusa.com.

ATTENTION:
If you have any information regarding the location of a 2006 Audi A3 with VIN WAUZZZ8P65A045963, please contact Audi of America at 1-866-657-3268.
Audi

WANTED
FOR QUESTIONING
Regarding the Theft of
2006 Audi A3
If you have any information regarding this individual please contact Audi of America at
1-866-657-3268

StrawberryFrog, New York

Microsoft: Idea Wins

In order to get some attention around the launch of a useful but boring product – Microsoft's Office Accounting software – StrawberryFrog created the competition Idea Wins, which set out to find the best new business ideas in America. From the outset, the agency approached the concept in an unusual way, initially advertising the competition by delivering parachutes across the country with free copies of the software attached, along with a challenge to use it to bring business ideas to life. One such idea – Kyle Boné's invention of the Anti-shirt, which covers the areas that other T-shirts don't, and leaves naked the areas that it usually covers, in order to eliminate the 'farmer's tan' – was promoted online by a series of amusing films and via MySpace. Inspired entrepreneurs were then encouraged to log onto www.ideawins.com, where they could submit their own business ideas and download the software. The campaign received lots of coverage by the media before four finalists were chosen. The public voted online for the winning idea, and the winner was eventually revealed on NBC's *Today* show. Over a period of two months, over 1.5 million copies of the accounting software were downloaded, three times Microsoft's annual target for the product.

Farmer

KYLE BONE
AND
HIS INVENTION

Microsoft

Interview: Taylor Smith

Taylor Smith is global communications director at Xbox. He worked on the phenomenally successful Halo 3 Believe campaign (page 180), which involved the creation of fictional documentaries and a diorama sculpture of a fictional historical battle alongside film and cinema spots.

EW: **Do you feel that advertising is changing now? Is it important to approach consumers in lots of different ways?**

TS: Yeah, absolutely. Maybe it's just me, but we all seem to be living much more frantic lifestyles at this point and our attention spans are so much more fractured, between cell phones and email and work, and all the other things we do in our life. It's really hard for advertising to break through in the traditional ways. So it's really about telling an interesting, benefit-driven, connected story, because people just don't have time for sales pitches – these just bounce off people. We've got a lot more things at our disposal in terms of the ways in which we can get content out, the ways that we can have people interact and the ways we can get our fans together to talk about things. The upside of working at Xbox and working in an entertainment brand is that people actually seek us out. We aren't like the insurance companies of the world.... There are billions of fans seeking out information about us, so we view advertising and marketing more as content creation; how we can get fans who are already fans more excited and how we can get new fans into the fold by story-telling. They are pretty simple principles but they're not easy to do.

EW: **Do TV ads still have a place within your advertising? Is that something that's still important to you?**

TS: It's definitely still part of the equation. It's a medium that, even though it's relatively short, really works to move people. It's an emotional medium. But TV isn't the be all and end all – it's part of the equation, it's one of the things that we do, but in terms of getting quick reach with a lot of people and adding fuel to the buzz of something that we're trying to bring into the market-place, we feel that TV is absolutely critical. It's different, but the price is still the same and going up!

EW: **Are you putting more budget towards non-traditional advertising these days?**

TS: We are. We're allocating quite a bit of production money for stuff that's never going to get advertised in traditional media. The biggest contributing factor to the success of Halo was the combination of all the different facets – the television spots, that tied in with the web experience, that tied in with the films and all those sorts of stuff. We really just wanted to create an exhibit in an authentic way – it was about telling a story, and that story was reflected in terms that people get universally. People get museums, they get tributes to battles and tributes to heroes. That's a pretty approachable way to talk about something that in the past could be perceived as violent, gory and aggressive. We wanted to use more universal and human emotional terms so we took a historical view on it.... We wanted to tell the story from a man's perspective, from a human perspective and to do it in terms that people could get all over the world, and get whether they were fans of it or not.

EW: **How much do blogs affect you? Do you worry about the fact that people can now so easily be negative about brands online? Or are we past that stage?**

TS: I think that stage is a stage we're going to be living with forever at this point. It's a soapbox and anyone can say whatever they choose to. What's really interesting is the dialogue and the debate that you get on things. People have really high expectations of what we're doing and how we're going to do it and so when you do something great they embrace it and get thrilled about it, but when you do something that's kind of mediocre they just hammer you. It's really interesting to see the dialogues between the two – sometimes you have stuff that's kind of polarizing, some people love it and other people hate it, and they kind of go at it in these forums. There's a lot of organized forums around gaming and entertainment – there are so many destinations to go to where you can find people who want to talk about this stuff on the web. So the bar's high – you've got to be really careful that you do stuff that's quality, otherwise you just get whipped by it.

EW: **People are saying that advertising is being very influenced by the gaming culture – would you agree with this?**

TS: I believe that. It's around trying to create experiences. Whether those are digital experiences that might take more of a literal game-type approach – the digital world creates a level of interactivity with things and that interactivity often takes the form or structure of a game. I think that's good – it's interesting for everyone involved.

EW: **And has the relationship you have with advertising agencies changed with these developments? Does it affect the agencies you choose to work with?**

TS: What it really means to me is you've got to have talented agencies that have the backbone and structure of any good agency, but, even more than that, they've got to be really willing to be progressive and tell good stories and not think about things in a one-dimensional sort of way. We need to think about things in three dimensions and have ideas that work their way through all sorts of different media, and have a really good understanding and passion for the space, so we can create things that not only gamers are going to like but are going to bring new people into the category as well. Really, I think that some of the people who are doing the best work in the industry are sort of thinking about it similarly: How do you create experiences, how do you have content that is interactive and more long term? Those are challenges that we're all trying to figure out in different ways.

EW: **Do you feel that agencies now have to have a broader offering – have events departments, a digital department etc.? Or is that not a priority for you?**

TS: I feel that different things work well in different cases. Sometimes agencies have a particular area of speciality – whether that be events or digital or traditional advertising formats or PR. Sometimes they can partner well with other groups and then you get the best of both worlds. Other times its much better to let the agency have its own connective core. It can work both ways. Clearly agencies are trying to provide a one-destination place in terms of capabilities, and I like the theory of that, as long as the people and the talent and the capabilities are really strong throughout. That's a great situation from a client perspective – for the client not to have to be the central hub, so that the agency can be more of a central hub. But that doesn't always work as well sometimes. There's nothing easy about doing integrated marketing; everything about it is exponentially harder, it takes all that much more collaborative planning and discussion and keeping everyone up to speed and things like that. And we execute programmes at a global scale, so that's not only a coordination within a single market, that's coordinating all the marketing leads across 30 major markets.

McCann/T.A.G., San Francisco

Microsoft Xbox: Halo 3 Believe

In a bid to reach new audiences for the Halo franchise for the release of Halo 3, a futuristic human versus aliens science fiction video game, McCann and T.A.G. in San Francisco came up with this complex integrated campaign that utilizes both film and online advertising. They created a large diorama that documented a historic battle, which was filmed for TV and cinema spots. An interactive flythrough tour of the diorama was then also placed online. It was all intended to present Halo as a story with real emotion. 'Our objective was to use every medium we could to communicate the simple idea that Master Chief [the hero of the game] is a true hero to all humankind,' says John Patroulis, creative director at T.A.G.

'The goal was to make this the biggest title launch in Xbox history,' Patroulis continues. 'And we went about it by executing a global campaign that used absolutely no game footage, starred either plastic figures or old men in its films, used classical music as its soundtrack, and almost never showed Master Chief.' Halo 3 became the fastest pre-selling game in history and made $170 million (£116 million) in sales on its first day, the biggest launch in entertainment history.

Far left: Photograph of the diorama that was created for the Halo 3 campaign. Left: Stills from the Halo 3 Believe TV and cinema ad campaign that was filmed within the diorama.

'The ability to really move people is limited in a 30- or even a 60-second TV spot, but the chance of something that's more interactive or longer format … that's the same feeling you get as after you've read a book or seen a movie, that you've gone through a story or an experience and that's what moves people.'

Taylor Smith, global communications director, Xbox

BURGER
KING

Crispin Porter + Bogusky/Pitch, USA

Burger King: Xbox King Games

Crispin Porter + Bogusky and Pitch plugged into the popularity of computer games in this campaign for Burger King, with Microsoft partnering the fast food chain to create three Xbox video games that featured the Burger King character 'The King'. The games, which were designed in-house at Crispin Porter + Bogusky, were sold in store for a limited period for just $3.99 (£2.70) with the purchase of a BK Value Meal. The games also featured other characters that had recently appeared in advertising for Burger King. In only five weeks, 2.4 million games were sold.

BBDO New York/Big Spaceship, New York

HBO: Voyeur

The HBO Voyeur campaign was intended to articulate US TV channel HBO's ability to tell great stories, and to tell them across a number of media platforms. To do this, BBDO New York and Big Spaceship created a campaign that played out online, on mobile phones and on TV. The story began with a film that took viewers inside a number of New York apartments, *Rear Window*-style. This was first revealed to a live audience by the use of a high-definition projection that was presented on a large blank wall in New York, giving the illusion that the audience could see into the protagonists' life-sized homes. This experience was then replicated online, and users could zoom into each of the apartments to watch the events taking place in closer detail. Users could also zoom out and look at the New York skyline, where new stories could be discovered. In one of the stories an FBI agent was murdered in an apartment, and viewers were then directed to HBO On Demand where a film, *The Watcher,* revealed what happened to a voyeur who is caught watching by the killer. Clips could also be downloaded to iPods and PSPs, while a partnership with telephone company AT&T meant that new tips and clues to the stories could be sent out to mobile phones. Millions of voyeurs visited the website during the campaign.

Myreson
FUNERAL HO

Images from the HBO Voyeur website.

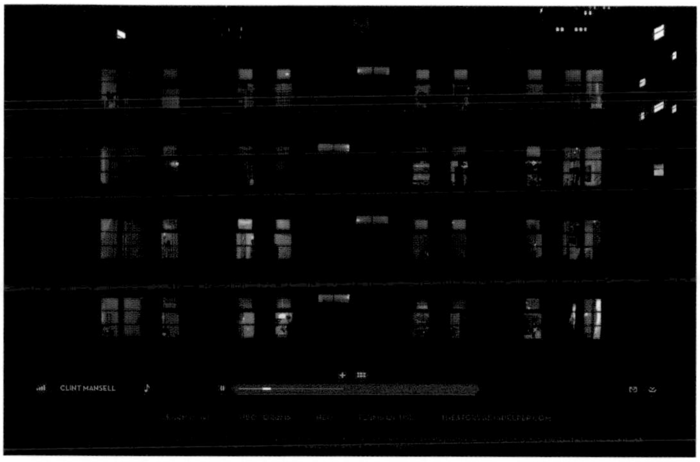
CLINT MANSELL

CLINT MANSELL

CLINT MANSELL

SUPERSONIC

AKQA, London

Nike: Supersonic

Nike Supersonic was conceived by AKQA to get young Londoners excited about running. The brand already held the hugely successful yearly Run London event, which was extremely popular among 30-something Londoners, but Supersonic was deliberately pitched at a younger audience. Supersonic invited London's youth to prove their speediness in a series of three 100-metre trials held across the city, with the top-scoring entrants winning three tickets for themselves and two friends to an event mixing running and music – a 1-K floodlit race through Battersea Park with an after party featuring live performances from Dizzee Rascal and The Enemy. Runners' times were recorded on an online leaderboard and 1,000 runners ran in the final. All the runners in the final received an iPod nano and Nike + iPod Sport Kit, and the fastest man and woman also won three tickets each to any worldwide sporting event. In addition to press and online coverage of Supersonic, Channel 4 also aired a 30-minute TV show of the event.

NIKE.COM
REGISTER
MY ACCOUNT
NEWSLETTER
Get connected to your running experience. Relive your runs. Track your progress.
NIKE+ USERS:
• Log in
Runs
Compare: Distance Time By: Run Week Month See All Runs
RUN TOTALS 10/22/06 at 8:45am
4.5mi DISTANCE
0.35'12":65 TIME
6'23"/mi PACE
589 CALORIES
09/08 09/09 09/10 09/12 09/13 09/14 09/16 10/04 10/06 10/09 10/22 10/23
My Runs
Products
Community
21,527,138mi
Sport Music
Support
COUNTRY SELECTOR
STORE LOCATOR
CUSTOMER SERVICE
PRIVACY/TERMS OF USE
©2007 NIKE ALL RIGHTS RESERVED

R/GA, New York

Nike: Nike+

The Nike+ website, www.nike.com/nikeplus, which is aimed at runners, allows users to upload their personal running times, track their individual progress, compare runs and interact with a wider community of passionate runners from over 23 countries. There are also forums on the website where runners can support, challenge and provoke each other.

To further enhance its users' experience of the site, Nike joined forces with Apple to create the Nike + iPod Sport Kit, which allows runners to attach a small accelerometer to a shoe, where it communicates with the user's iPod and stores information such as the runner's workout duration, distance travelled, pace and calories burned. In addition to the Apple tie-up, Nike has released its own SportBand kit, which also records the user's stats. Both the Nike + iPod Sports Kit and SportBand kit can be synced to the Nike+ website, where all the runners' facts and figures can be uploaded.

Challenge your friends.
My Runs
Products
Community
Sport Music
Support

Google
My Runs
Products
Community
Sport Music
Support

Fallon, London

Sony Walkman: Music Pieces

To advertise a new Sony Walkman digital media player, Fallon created an epic TV spot, entitled Music Pieces, which gathered together 128 musicians in the Alexandra Palace Theatre in London. Each was given just one note to play in a piece of original music composed for the commercial by Peter Raeburn. Thirty-two electric guitars and 32 drums, among many other instruments, featured in the spot.

The finished ad and a behind-the-scenes film were then placed on www.walkmanproject.com, and visitors to the site were encouraged to join in with the orchestra by uploading clips of themselves playing the track or singing along with the song. The site also offered the opportunity for users to mix tracks made by other people and upload those.

Home
What's it all about?
Record your track
Mix it up
Walkman® range
The Walkman® Project
FIND OUT MORE
RECORD YOUR TRACK
MIX IT UP
WATCH OUR TV AD
Latest news
Explore the Walkman® range
SONY

Above: Stills from the Sony Walkman Orchestra TV spot. **Left:** Image from the website.

GT Tokyo

Microsoft Xbox: Big Shadow

GT Tokyo drew on a certain function within the Xbox game, Blue Dragon – where the protagonist's shadow becomes a dragon when he fights – for its promotion of the game in Japan. Focusing on the primordial human experience of shadows, the agency projected magnified shadows of ordinary people against buildings in Shibuya, Tokyo, and created a system whereby they could play with them. The projected shadow could suddenly change into the shape of a dragon, adding to the fun.

Technology formed the backbone of the project – the 'shadows' cast were not real, but were projections of images captured by a video camera and manipulated with a specially developed program before being cast onto the wall by four powerful projectors. This combination of technology enabled the 'shadows' to morph into shapes such as the dragon shadow images. The dragon would appear when participants performed certain actions, such as raising their arms over their heads. Minotaur and phoenix shadows were also programmed to appear alongside projections of a giant hand, a foot and a cup of water. Extra shadows could be added to the on-site wall projection in real time via the internet. All the relayed images were then archived online, where users could view them as a sequence of still images arranged along a time axis.

ABC·MART
カラオケ
歌広場
ABC·MART
24
OPEN
炭火
BAR

GNUF.COM

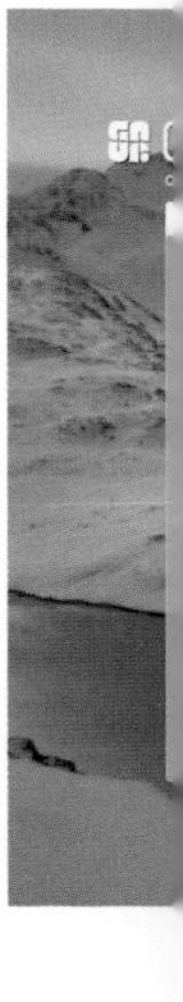

Above: Photographs of the dice being prepared and then transported to Greenland for the dice roll. **Far right:** Images of the competition as featured on the www.gnuf.com website.

ACNE, Stockholm

Gnuf.com: The World's Greatest Dice Roll

Swedish company ACNE created an unusual event to launch www.gnuf.com, a new gaming website. In an attempt to position the website away from the traditional associations of gambling – strippers, bling and Las Vegas – ACNE created a major offline event, which could be interacted with online. The company arranged for two enormous half-ton dice to be thrown down a snow-covered mountain in Greenland. The event was filmed and footage of it was placed online. Visitors to the site were encouraged to bet on the outcome of the dice, and the length of time they took to tumble down the mountain, for the chance of winning a holiday to Greenland.

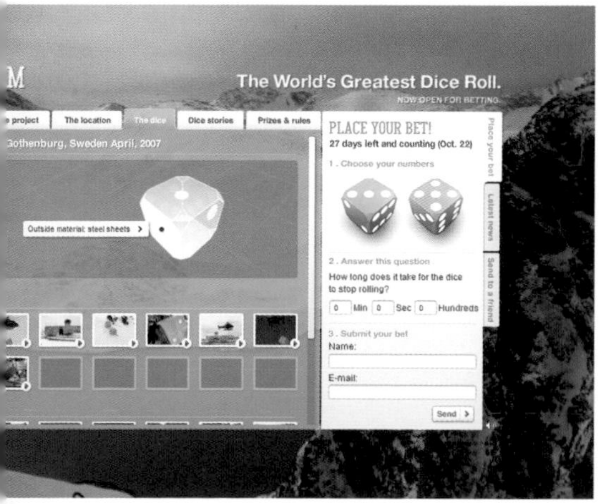
The World's Greatest Dice Roll.
NOW OPEN FOR BETTING
The location
The dice
Dice stories
Prizes & rules
Gothenburg, Sweden April, 2007
Outside material: steel sheets
PLACE YOUR BET!
27 days left and counting (Oct. 22)
1. Choose your numbers
2. Answer this question
How long does it take for the dice to stop rolling?
Min
Sec
Hundreds
3. Submit your bet
Name:
E-mail:
Send
Place your bet
Latest news
Send to a friend

Close

MIND THAT CHILD

'Assumptions have gone out the window, and that puts the emphasis back on creativity. You can't just assume that by spending money on certain media that you'll get the audience. It's no longer about who's got the deepest pockets but who can find the best connections.'

David Droga, founder and creative chairman, Droga5

Chapter Five: Self-initiated

Advertising agencies don't just make ads. Advertising creatives have always embarked on other artistic ventures outside of their work in the agency, and now these extra-curricular activities are increasingly being brought in-house. As clients demand ever more unusual and creative solutions to approaching new audiences, it is now an advantage if an agency shows that it can create art, design products and websites, run a record label or publish books and comics. And of course it keeps the creatives very happy too. This chapter looks at some outstanding pieces of work from agencies that are not produced for clients, but are made simply for the love of being creative.

Mother, London

Mother Comics

Mother advertising agency formed its comic publishing arm, Mother Comics, in 2008. Its first offering was *Four Feet From A Rat*, a four-part comic that was distributed with copies of *TimeOut* magazine during 2008. *Four Feet From A Rat* is based on tales of London life and there is much that is familiar to Londoners – a pigeon mafia makes an appearance, and one story is set on the Routemaster buses, all of which are driven by zombies. Mother worked with graphic novel publishers Mam Tor to create the comic, who helped the ad agency to commission the artists who worked on it.

MOTHER COMICS
PRESENTS
FOUR FEET FROM A RAT
FFFAR_01
MARCH
08
MAM TOR
Publishing

HOP ON, HOP OFF.
HOP ON
They're not manic depressives they're bloody zombies.
What the hell is it? Prozac? They almost look cheerful.
I'm gonna puke!
Ok, lets go...oh shit
HOP. OFF.
I don't care. We need to get the hell out of here.
RUN DARREN!!!
GET IN THE BUS LANE...

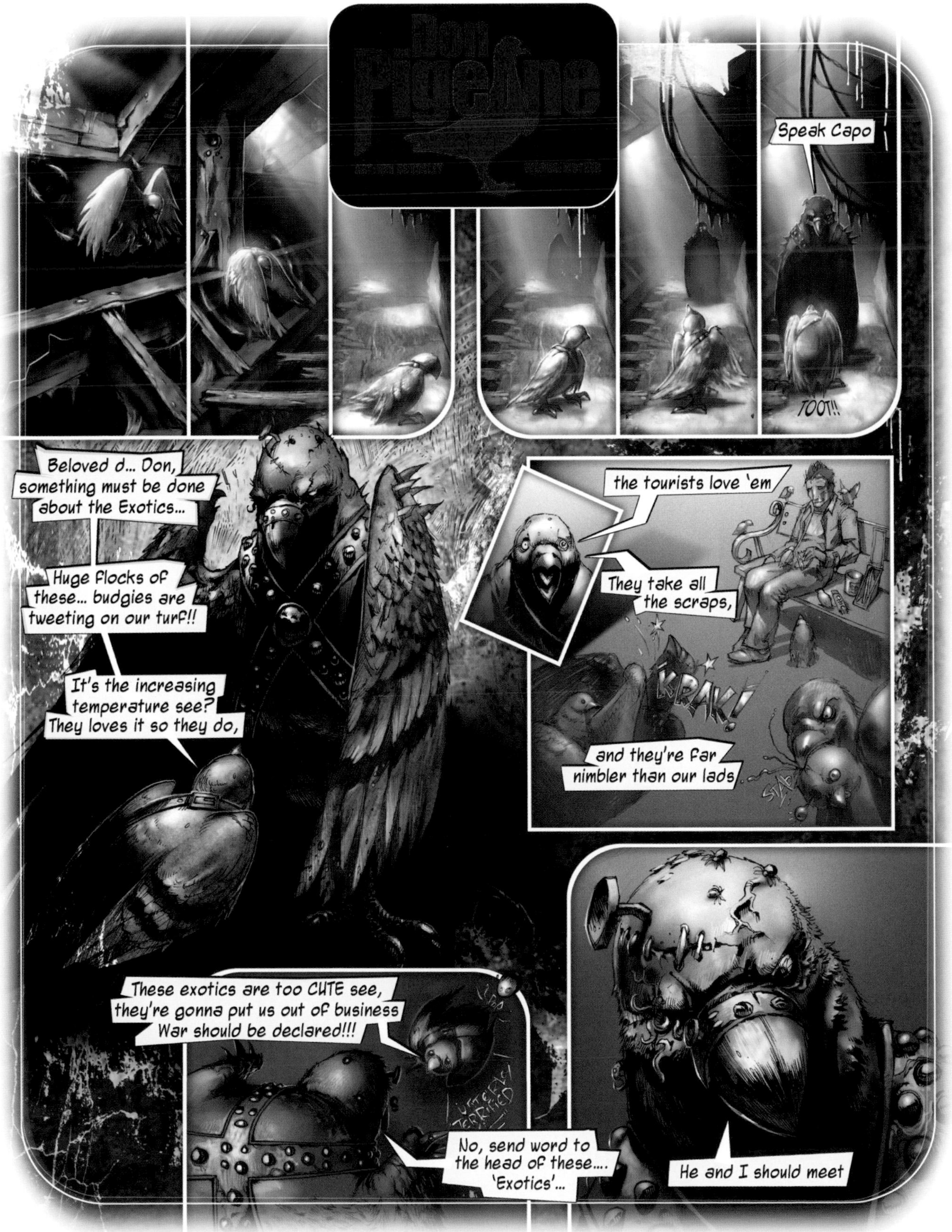

Don Pigeone
Speak Capo
TOOT!!
Beloved d... Don, something must be done about the Exotics...
Huge flocks of these... budgies are tweeting on our turf!!
It's the increasing temperature see? They loves it so they do,
the tourists love 'em
They take all the scraps,
KRAK!
and they're far nimbler than our lads
These exotics are too CUTE see, they're gonna put us out of business War should be declared!!!
No, send word to the head of these.... 'Exotics'...
He and I should meet

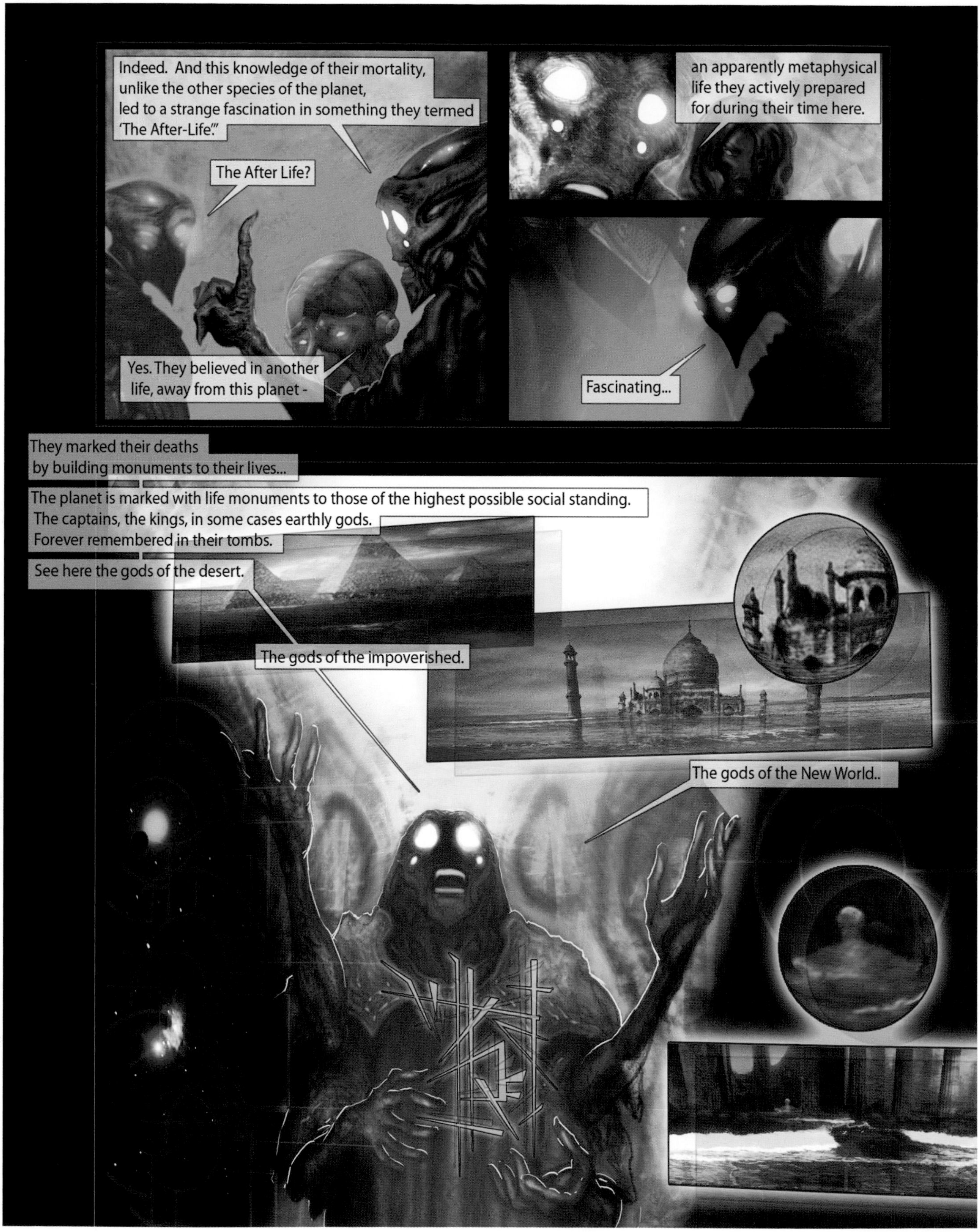
Indeed. And this knowledge of their mortality, unlike the other species of the planet, led to a strange fascination in something they termed 'The After-Life'."
The After Life?
Yes. They believed in another life, away from this planet -
an apparently metaphysical life they actively prepared for during their time here.
Fascinating...
They marked their deaths by building monuments to their lives...
The planet is marked with life monuments to those of the highest possible social standing. The captains, the kings, in some cases earthly gods. Forever remembered in their tombs.
See here the gods of the desert.
The gods of the impoverished.
The gods of the New World..

‘It seems like a natural evolution.... Everything is just little bits and they’re imperceptible and the next thing you’re developing digital solutions for clients and you’re creating films and you’re creating comic books. I don’t think you’re necessarily conscious that there is a big revolution going on within the agency, and that’s how it should be, I think.’

Robert Saville, co-founding partner and creative director, Mother

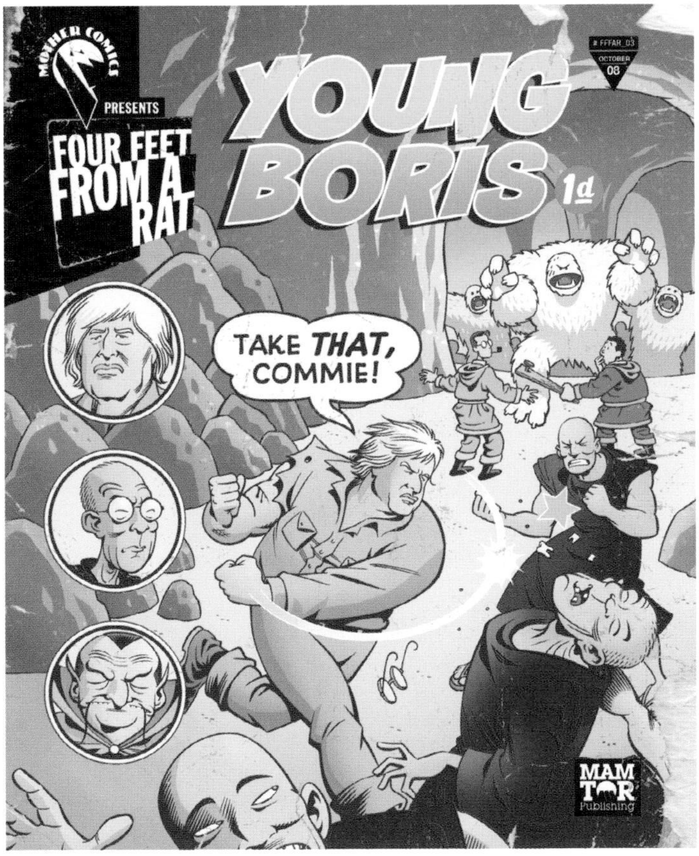
MOTHER COMICS
PRESENTS
FOUR FEET FROM A RAT
FFFAR_03
OCTOBER 08
YOUNG BORIS
1d
TAKE THAT, COMMIE!
MAM TOR Publishing

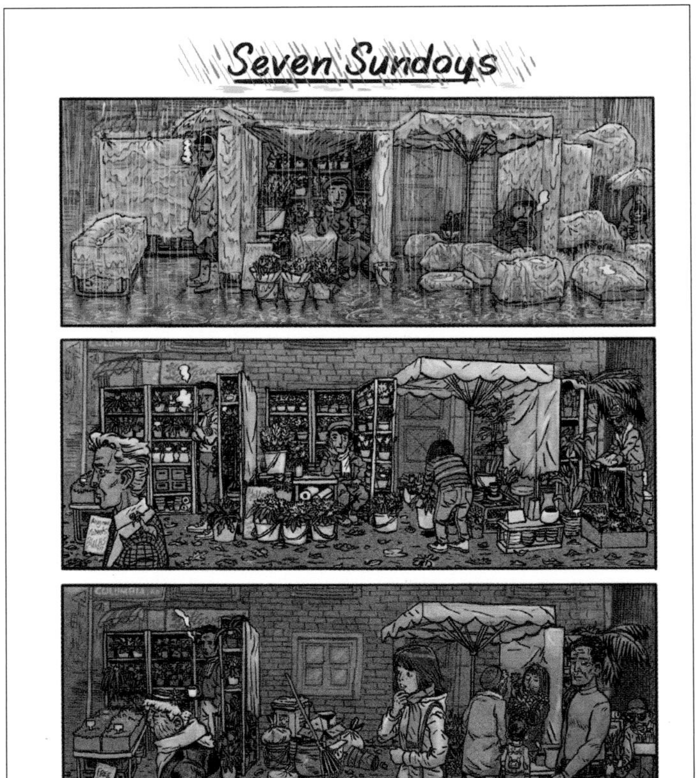
Seven Sundays

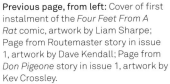

Previous page, from left: Cover of first instalment of the *Four Feet From A Rat* comic, artwork by Liam Sharpe; Page from Routemaster story in issue 1, artwork by Dave Kendall; Page from *Don Pigeone* story in issue 1, artwork by Kev Crossley.

This page, from left: Page from *Crane Gods* story in issue 1, artwork by Liam Sharpe; Cover of issue 3, artwork by Roger Langridge; Page from *Seven Sundays* story in issue 3, artwork by Ralph Niese.

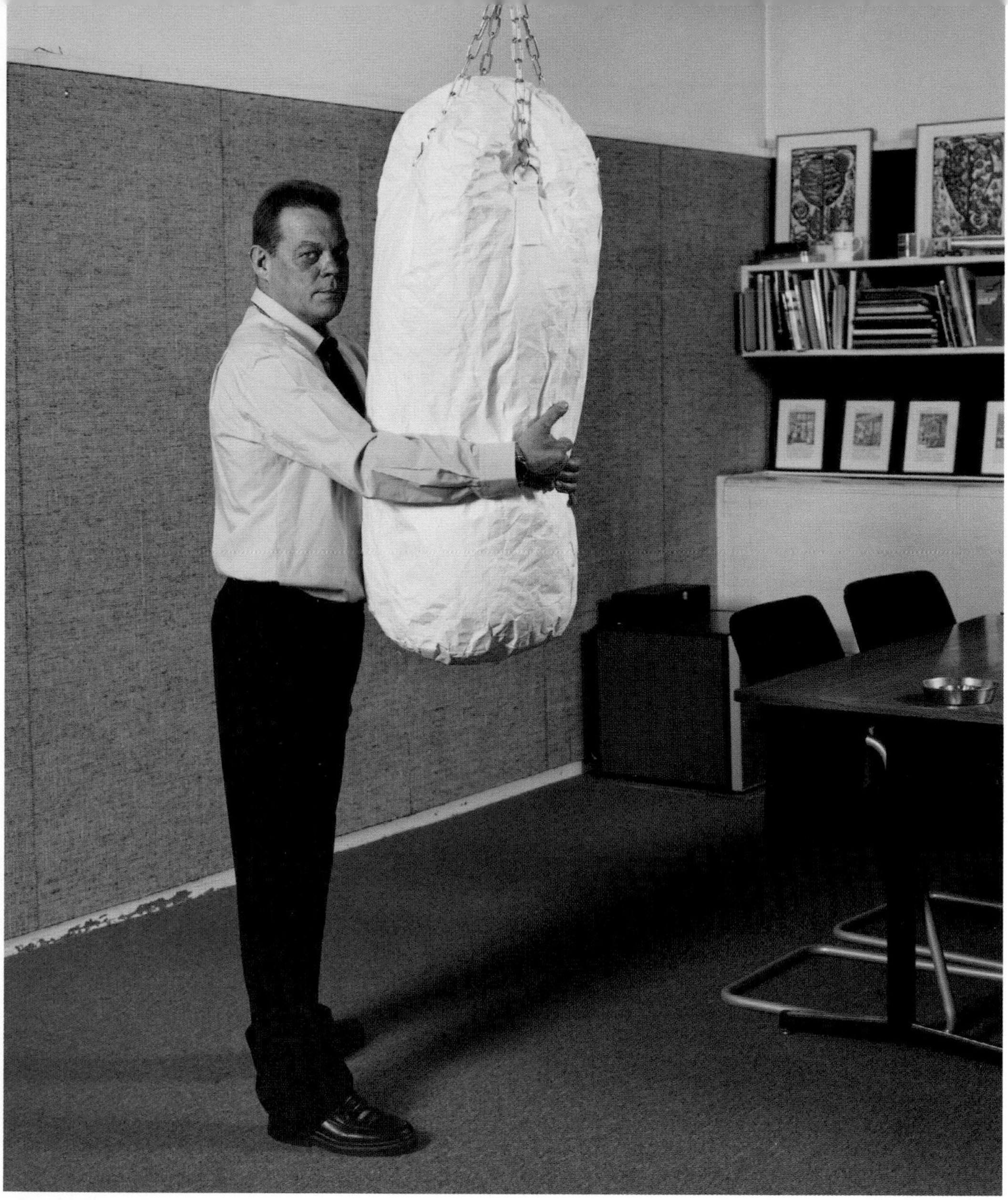

KesselsKramer, Amsterdam

do box

do is a series of eclectic products from the KesselsKramer agency, all of which involve the participation of the consumer. The do box, for example, offers a lateral approach to one of the most important topics of our times, recycling. The product consists of a punch-bag, which, instead of bulking out with the more conventional padding of foam or sand, users are encouraged to fill with rubbish such as old clothing. Once full, the bag can be used to take out its owner's frustrations on the planet's environmental problems (or any other worries they may have) by punching hard. The do box is sold through KesselsKramer's website, as well as through the KK Outlet, a shop contained within the agency's London office.

Droga5, New York/
Smuggler, Los Angeles

Honeyshed

Honeyshed was a shopping and entertainment website aimed at 18–35-year-olds, which operated from 2007–9. What made it unusual was that it was the brainchild of advertising agency Droga5 and production company Smuggler. The website was essentially a trendy version of a shopping channel, and saw a selection of hip young presenters sell various products to visitors to the site in quirky and amusing ways. What set Honeyshed apart was its irreverent approach and the range of products on the site, which were all chosen by its creators. The goods on the site were largely focused around entertainment and fashion, and there was also a selection of free 'fun shit' films to watch and play with, which aimed to encourage people to return to the site, and then in turn do some shopping. Honeyshed closed in 2009 as a result of economic pressures.

HONEYSHED

HONEYSHED
HONEYSHED

HONEYSHED

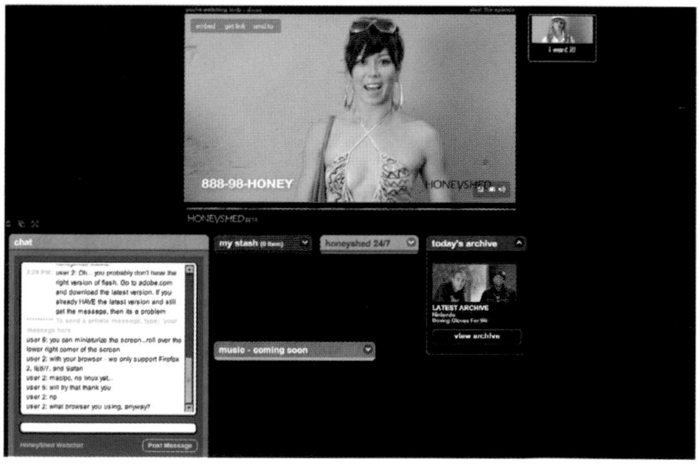
888-98-HONEY
HONEYSHED
chat
my stash
honeyshed 24/7
today's archive
LATEST ARCHIVE
view archive
music - coming soon
Post Message

BETC Euro RSCG, Paris

BETC Design, Art and Music Projects

Since its launch in 1994, BETC Euro RSCG in Paris has been making work in creative disciplines that fall outside the usual remit of an advertising agency. The agency has its own design arm, which has created such iconic designs as the Parisian Metro rubbish bin (1994), and has produced work for clients such as Air France, for which it designed the airline's business class seat in 2003. BETC also has its own art gallery, Passage du désir, in the basement of its main building, which has shown acclaimed international artists such as Rineke Dijkstra, Darren Almond and Joana Vasconcelos. In addition, the agency regularly holds its own club nights, Panik parties, in cities all over the world. These activities form a central part of BETC's output, alongside its more traditional advertising work for brands.

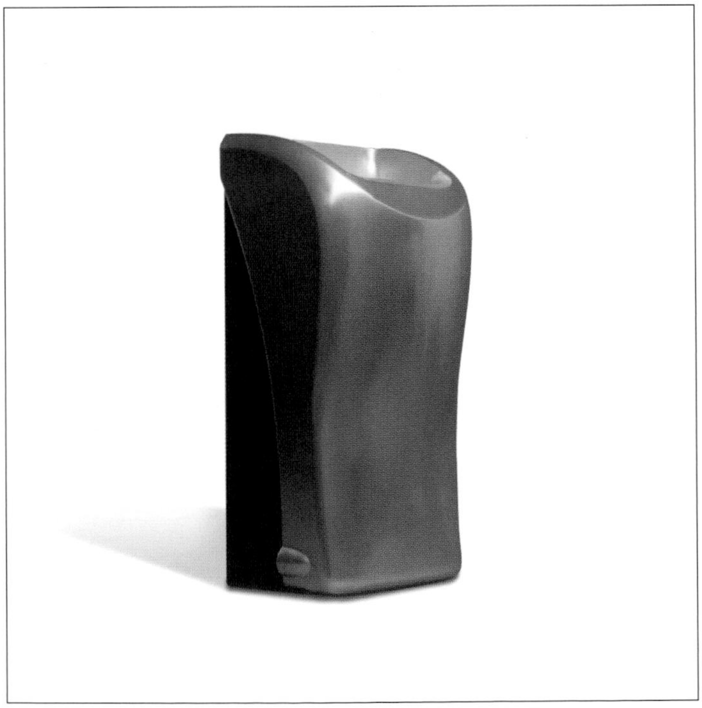

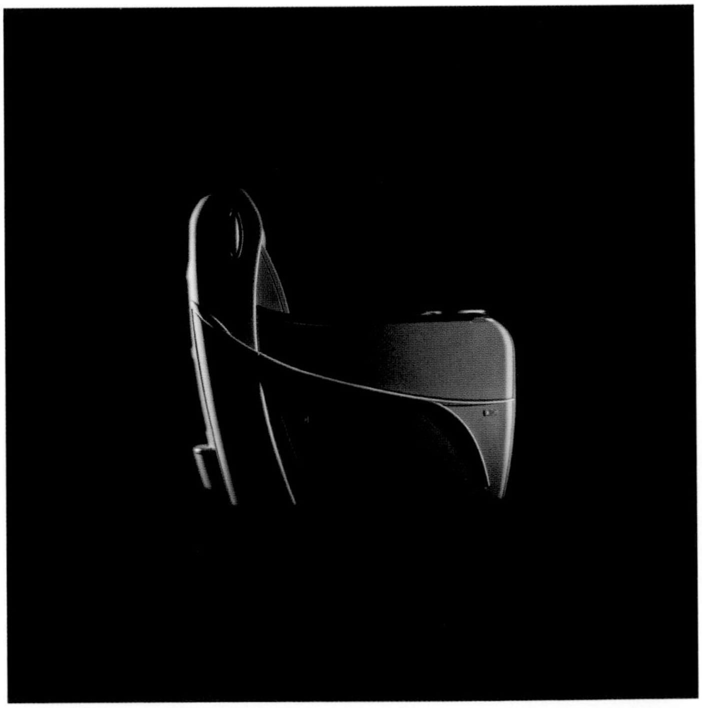

PASSAGE DU
DESIR

ALEX MACLEAN

Far left: RATP bin, designed for the Paris Metro in 1994; Air France business class seat, designed in 2003. **Above:** Images from exhibitions held at the Passage du désir, the contemporary art gallery within BETC's main Paris offices. **Left:** Flyer for Panik club night.

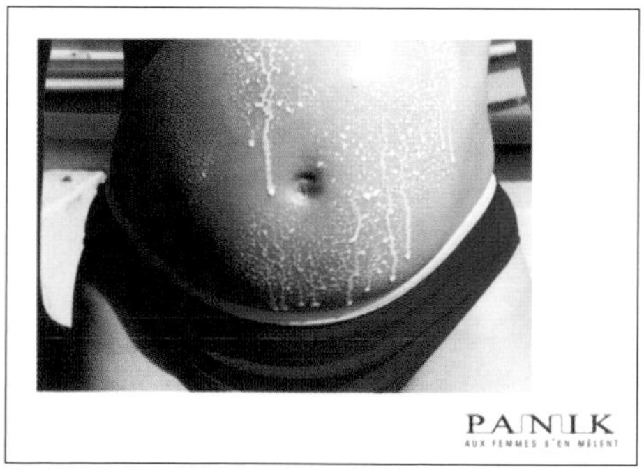
PANIK

Interview: Erik Kessels

Erik Kessels is co-founder and president of KesselsKramer advertising agency, with offices in Amsterdam and London. The agency is acclaimed for its highly creative advertising work for Nike, Audi, Levi's, Diesel and Hans Brinker Budget Hotel (page 98). Alongside making ads, the agency has its own publishing arm (page 206), and has also produced eclectic products (page 200) for sale online and through the KK Outlet, London.

EW: **When you started out, did you know that you wanted to do very creative work?**

EK: It was purely from instinct. Johan [Kramer] and I had some clients on our own and we worked very directly with them, and it was very easy, so when we were setting up an agency we thought 'Why is it not possible there?' That's why we started and at that time we found that clients were more willing to talk directly to the people who made the work, and who came up with the ideas. That was already slowly changing. Some clients also had a marketing education so they knew a lot about marketing – the only thing they were lacking was an idea and somebody who could make that step between their problem and a good idea.

EW: **Were clients pleased about this?**

EK: The clients that we were worked for were pleased. But it's not for everybody. There are still clients now that want to be taken out for lunch, or want to be pampered. We have a very intense relationship where we both work and keep each other inspired – the client and the agency – and sometimes you don't feel that barrier any more. It's still difficult sometimes, though.

EW: **People know more now.**

EK: Yes and in that sense it's quite liberal and democratic. You have to have a very good idea now – that's the only thing that designers and film-makers and agencies can offer.

I think what a lot of agencies forget is that talking to a client, and having a good relationship with a client, that's already 80 per cent of the job. I've been raised with the fact that you make work, and the tension builds up in the agency, and then the client hasn't seen anything for weeks, and everybody is nervous, and the client is nervous. And then they show it. There's no communication. They call themselves communication agencies but there's no communication. I've made the most stupid mistakes in meetings, it's embarrassing. But I've shown that I'm human, and they've sympathized with that fact. There should be a level of respect.

EW: **In terms of the 'idea', what do you think about buzz words such as branded content, or of viral taking over from TV?**

EK: It's totally not interesting in a way. Because then you're talking about the surface – it's not interesting. There's a problem, you solve it with a strong idea and then whatever medium fits best with it, that's fine.

EW: **What drew you to go into advertising?**

EK: I was trained as an illustrator, so I was also doing jobs, but I found that too lonely, the whole thing. Then I worked as a visualizer in an agency and I found the whole atmosphere very nice. Then I became an art director and it slowly went like that. Which now is also completely different – people come from school and they immediately start off. They're not trained gradually any more.

EW: **Do you think that's a negative thing?**

EK: It has both sides because young people now, it's amazing how much they know when they're 21. I didn't know shit! When I arrived in Amsterdam ... I didn't know anybody, or the people that I liked, it just didn't occur to me. But nowadays they know everything; that's sometimes a disadvantage because they're so ... now sometimes people in their mid-twenties have a mid-twenties crisis because they're so full of energy, so full of images and choices. Another thing that is difficult for them is they become professional too soon. They are professionals very quickly – where is the amateur in them, somebody who's very passionate? In the creative world I like that the most. For instance, when I do things myself, it's always a fine line. People call you professional, but when you make things sometimes you think 'Oh god, this is horrible'. There's this line of risking things and sometimes making things even worse than your mother would make them.... But that's a nice process I think.

EW: **Is there a KesselsKramer type?**

EK: When I hire new creatives, that's really what I look for. Lately there was one guy who came and was perfect, I was really impressed by the work and I was even jealous, the guy was 22. Then I started to talk with him more on a personal level on why he would do this, and he said that he'd looked at this agency and that agency and here was where he most wanted to work, and he started to slag off a little the other agencies ... and after the conversation he was a completely different person in my mind. I like people more that have a certain naïvety in them or a bit of shyness because nobody can be perfect. Plus I like it when people have other passions as well. There was a German girl, and I hired her because she knitted a fashion collection for penguins. And it's not just for fun – penguins in Western zoos they really need protection when it gets very cold, otherwise they'll freeze. Normally they have a little bandage around them to keep them a bit warmer, but she thought 'why not make sweaters for them', so she made a collection of sweaters and the zoo accepted it, and the penguins wore them and it was an attraction in the newspaper. There you have a job where she combined everything.

EW: **You do a lot of these side projects at KK. How do they come about?**

EK: When people have the energy for it and they propose it. Same way that I do things sometimes. It's not like I'm busy with them the whole day, I'm busy with doing campaigns and other work but there are always these off moments. It's sometimes nice with your work to take a little side street and it brings you to a different place. And other people also come with these ideas and we try to see if we can interest somebody in them. Because the books that we do and some of the products ... none of it is pre-paid by us. We paid a bit on the first book that we made but after that we've followed the same route as a normal publisher – we're not that big, but I believe in it. When you pay £10K for a book to just produce it, that's not good. I believe you have to be in that world. One time I had an idea on my table for a year and a half and nobody picked it up. In the end it happened that somebody did but some ideas are binned.

It's a dangerous line, when you're an advertising agency and you do these things out of the company profit. Because we've built it up slowly, now we have more trust in it.

EW: **Where do you see advertising going in the future?**

EK: The surroundings have changed around us, with the arrival of the internet. But, to be honest, sometimes when I see work or procedures, nothing has changed at all in the last 15 years, really nothing. Even with the arrival of the internet it hasn't changed. A lot of advertising just says very loudly: 'I'm advertising, look at me, I'm advertising.' Which has some good sides because otherwise there would be complete chaos and it would always mislead you. I think the big change is that more and more all the luxury and the mystique is being taken away. If you have a very good idea, you can take it very far. When you have a very good idea, there are no limitations.

KesselsKramer, Amsterdam

'In Almost Every Picture' Books

'In Almost Every Picture' is a series of books published by advertising agency KesselsKramer. Each book documents a body of photographs of one subject, usually found imagery of a person or people unknown, which was never intended for public display. The photographs are intimate, often banal but always strangely fascinating. What unites them is a repetitive theme running through 'almost every picture' of each series. Published annually, and edited by Erik Kessels in collaboration with others, the books have included a collection of photographs taken by a husband of his wife and found on a flea market in Barcelona, a series of photographs of a woman taken every year at a shooting gallery in Germany, and a collection of photographs featuring a particularly photogenic Dalmatian dog. There are stories within all the 'In Almost Every Picture' books, yet many of the narratives are only hinted at, with the viewers left to speculate on what the lives within these images might have been.

‘It’s definitely a restless time at the moment. It’s a very democratic time as well, I think, because there are no rules any more.’

Erik Kessels, co-founder and president, KesselsKramer

Far left, top: From ‘In Almost Every Picture’ 1, a series of photographs taken by a husband of his wife during the years 1956 to 1968. **Above:** Images from ‘In Almost Every Picture’ 5, which starred a photogenic Dalmatian dog. **Left:** Covers of the first six books.

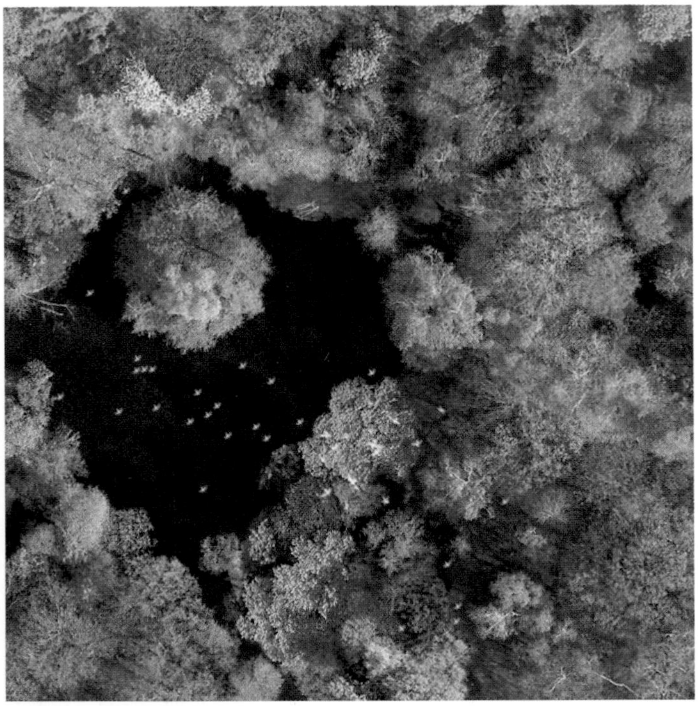

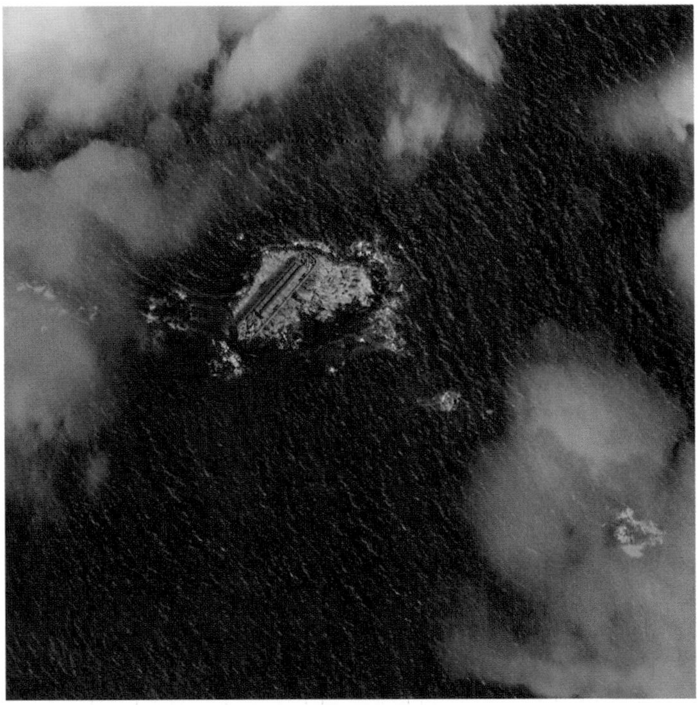

The Glue Society, Sydney

The Glue Society Art Projects

As well as writing and directing work for clients, The Glue Society in Sydney has completed a number of fine art projects, making it one of the few advertising agencies to achieve success and respect within the art world. The first of these projects came about in 2006 when the company was invited to contribute a sculpture to the annual 'Sculpture By The Sea' exhibition on the walk between Bondi and Tamarama in Sydney. The Glue Society created *Hot With A Chance Of A Late Storm*, a sculpture of a melting ice cream van. The piece won both the public and the children's prize at the exhibition as well as international news coverage. Following this, The Glue Society was commissioned to produce a series of artworks for the 2007 Pulse art fair in Miami. This time, the company made 'God's Eye View', a group of images that used reworked Google Earth aerial photographs to re-imagine four scenes from the Bible, entitled *Moses, Eden, Cross* and *Ark*. The images were displayed on lightboxes on the floor at Pulse, so the audience had to look down at them. The artworks received international news coverage. The Glue Society continues to make art projects alongside its commercial work.

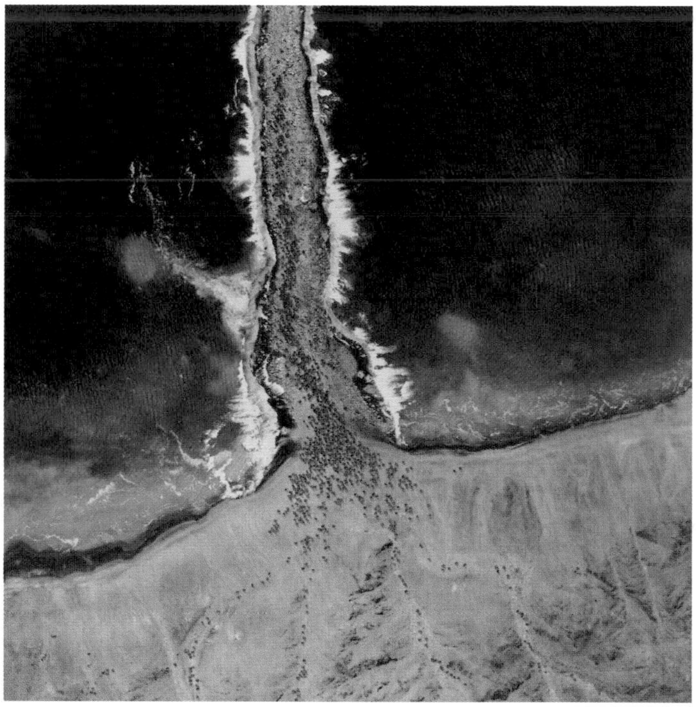

From far left: 'God's Eye View' artworks by The Glue Society. *Eden*, *Ark*, *Cross* and *Moses*. The series appeared in the 2007 Pulse art fair in Miami.

MIND THAT CHILD
Extra Cream ICE

Hot With A Chance Of A Late Storm, a sculpture created by The Glue Society in 2006 for the annual 'Sculpture By The Sea' exhibition in Sydney.

Interview: *Carl Johnson*

Carl Johnson is co-founder of Anomaly, New York, a new form of company within the advertising industry. As well as creating marketing and advertising solutions for brands, it goes into partnership with its clients to create new products and intellectual property (page 214). The agency has been seen by many as a model for the future.

EW: **Would you agree that advertising is going through a period of change? What's causing this?**

CJ: Advertising is undergoing a phenomenal period of change driven primarily by technology and the consequent media fragmentation. The web is as important an 'invention' as the wheel. Nothing will ever be the same again and it has created vast new opportunities to reach both massive audiences and individually named prospects; it has unleashed the creative power of all of us and it has facilitated more meaningful conversations between brands and consumers rather than blunt one-way 'messaging'.

Finally, and crucially, web-driven transparency has brought into the full glare of the public eye everything a brand or company does with the positive impact on making better products and services – or else!

These changes have created opportunities at every turn for those nimble enough and bold enough to capitalise on them. It is also disrupting conventional thinking, structures and business models, leaving whole industries – such as the music business – floundering, and agencies and their clients desperately seeking solutions. Things couldn't be better.

EW: **Do you think it is important now for advertising companies to offer a variety of skills across all media? What do you see as the pitfalls of this level of diversifying?**

CJ: It is not important, it is essential, if, of course, you want to be at the upfront part of the brand and business development debate. For genuine objectivity an agency must have an open mind or it limits itself to the end part of the conversation with a client, as the craft executor of someone else's strategic decisions.

However, agencies also have to be honest about what they can and cannot do to a high level, and be wide open for collaboration with other creative businesses. This shift is crucial and a real cultural challenge to many 'territorial' agencies more intent on protecting their turf than building bigger, better solutions.

EW: **Has the office set-up/style of working within agencies changed too, in your experience?**

CJ: Yes for sure, certainly in the good ones. They are more open, more collaborative, more messy, less structured, more fun ... and noisier! I used to be a cynic regarding the importance of environment and am now a complete advocate of its central importance to culture and creative thinking.

EW: **Do you feel that the relationship with your clients has evolved due to the changes in the industry?**

CJ: We don't think about it like this. If you're good they like and value you – if you're not, they don't.

EW: **How have clients reacted to the intellectual property work that you do – do you think that this is the kind of work that many ad agencies will begin to do?**

CJ: It intrigues most clients but at minimum it positions us clearly outside the conventions of the industry and gives us permission to have a different conversation about how we both can create value for them and receive appropriate compensation in return. At best they realize that we are more grounded and more commercial than 'agencies' normally are because we are used to having our own money at stake rather than simply spending someone else's. Most surprising is how difficult some large companies find it to be entrepreneurial as their 'processes' or 'rules' prevent them taking advantage of clear business opportunities.

What is fantastic is that we have been inundated with opportunities to collaborate with individuals and companies – budding entrepreneurs, media organizations, sports franchises, celebrities and venture capitalists. These collaborations are exciting, dynamic and profitable. They also constantly develop our knowledge and connections far beyond those an agency would typically have.

With regard to other agencies doing this sort of thing, the real distinction is between those 'playing at it' and those that mean it. Anomaly was created for this express purpose and it is central to our decisions, staffing, focus and business strategy. Our key metric in determining the realization of our vision for Anomaly relates to success in this area. Becoming a large, growing 'holistic communications agency' would not be success for us.

Anomaly, New York

Anomaly IP

New York-based agency Anomaly has created an unusual model within the advertising/marketing industry. Rather than simply making ads to promote finished products for brands, it instead sets out to work with companies and new talent to create new intellectual property (IP), which it then also markets, often in unusual ways. Examples of Anomaly's IP projects include a partnership with Eric Ripert, the head chef and co-owner of Le Bernardin; EOS, a line of women's shaving and skin products; and identitee, a new range of T-shirts for music lovers. These projects offer a hint of the way in which advertising agencies may develop, actively investing in and developing brands, as well as offering advertising and marketing solutions for them.

eos
the evolution of smooth.™
ultra moisturizing
shave cream
island blue
with natural aloe, oat & antioxidants
7 FL OZ (207 mL)
eos
the evolution of smooth.™
ultra moisturizing
shave cream
pomegranate raspberry
with natural aloe, oat & antioxidants
7 FL OZ (207 mL)
eos
the evolution of smooth.™
ultra moisturizing
shave cream
vanilla bliss
with natural aloe, oat & antioxidants
7 FL OZ (207 mL)

AVEC ERIC

AVEC ERIC
RASPBERRY CLAFOUTI
GET TOASTED
HOME
VIDEOS
RECIPES
LINKS
GET TOASTED
DINNER SOCIAL
MARKET TABLE SCHEDULE
PRESS
CONTACTS
LE BERNARDIN
SPONSORS
OLYMPUS
PRODUCED BY
ALSO BY ERIC
DINNER SOCIAL
PHOTO CONTEST
OLYMPUS

A2

Jung von Matt, Hamburg

nextwall

Jung von Matt created nextwall, a graffiti wall 30 metres (98 feet) long in the Karo district of Hamburg, as 'a creative laboratory for combining street art with digital media'. Five graffiti artists – Daim, Tasek, Daddy Cool, Desur and Seak – worked on the wall over five days in April 2007, and the creation of the artwork was broadcast live over the internet. Jung von Matt has since used the wall to try out various creative multimedia ideas with which passers-by can interact. These include a mobile phone guide that explains details of the graffiti to the user, and QR Codes (Quick Response Codes – a development of bar codes), which, when photographed using a mobile phone, activate additional 'wall' features on the phone.

Richard Buter

Wieden + Kennedy Tokyo

W+K Tokyo Lab

W+K Tokyo Lab is a record label launched by Wieden + Kennedy Tokyo in 2003. It mixes music with visuals, with all the CDs released being accompanied by a DVD of music videos for each song. The label therefore often works with musicians with a strong visual component to their work. In the past, these have included Hifana, Takagi Masakatsu and DJ Uppercut.

The label is run by a small group of people at the agency who work on it alongside their usual client work. 'We don't function like a traditional music label, because we are a creative company,' +cruz, director of Tokyo Lab, says. 'Our objectives lean towards creating new ways of experiencing music and visuals. So there are fewer layers, the people who run the label are the same people who create the entire music experience. We ourselves become equal artists with the musicians we sign and collaborate with.'

'W+K Tokyo Lab was founded as an outlet for creativity, beyond client-based work. It's a way for us to be active participants in the culture we exist in, rather than observe from afar.'

+cruz, director, W+K Tokyo Lab

HIFANA

JEMAPUR
EVACUATION

HIFANA

BEAT BOX
CHAMP

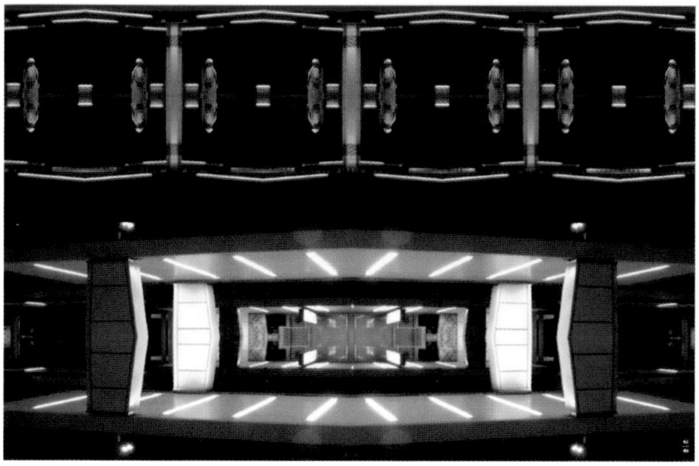

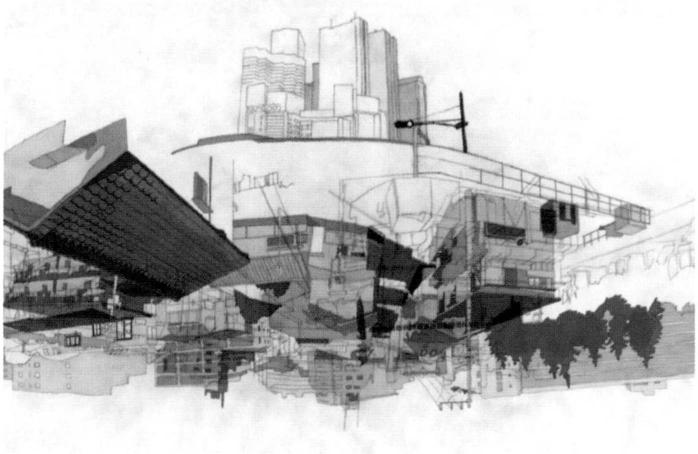

Far left, clockwise from top left: Cover of *Channel H* by Hifana; Cover of *Pieces Tokyo Club Mix* by UC aka DJ Uppercut; Cover of *Connect* by Hifana; Cover of *Evacuation* by Jemapur. **Above, clockwise from top left:** Still from video for CD/DVD release of *Digital Breath* by Afra; Still for video for CD/DVD release of *Channel H* by Hifana; Artworks for *Tokyo Ten* book by Toshiko Kimura, Takagi Masakatsu, Erica Dorn and Kosai Sekine. **Left:** Covers of *Tokyo Ten* book release, which celebrated five years of Tokyo Lab.

Credits

Chapter One: Digital

Uniqlo: Uniqlock
Agency: Projector
Creative director: Koichiro Tanaka
Art director: Takayuki Sugihara
Director: Yuichi Kodama
Producer: Takaharu Hatori
Interactive designers: Keiichi Tozaki, Yukio Sato
Music: Fantastic Plastic Machine
Choreographer: Air:man

Orange: Unlimited
Agency: Poke
Creative director/Partner: Nik Roope
Creative director/Partner: Iain Tait
Partner: Nick Farnhill
Project lead: Alex Light
Project manager: Karen Slade
Design director: Nicky Gibson
Art director: Julie Barnes
Designer: Dom Baker
Designer/Illustrator: Simon Cook
Illustrator/Animator: Rex Crowle
Generative artist/Designer: Marius Watz
Flash developer/Animator: Caroline Butterworth
Flash developer/Animator/Designer: Richard Dee
Technical director: Igor Clark
Creative services director: Steph Mylam
Flash developer/Technical lead: Derek McKenna
Developer: Andrew Knott
Developer: Marc Rice
HTML developer: Jolly Auounsson
Composer/Sound designer: Nick Ryan

Adobe: Layer Tennis
Agencies: Coudal Partners/Goodby, Silverstein & Partners
Concept, creative and administration: Coudal Partners
Production: Goodby, Silverstein & Partners
Executive producer: Sidney Bosley
Strategy: Sidney Bosley, Dharnesh Kaur, Jenny Yumiba
Account management: Megan McShane, Julie Florence, Brian Dunbar, Amanda Sims
Sponsored by Adobe

Adobe: Flash on
Agency: Big Spaceship

Sony Japan: Rec You
Agencies: Dentsu Inc/GT Tokyo
Production: NON-GRID Inc/Pictures Inc/Puzzle Inc
Executive producer: Koshi Uchiyama
Creative director/Planning/Art director: Naoki Ito
Agency producer: Yasuhisa Kudo
Client supervisor: Zen Tachikawa
Account executives: Harunobu Deno, Kenkichi Shimizu, Tomoyasu Katagai, Tetusfumi Nishikawa
Media planner: Takuya Fujita
Producer: Yuki Morikawa
Directors: Qanta Shimizu, Daima Kawamura, Hiroshi Koike
Media architect: Yukinori Nakayama
Production manager (web): Masaki Endo
Designers: Kohei Kawasaki, Ayako Kamikanda
Flash and programming: Keita Kuroki
System engineers: Hiroyuki Hanai, Hisafumi Matsushita, Takuho Yoshizu, Noriko Matsumoto
Producer (movie): Atsuki Yukawa
Production managers (movie): Soyogi Sugiura, Naoki Ishikawa
Cameraman chief: Taichi Yoshida
Cameraman: Taro Hirano
Visual effects editor: Takayuki Ikebe
Editor: Jun Kitajima
Coordinator: Yuji Iwaya
Music artists: Tokio Noguchi, DJ AKI

Burger King: Simpsonize Me
Agencies: Crispin Porter + Bogusky/PITCH
Co-CEOs: Jon Banks (PITCH), Kim Thomsen (PITCH)
VP marketing: Juergen Dold (Equity Marketing)
VP adult marketing: Linda Price (Equity Marketing)
SVP creative director: Mikko Meronen (Equity Marketing)
VP creative directors: Rob Reilly, Bill Wright, David Wagner (Equity Marketing)
Interactive creative director: Jeff Benjamin
Senior art director: Nancy Kadowaki (Equity Marketing)
Art director: Neil Heymann
Designer: Daisy Chavoshi
Flash designer: Ken Slater
Director of integrated production: David Rolfe
Executive integrated producer: Winston Binch
Integrated producer (interactive): Myke Gerstein
Interactive technical director: Scott Prindle
Interaction director: Matt Walsh
Technical producer: Rick Valdez
Senior design technologist: Mat Ranauro
Design technologist: John Gerweck
Senior interactive designer: Julia Hoffmann
Quality assurance: Stewart Warner, Ken Goldfarb, Manav Rattan
Senior metrics manager: Darren Caldwell
Development partner: Cortona, Betaface

BBC Radio 1: Musicubes
Agency: Agency Republic
Client: James Wood, BBC Radio 1
Creative directors: Gavin Gordon-Rogers, Gemma Butler
Flash developer: Robin Wong
Project management: Sam Court
Planning: Tim Millar

Nike: The Chain
Agency: LBi
Creative director: Lars Cortsen
Copywriter: Thomas Robson
Art directors: Rasmus Frandsen, Kristian Grove Møller
Agency producers: Simon Ryhede, Michael Amsinck
Account director: Bettina Sherain
Technical producer: Jesper Arvidson

Red Bull: Red Bull Flugtag Flight Lab
Agency: less rain
Creative direction/design: Carsten Schneider, Lars Eberle
Interaction design/Papervision3D lead: Patrick Juchli
Technical direction/Website development: Oliver List, Thomas Meyer
Website programming: Birk Weiberg, Max Kugland, Will Kuo
PaperDude: Luis Martinez
Sound: Taeji Sawai
Illustration: Hawken King
Intro video: Juan Romero
Flight Lab widget/Facebook app programming: Will Kuo

BMW: Unstoppable GPS Drawing
Agency: 180 Amsterdam
Executive creative directors: Andy Fackrell, Richard Bullock
Creative director: Sean Thompson
Senior art director: Martin Terhart
Art director: Benjamin Bartels
Copywriter: Ulrich Luetzenkirchen
Executive producer: Claire Finn
Digital producer: Peter Bassett
Content producer: Sandra Durham
Production company : ManaMedia
Director: Thomas Leach
Executive producer: Dani Kiwi Meier
Editorial company: U-Turn Content Production
Editors: Fiona Fuchs, Charlie Castleton
Producer: Lucy Salter
Digital production: K! Digital, Ubilabs

Scion: Scion Speak
Agency: StrawberryFrog,
Executive creative director: Kevin McKeon
Creative director: Chaz Mee
Art director: Phil Conway
Copywriter: Paul Watcher
Illustrator/designer: Tristan Eaton, Thunderdog Studios
Agency producer: Katie Lewis
Director: Chris Coots, StrawberryFrog
Web production: Freedom

California Milk Board: Get the Glass
Agency: Goodby, Silverstein & Partners
Co-chairman, executive creative director: Jeff Goodby
Creative directors: Pat McKay, Feh Tarty
Interactive creative director: Will McGinness
Associate interactive creative director: Ronny Northrop
Senior art director: Jorge Calleja
Senior copywriter: Paul Charney
Copywriter/Art directors: Jessica Shank, Katie McCarthy
Art director: Brian Gunderson
Creative coordinator: Asya Soloian
Director of interactive production: Mike Geiger
Senior interactive producer: Heather Wischman
Associate Interactive producer: Kelsie Van Deman
Broadcast producer: Michael Damiani
Account director: Martha Jurzynski
Assistant account manager: Ashley Weber
Production company: North Kingdom
AD/Designer: Robert Lindström
Creative director/Producer: David Eriksson
3D design: Mathias Lindgren, Daniel Wallström
3D character design: Lucian Trofin
Flash design: Mikael Forsgren, Kenny Lindström
Lead Flash development: Klas Kroon
Flash development: Hans Eklund, Buster Blom
Graphic design: Charlotta Lundqvist
Illustration: Anton Eriksson
Set/Model design: Ted Kjellsson
Post production: Tomas Westermark
Producer/project manager: Annelie Jönsson

Sony Pictures: 30 Days of Night
Agency: Big Spaceship

Hewlett Packard and Fútbol Club Barcelona: Showtime
Agency: Herraiz & Soto
Art director: Ignasi Tudela
Copywriter: Conchita Fornieles
Creative developer: Arnau Bosch
Creative developers (website): Sergi Cullell, Sergio Puertas
Planner: Oliver Henares
Media planner: Noemí Martinez
Account managers: Marcelí ZuaZua, Robert Arán

NBC Universal: The Ultimate Search for Bourne with Google
Agency: Big Spaceship

Nike: PHOTOiD
Agency: AKQA
Chief creative officer: Daniel Bonner
Creative director: Duan Evans
Associate creative director: Nick Bailey
Art director: Davor Krvavac
Motion graphics director: Greg Mullen
Motion graphics production: Jim Birchenough
Interactive designer: Johnny Slack
Senior account director: Geoff Northcott
Mobile strategy director: Jonathan Hum
Digital project manager: Joel Godfrey
Mobile technical producer: Andrew Burgess

adidas: Impossible is Nothing
Agency: Netthink
Director general: Alejandro Estevez Zurita
Creative director/art director: Mario Sánchez del Real
Copywriter: Jesús Henares
Art director: Quico Rubio
Programming: Iván Gajate
Technical director: David López, Mesas
Client services director: Manuel G. Cordero
Account director: Iván Ramos
Account manager: Elena Pozuelo
Account executive: Paula Páramo

Arcade Fire: *Neon Bible*
Director/Actionscript programmer: Vincent Morisset
Effects/Post: Olivier Groulx, Vincent Morisset
DOP: Christophe Collette
Stylist: Renata Morales
Production manager: Michael Leger
Production: Jean-Luc Della Montagna, Nú Films

Chapter Two: Branded

Microsoft: Zune Arts
Agency: 72andSunny
Creative directors: Glenn Cole, Bryan Rowles
Copywriters: Sean Vij, Louise Shieh, Charlie Stephenson
Executive producer: Sam Baerwald
Producer: Elisa Orsburn
Designer: Jeff Beberman, Katie O'Shea
***Mother Like No Other* film**
Director: Yves Geleyn
Production company: Hornet Inc
Executive producer: Michael Feder
Producer: Hana Shimizu
Editor: Joe Suslak
Sound design: Huma-Huma
3D artist: Erwin Riau
Mix: Lime Studios, Lorren Silber
Music: The Bird and the Bee
Music Label: EMI/Blue Note Label Group
Music Publisher: EMI Publishing
***Intergalactic Swap Meet* film**
Director: againstallodds, Derek Picken
Designers: Derek Picken, Niklas Rissler
Illustrators: Niklas Rissler
***Tickle Party* film**
Design/directors: FriendsWithYou, Samuel Borkson & Arturo Sandoval III
Co-director: Orilo Blandini
Music: Santogold
Sound FX: Pon Poko
***Endless Cookie* film**
Directors: SSSR
Production company: Passion Pictures
***Le Cadeau Du Temps* film**
Director: Cory Godbey
Production company: Portland Studios, Inc
***Masks* film**
Directors: Jonathan Garin, Naomi Nishimura

Production company: Panda Panther
Executive producer: Lydia Holness
Assistant producer: Natsu Takahashi
Designers: Elisa Riera Ruiz, Ari Hwang, Jonathan Garin, Naomi Nishimura
Lead 3D animators: Jonathan Garin, Matt Connolly
3D animators: Chad Yapyapan, Ajit Menon, David Hill, Bill Burg, Han Hu, Peter Karnik, Eric Wagner, Eugen Sasu
3D artists: Guy Manly, Ari Hwang, Shu Chen, LiPaul Liaw, Roger An, Naomi Nishimura
Compositing: Naomi Nishimura, Jonathan Garin
Props and art department: Keiko Miyamori, Natsu Takahashi, Jonathan Garin, Naomi Nishimura
Music: Black Angels
Label: Light in the Attic Records

Sony Ericsson Xperia: *Who Is Johnny X?*
Agency: Dare
Associate creative director/art director: Matt Firth
Art director: Fabiana Xavier
Scriptwriters: Carina Martin, Stuart Douglas, Richard Martin
Copywriters: Nicky Palamarczuk, Vickie Ghose, Amy Gould
Production company: Nice Shirt Films
Director: Stuart Douglas
Producer: Richard Martin
Editors: Ted Guard and Jonnie Scarlett, The Quarry
Post production: Jon Hollis
Telecine: Tareq Kubaisi, Ian Vic Parker
Music: Kevin Sargent
Sound design: 750 mph
Interactive film producer: Jo Rae-Chodan
Agency producer: Lee Charlton
Designer: Ricardo Scappini
Media agency: MEC
Clients: Cathy Davies, Leigh Taylor, Catherine Cherry

Kit Kat: Ultimate Break
Agency: JWT Paris
Creative directors: Ghislain de Villoutreys, Olivier Courtemanche
Creative director/Art director: Xavier Beauregard
Copywriter: Hadi Hassan
Assistant art director: Yan-Gaël Cobigo
Agency producer: Elisabeth Boitte
Director/3D animation: AKAMA
Production company: WANDA
Producer: Claude Fayolle
Music: Xavier Berthelot

Schweppes: Schweppes Short Film Festival
Agency: Publicis Mojo
Executive creative director/copywriter: Nick Worthington
Copywriter: Karl Fleet
Art directors: Mikhail Gherman, Tony Bradbourne
Agency producer: Jodi Hari
Account handlers: Marcelle Ross, Graham Ritchie
Planner: Martin Yeoman
Interactive producer: Brendan Shivnan
Head of digital: Andre Louise
Production company: Sweet Shop
Directors: Kezia Barnett, Melanie Bridge, Noah Marshall, James Pilkington
Clients: Evgenia Stoichkova, Elif Tokat, Duygu Alptekin, Vassil Tzvetannor

adidas: adicolor
Agency/Digital studio: Idealogue
Creative directors: Jacqueline Bosnjak, Mark Beukes
Executive producer: Sara Seiferheld
Music partner: Q Department
Directors: Roman Coppola & Andy Bruntel, Neill Blomkamp, PSYOP, HAPPY, TRONIC, Saiman Chow, Charlie White

eckō Unltd: Still Free
Agency: Droga5
Creative chairman: David Droga
Creative director/Art director: Duncan Marshall
Writer: Jeski Takaharo
Producer: Sally Ann Dale
Director: Randy Krallman
Executive producers: Patrick Milling Smith, Brian Carmody
Producer: Allison Kunzman
2nd Unit: Brian Beletic, Ben Mor
Editors: Maury Loeb, Robert Ryang

Cadbury Dairy Milk: Gorilla
Agency: Fallon
Group account director: Chris Willingham
Senior planner: Tamsin Davies
Executive creative director: Richard Flintham
Creative director/Copywriter/Art director: Juan Cabral
Agency producer: Nicky Barnes
Editor: Joe Guest
Production company: Blink Productions
Producer: Matthew Fone
Post production: Moving Picture Company/Golden Square
Audio post production: Wave Studios
Client: Phil Rumbol

Honda: Jump
Agencies: Wieden + Kennedy London/4 Creative
Director: Tim Van Soren
Art directors: Tom Tagholm, Craig Hanratty
Copywriters: Tom Tagholm, James Springall
Production company: 4 Creative/North One Television
Producers: Charlie Read, Keeley Pratt, John Nolan
Photographer/Cameraman: Tony Danbury, Gary Wainwright
Clients: Ian Armstrong, Harry Cooklin

adidas Originals: Celebrate Originality
Agency: 180 Amsterdam/180 LA (180/TBWA alliance)
Executive creative directors (Amsterdam): Richard Bullock, Andy Fackrell
Executive creative director (LA): William Gelner
Creative director/copywriter (LA): Tyler Hampton
Art directors/Copywriters (Amsterdam): Samuel Coleman, Dario Nucci
Art director (Amsterdam): Stuart Brown
Art director (LA): Erwin Federizo
Copywriter (Amsterdam): Niklas Lilja
Executive producer (Amsterdam): Cedric Gairard
Executive producer (LA): Peter Cline
Agency producer (Amsterdam): Cat Reynolds
Director of digital (Amsterdam): Pierre Wendling
Senior digital creative (Amsterdam): Lyall Coburn
Digital producer (Amsterdam): Peter Bassett
Art buying (Amsterdam): Kristina Floren
Photographers: Adam Broomberg & Oliver Chanarin
Production companies: Stink London, @radical.media
Directors (Stink): Martin Krejci, James Brown, Henry-Alex Rubin, Ben Dawkins
Director (@radical.media): McCoubrey Brothers
Executive producer (Stink): Daniel Bergman
Executive producer (@radical.media): Donna Portaro
Producer (Stink): Molly Pope

Nike: *Dare*
Agency: Wieden + Kennedy China
Executive creative director: Frank Hahn
Copywriters: Dean Wei, Achilles Li
Production company: @radical.media
Executive producers: Jon Kamen, Justin Wilkes
Producer: Ben Schneider
Production services: Gung Ho
DOPs: Sandra Schaede, Ralf Schmerberg
Editors: Martin Swann, Ting Poo
Original music: Rudolf Moser
Graphic designer: Dong Wei
Agency executive producer: Bill Davenport
Agency producers: Kerli Teo, Xiao Lin
Account handlers: Raino Cao, Jason White
Advertiser's supervisors: Ginger Zhu, Shannon Ellis
Director: Ralf Schmerberg
Music: Rudolf Moser

Dove: *Evolution*
Agency: Ogilvy & Mather
Directors: Yael Staav, Tim Piper
Copywriter/art director: Tim Piper
Art director: Mike Kirkland
Creative directors: Janet Kestin, Nancy Vonk
Agency producer: Brenda Surminski
Production company: Reginald Pike
Producer: Jennifer Walker
Animator: Kevin Gibson
Editor: Paul Gowan
Lighting camera-person: Tico Poulakakis
Sound designer: David Hayman
Music composers: David Hayman, Andrew Harris
Account handlers: Aviva Groll, Sarah Kostecki, Hayley Schipper
Marketing manager: Mark Wakefield
Brand manager: Stephanie Hurst
Photographer: Gabor Jurina
Digital retoucher: Edward Cha
Post production producer: Stefani Kouverianos
Graphics: Kevin Gibson, Terry Rose, Andy Hunter
Dove is a registered trademark owned by Unilever Canada Inc.

Smooth E: *Love Story*
Agency: Jeh United
Executive creative director/creative director/copywriter/art director: Jureeporn Thaidumrong
Production company: Phenomena
Director: Thanonchai Sornsrivichai

Burger King: Whopper Freakout
Agency: Crispin Porter + Bogusky
VP creative directors: Rob Reilly, Bill Wright
Interactive creative director: Jeff Benjamin
Associate creative director/copywriter: Ryan Kutscher
Sr. art director: Paul Caiozzo
Art directors: Andy Minisman, Dan Treichel, Julia Hoffman
Copywriters: Omid Farhang; Nathan Dills
VP director of integrated production: David Rolfe
Executive integrated producer: Chris Kyriakos
Executive integrated producer (interactive): Winston Binch
Integrated senior producer (interactive): Harshal C. Sisodia
Sr. interactive designer: Thomas Rodgers
Production company: Smuggler
Director: Henry-Alex Rubin
Executive producers: Patrick Milling Smith, Brian Carmody, Lisa Rich
Head of production: Allison Kunzman; Laura Thoel
Producer: Drew Santarsiero
Director of photography: Learan Kahanov
Editorial company: Rock Paper Scissors
Editors: Adam Pertofsky, Chan Hatcher, Matt Murphy, Wyatt Jones
Assistant editors: Dan Aronin, Gabriel Britz, Neil Meiklejohn
Executive producer: Crissy DeSimone
Producer: Tricia Sanzaro
Music: Amber Music
Composer: Eugen Cho
Producer: Kate Gibson
ECD: Michelle Curran
Executive integrated music producer: Bill Meadows
Development partner: RED Interactive
Design/animation: Lifelong Friendship Society
Executive producer: Dan Sormani
Post production: RIOT
Fire artist: Mark Dennison
Inferno artist: Andy Davis
Executive producer: Stephanie Boggs
Producer: Shawna Drop
Audio post: Lime Studios
Audio engineers: Dave Wagg, Rohan Young, Loren Silber, Mark Meyuhas
Producer: Jessica Locke
Technical director: Scott Prindle
Associate technical director: Matthew Ray
Interaction director: Matthew Walsh
Interaction designer: Michael Tseng
Quality assurance: Stewart Warner, James Luckensow

Random House Canada: *The Gum Thief*
Production company: Crush
Creative director: Gary Thomas
Producer: Patty Bradley
Directors: Gary Thomas, Adrian Lawrence, Chris Rolf, Stefan Woronko
Online/compositing: Greg Dunlop
Sound design: Dave deCarlo, Sons and Daughters
Client: Sharon Klein

Aliph: Jawbone
Agency: Anomaly

Eurostar: *Somers Town*
A Tomboy Films Production in association with Mother Vision
Executive producers: Greg Nugent (Eurostar), Nick Mercer (Eurostar), Robert Saville (Mother)
Producer: Barnaby Spurrier
Associate producer: Zoe Bell
Director: Shane Meadows
Screenplay: Paul Fraser
Creative development: Ben Mooge, Markus Bjorman, Augusto Sola, Gustavo Sousa
Media agency: Vizeum Connections
Distribution company: Optimum Releasing
Production companies: Tomboy Films, Big Arty Productions
Editor: Richard Graham
Post production: The Mill
Music: Gavin Clark
DOP: Natasha Braier

adidas: *Power Within*
Agency: 180 Amsterdam
Creative directors: Sean Thompson, Dean Maryon
Book design: Alan von Lützau, Julian Wade, Emile Wilmar, 180 Design
Photography: David Turnley
Book production: Marlon Lee, David Corfield

Athlete artwork photography:
Maarten Wouters
Editing staff: Richard Bullock, Leigh Bullock, Pamela Villaflores, Sean Thompson
Written by Dean Maryon, Sean Thompson and 180, with the athletes
Published by 180 Amsterdam

Hans Brinker: Budget Hotel Collection
Agency: KesselsKramer
Creatives: Jennifer Skupin, Christian Bunyan

Amsterdam Partners: I Amsterdam
Agency: KesselsKramer
Creatives: Erik Kessels, Tyler Whisnand, Patrick van der Gronde
Photographers: Theo Baart, Koos Breukel, Patxi Calvo, Roy Cymbalista, Hans Eijkelboom, Tim Georgeson, Martijn van de Griendt, Maaike Koning, Dana Lixenberg, Hans van der Meer, Dorothée Meyer, Diana Monkhorst, Bianca Pilet, Johannes Schwartz, Bert Teunissen, Auke Vleer, Gerard Wessel, Henk Wildschut, Hans Wilschut, Manfred Wirtz
Publisher: Uitgeverij Podium

Chapter Three: Ambient

Onitsuka Tiger: Made of Japan
Agency: Amsterdam Worldwide
Executive creative director: Richard Gorodecky
Creative director: Andrew Watson
Creative team: Gillian Glendinning, Jasper Mittelmeijer
Planner: Simon Neate-Stidson

Porta Hnos: 1882
Agency: Madre
Production companies: Nunchaku Cine, Amautalab, Madre
Directors: Nicolás Kasakoff, Martín Jalfen, Javier Lourenco
Post production: Che Revolution Post, Amautalab, La Cúpula
Sound: No Problem, NorOeste, La Casa Post Sound
Music: Animal Music, NorOeste
Photographers: Daniel Maestri, Diego Vazquez, Gisela Filc, Karin Idelson, Florencia Bohtlingk, Juan Reos, Diego Valiña, Yanina Szalkowics, Clara Jarvis, Guillermo Tragant, Mariano Blatt, Ignacio Iasparra, Oscar Carlson, Juan Allari, Diego Bianchi, Juan Moralejo, Guillermina Baiguera, Adrián Salgueiro
Installation production company: Furia
Installation artistic director: Darío Pedreira
Clients: José Castro, Inés Porta

The National Gallery, London: The Grand Tour
Agency: The Partners
Art directors: Jim Prior, Greg Quinton
Design director: Robert Ball
Project managers: Donna Hemley, Andrew Webster
Designers: Kevin Lan, Paul Currah, Jay Lock
Copywriter: Jim Davies
Interactive Agency: Digit
Clients: Danielle Chidlow (The National Gallery), Dan Gates (Hewlett Packard)

The New Zealand Netherlands Foundation: World Press Photo
Agency: Clemenger BBDO
Executive creative director: Philip Andrew
Deputy creative director/art director: Mark Harricks
Writer: Srinath Mogeri
Typographer: Chris Chisnall
Editor: Jason Martin

Discovery Channel: *London Ink*
Agency: Mother
Creative: Mother
Sculpture production: Asylum
Tattoo design: Louis Malloy

Nokia: UNITY Lights
Agency: Wieden + Kennedy London
Creatives: Darren Wright, Lucy Collier
Architectural installations: United Visual Artists
Design and development installations: P2 Group
Rigging: Piggott's

Anheuser-Busch: The Bud Booth
Agency: Fallon
Executive creative director: Richard Flintham
Head of art & design: Mark Elwood
Art director: Chris Bovill
Copywriter: John Allison
Group account director: Alex Best
Account director: Jonathan Pangu
Agency planner: Steph Newman
Agency producer: Rob Punchard
Production company: Fallon
Design: Sam Tidman
Client: Vicki Kipling

42Below: Because We Can
Agency: The Glue Society
Direction/art direction: The Glue Society
Photography: Derek Henderson and The Glue Society
Client: Paul Dibbayawan

IKEA: Curtain
Agency: Jung von Matt
Creative directors: Arno Lindemann, Bernhard Lukas
Art director: Jonas Keller
Copywriter: David Leinweber
Account managers: Bent Rosinski, Laura Krell
Graphics: Lisa Port

UNICEF: Action Price Tag
Agency: Jung von Matt
Creative directors: Doerte Spengler-Ahrens, Jan Rexhausen
Copywriter: Sergio Penzo
Art director: Pablo Schencke
Agency producer: Jule Cramer
Account managers: Karoline Huber, Gero Quast

Nike: Barrio Bonito
Agency: BBDO Argentina
Executive Creative Directors: Gonzalo Vecino, Pablo Alvarez Travieso
Account director: Nicolás Pimentel
Account executive: Alejandro Gowland
Agency producer: Vicky Ferreira Novo
Client: Gino Fisanotti

Chapter Four: Integrated

WWF: Earth Hour
Agency: Leo Burnett Worldwide/ Arc Worldwide

UNICEF Tap Project
Agency: Droga5
Creative chairman: David Droga
CEO: Andrew Essex
Executive creative director: Ted Royer
Senior art director: Ji Lee
Director of creative innovation: Maggie Meade
Director of print services: Jennifer Candelario
Animation design: Paul McGreiver
Retouching: Van Studivant, Rob Lugo
Production assistant: Matt Rutherford
Photographer: Doug Lohmeyer
Web design: Barbarian Group
Editor: Final Cut

NYC Department of Education: Million
Agency: Droga5
Creative chairman: David Droga
Executive creative directors: Duncan Marshall, Ted Royer
Creative director: Ben Nott
Creatives: Cam Blackley, Matty Burton
Digital producer: Craig Batzofin
Project manager: Julia Albu
Producer: Thomas Beug
Creative director of media: Scott Witt

Specialized: Innovate or Die
Agency: Goodby, Silverstein & Partners
Co-Chairman, Creative director: Rich Silverstein
Creative director: Randy Stowell
Senior art director: Frank Aldorf
Art director: Wyeth Koppenhaver
Copywriter: Nick Prout
Broadcast producer: Timothy Plain
Interactive producers: Erin Dahlbeck, Jonathan Percy
Graphics producer: Alison Plansky
3D animator/compositer: Colin Trenter
Motion designer: Chris Kelly
Account managers: Ashley Weber, Zöe Kretzschmar
Flash production company: KNI

Sony: Vaio Online Script Project
Website:
Agencies: Fallon/Dare
Creative directors: Flo Heiss, James Cooper (Dare)
Art directors: Matt Firth, Vicky Ghose (Dare), Andy Lockley (Fallon)
Copywriters: Andy Lockley (Fallon), James Cooper (Dare), Carina Martin (Dare)
Designer: Matt Firth (Dare)
Programmers: Ryan McGrath (Dare), Jim Tann (freelance)
Directors/photographers: Blinkk
Production company: OneSix7 Productions Ltd
Post production: Rushes
Composer: Ian Williams
Technical director: Jake Morris
Group account director: Deborah D'Souza
Planner: Elaine Miller
Clients: Emily Young, Kirsi Stewart
Animation:
Production company: Sherbet
Executive producer: Jonathan Bairstow
Producer: Rachel Matchett
Designer/director: Laurie J Proud
Original Music & Effects: Barney Quinton

Absolut: Absolut Machines
Agencies: Absolut/Greatworks
Lead agency: Greatworks
Designers: Dan Paluska and Jeff Lieberman; Teenage Engineering

Tate Modern: Tate Tracks
Agency: Fallon
Executive creative director: Richard Flintham
Copywriter/Art director: Juan Cabral
Head of design: Hugh Tarpey
Account directors: Chris Kay, Irenie Ekkeshis
Senior planner: Alex Sullivan
Client: Will Gompertz

Absolut: Absolut Label
Agency: KesselsKramer
Creatives: Karen Heuter, Dave Bell, Neil Aitken, Keith Gray, Jennifer Skupin
Production: Lucie Tenney
Photography: Carmen Freudenthal, Elle Verhagen, Elspeth Diederix, Sofia Sanchez, Mauro Mongiello

Liberty Mutual: The Responsibility Project
Agency: Hill Holliday
Chief creative officer: Kevin Moehlenkamp
Group creative director: Ernie Schenck
Copywriter: Neal Hughlett
Art director/Illustrator/Artist: Eric Shi (Purse Snatch print ad)
Art buyer: Nancy Bagdonas
Print production: Pam Neilson, Dave Majeau
Blog editor: Kathy McManus
Production company (Lighthouse film): Exopolis
Executive producers: Ernie Schenck, Bryan Sweeney, Scott Hainline
Directors: Charlie Short, Ming Hsuing

Sci Fi Channel: Adopt Sci Fi
Agency: BETC Euro RSCG
Creative director: Stéphane Xiberras
Copywriter: Arnaud Assouline
Art director: Benjamin LeBreton
Production company: Quad
Executive production Romania: Domino Prod
Director: Reynald Gresset

ABC TV: *The Chaser's War on Everything*
Agency: The Glue Society
Writers: James Harvey, Jonathan Kneebone
Art director: James Dive
Logistics: Simon Ludowyke

Court TV: *Parco P.I.*
Agency: Amalgamated
Creative directors: Jason Gaboriau, Doug Cameron
Art directors: Tommy Noonan, Laura Potsic
Copywriters: Tommy Noonan, Jon Yasgur, Laura Potsic, Amy Mirwald
Designers: Faun Chapin, Heather Lasche

eBay: You Are eBay
Agency: BETC Euro RSCG
Production company: Cosa Production
Director: Denis Thybaud
Film Peinture "Gaëlle veut tu m'epouser": Michael Forest
Film Guitare: Pacôme Vexlard
Creative director: Stéphane Xiberras
Copywriter: Olivier Apers
Art director: Hugues Pinguet

Speight's: The Great Beer Delivery
Agency: Publicis Mojo
Executive creative director: Nick Worthington
Creative team: Nick Worthington, Lachlan McPherson, Guy Denniston, Karl Fleet
Team leader: Tom Davidson
Account director: Luke Farmer
Account executives: Juliet De Chalain, James Blair
Head of planning: Martin Yeoman
Media planner: Emma Whyte
Head of channel planning: Steve Clark
Executive agency producer: Corey Esse
Agency producer: Sacha Loverich
Online producer: Paul Shannon
Editor: Justin Harwood
Film company: RJ Media, Filmgraphics
Film company executive producer: Richard Scotts
Onboard producer/director: AJ Johnson
Onboard editor/technician: Gavin Brennan
Onboard cameraman: Abe Raffills
Film company production manager: Lisa Fardy
Launch TVC director: Jono Nyquist
Launch TVC producer: Phil Wade
Launch TVC editor: Drew McPherson

Designer: Lorenz Perry, Mark van der Hoeven
Print production: Brendon Eastlake, Roger Doré
Clients: Sean O'Donnell, Jessica Venning-Byran

Converse: Connectivity
Agency: Anomaly

Unilever: Axe 3
Agency: Vegaolmosponce
Executive creative director: Hernan Ponce
Integrated communications director: Gonzalo Vidal
Creative directors: Rafael D'Alvia, Sebastian Stagno
Integrated creative director: Marcela Augustowsky
Art directors: Diego Sanchez, Angel Castiglia
Copywriters: Matias Corbelle, Facundo Romero
Client services director: Vanina Rudaeff
Brand director: Nestor Ferreyro
Brand executive: Constanza Vanzini
Integrated brand director: Hernán Zamora
Integrated copywriter: Julián Ibarlucena
Integrated art director: Juan Manuel Blasco
Agency producers: Roberto Carsillo, Jose Silva
Production company: Blink Productions
Producer: Nick Glendinning
Directors: Lynn Fox
DOP: Ian Foster
Post production: The Mill
Offline editor: Joe Guest
Flame operator: Giles Cheetham
Telecine operator: Paul Harrison
Clients: Pablo Gazzera, Florencia Peña, Cristian Cores, Fernando Laratro, Javier Kolliker, Pedro Kudrnac

Virgin Mobile: Jason
Agencies: The Glue Society/Host
Creative director: The Glue Society
Creatives: Matt Devine, Luke Crethar
Director: The Glue Society
Production company: @radical.media

Audi: Art of the Heist
Agencies: McKinney/Campfire
Executive creative director (McKinney): David Baldwin
Group creative directors (McKinney): Dave Cook, Jonathan Cude
Executive producer/Partner (Campfire): Steve Wax
Partner/Director (Campfire): Mike Monello
Producer (Campfire): Jenn Mnn
Head writer/Co-director (Campfire): Brian Cain
Writers (Campfire): Gregg Hale, Ernie Larsen, Jim Gunshanan
Digital creative director (Campfire): Brian Clark
Clients: Stephen Berkov, Mary Ann Wilson, Jim Taubitz

Microsoft: Idea Wins
Website:
Agency: StrawberryFrog
Executive creative directors: Kevin McKeon, Tori Winn
Copywriter: Brian Platt
Art director: Jed Grossman
Director: GoodGuys
Production company: Driver
Agency producer: Becky Reagan
Interactive company: Struck
Anti-Shirt TV spot:
Executive creative directors: Kevin McKeon
Copywriter: Brian Platt
Art directors: Tricia Ting, Jed Grossman
Director: Tomorrows Brightest Minds
Production company: Driver
Agency producer: Becky Reagan
Post production: Final Cut
Sound design: Elias NY

Microsoft Xbox: Halo 3 Believe
Agencies: T.A.G./McCann Worldgroup San Francisco
Creative directors: Scott Duchon, Geoff Edwards, John Patroulis
Art directors: Nate Able, Tim Stier
Copywriter: Mat Bunnell
Agency producer: Hannah Murray
Group account director: Matt Stiker
Account team: Chris McDonald, Zach Rubin, Sue Luong
Group strategy director: Mike Harris
Production company: MJZ
Director: Rupert Sanders
Executive producers: David Zander, Lisa Rich, Marcia Deliberto
Line producer: Laurie Boccaccio
DP: Chris Soos
Miniature landscape: New Deal Studios
Miniature figurines: Stan Winston Studios
Editorial: Rock Paper Scissors/Peepshow
Editor: Andrea MacArthur
Assistant editor: Paul Plew
Executive producers: Cristina DeSimone, Liv Lawton
Producer: Tricia Sanzaro
Visual effects: Method
VFX director: Cedric Nicholas
Executive producer: Neysa Horsburgh
Production manager: Sue Troyan
Producers: Luisa Murray, Lisa Houck
Music: Frederic Chopin, Prelude in D flat Major, Op. 28, No. 15, "Raindrop"
Music company: Stimmung
Performer: Mike Lang
Mix: Loren Silber, Lime Studios

Burger King: Xbox King Games
Agencies: Crispin Porter + Bogusky/PITCH
Chief creative officer: Alex Bogusky
VP creative director: Rob Reilly
VP interactive creative director: Jeff Benjamin
Art directors: Aramis Israel, Mark Taylor
Copywriters: Ryan Kutscher, Jeff Gillette, Aramis Israel, Bob Cianfrone, Jake Mikosh, Rob Thompson
Designers: Mike DelMarmol, Alvaro Ilizarbe, Pres Rodriguez, Carlos Lange, Conor McCann, Joe Miranda, Jiwon Lee
Director of integrated production: Rupert Samuel
Integrated producers: Eric Rasco, Brian Rekasis, Jurgen Dold (Equity Marketing), Jessica Reznik
Integrated producer (art buying): Sheri Radel
Executive integrated music producer: Bill Meadows
Graphic design: Logan
Original music: Eduardo Alonso/PLUS Productions
Game developer: Blitz Games
Project manager: Chris Swan, John Jarvis, Eneko Bilbao
Microsoft program manager: Kevin Hathaway
Live action production company: Evolution Engine
Directors (live action): Aramis Israel, Dan Ruth, Eric Rasco
Executive producer (live action): Mitch Lawin
Producer (live action): Debi Landry
Director of photography (live action): Chris Bierlein
Post production (live action): PLUS Productions
Editor (live action): Michael Gersten
Co-CEOs/Creative directors: Jon Banks (PITCH), Kim Thomsen (PITCH)

HBO: Voyeur
Agencies: BBDO New York/Big Spaceship

Nike: Supersonic
Agency: AKQA
Chief creative officer: Daniel Bonner
Associate creative director and lead copywriter: Nick Bailey
Creative director: Duan Evans
Creative and art director: Rodrigo Sobral
Motion graphics designer: Greg Mullen
Group account director: Matt Bain
Senior account manager: Remi Abayomi
Technical manager: Stuart George
Project manager: Joel Godfrey

Nike: Nike+
Agency: R/GA
Executive creative directors: Kris Kiger, Nick Law, Richard Ting
Associate creative directors: Gui Borchert, Natalie Lam, Jill Nussbaum, Michael Spiegel
Copywriters: Josh Bletterman, Alison Hess
Designers: Jeff Baxter, Wade Convay, Gary Van Dzura, Ed Kim, Michael Reger, Elena Sakevich
Interaction designers: Claudia Bernett, Joe Tobens
Executive producer: Matt Howell
Group director, production: Sean Lyons
Producers: Brock Busby, Daniel Jurow, James Kuo, David Ross
Technology lead: Nick Coronges
Programmers: Aaron Ambrose, Noel Billig, Matthias Hader, Asako Kohno, William Lee, Michael Mosley, Michael Piccuirro, Geoffrey Roth, Ben Sosinski, John Tubert, Stan Wiechers
Quality assurance: Nauman Hafiz, Michele Roman, August Yang

Sony Walkman: Music Pieces
Agency: Fallon
Creative director: Juan Cabral
Creatives: Samuel Akesson, Tomas Mankovsky
Agency producer: Jo Charlesworth
Director: Nick Gordon
Production company: Academy
Editor: Final Cut
Post production: MPC
Group account director: Ben Cyzer
Account director: Nathalie Clarke
Account planner: Jo Hudson
Media buying: OMD
Soundtrack: Peter Raeburn
Client: Hugo Feiler

Microsoft Xbox: Big Shadow
Agency: GT Tokyo
Production companies: Projector Inc., NON-GRID Inc., IMG SRC Inc., ZOOLIB, tha ltd
Creative director: Koshi Uchiyama
Art director: Naoki Ito
Planners: Naoki Ito, Kensuke Senbo, Yugo Nakamura
Media Coordinator: Akinori Otani
Directors: Kensuke Senbo, Daima Kawamura
Technical directors: Jun Masuda, Takeru Kobayashi, Hirosi Kobayashi
Programmer: Takashi Maekawa
Director (website): Qanta Shimizu
Designer (website): Atsushi Fujimaki
Technical director (website): Daima Kawamura
Programmers (website): Makoto Yamaharu, Kenichi Takahashi, Tatsuya Murayama
Producer: Yasuhisa Kudo

Gnuf.com: The World's Greatest Dice Roll
Agency: ACNE Creative
Web production company: ACNE Digital
Film production company: ACNE Film

Chapter Five: Self-initiated

Mother Comics
Agency: Mother
Creative director/copywriter/art director: Mother
Designer: Jim Bletsas
Publisher: Mam Tor
Artists (issue one): Liam Sharpe, Kev Crossley, Chris Weston, Tom Muller
Artists (issue three): Ralph Niese, Roger Langridge, Dave Kendall, Chris Weston

do box
Agency: do/KesselsKramer
Design: Jennifer Skupin
Photography: Bianca Pilet

Honeyshed
Agency/Production company: Droga5/Smuggler
Chairman: David Droga
President: Patrick Milling Smith
Executive director: Brian Beletic
Head of programming: Kim Howitt
Chief technology officer: Devrin Carlson-Smith
Executive producer: Kelly Frazier
Production designer: Robbie Freed
Head writer: Vanessa Coblentz

BETC Design, Art and Music Projects
Agency: BETC Euro RSCG

'In Almost Every Picture' Books
Company: KesselsKramer Publishing
Collected and edited by Erik Kessels, with Andrea Stultiens (book 2) and Marion Blomeyer (book 5)

The Glue Society Art Projects
'God's Eye View':
Agency: The Glue Society
Lead artist: James Dive
3D modelling: Cream Studios
***Hot With A Chance Of A Late Storm*:**
Agency: The Glue Society
Lead artist: James Dive
Construction: Studio Kite

Anomaly IP
Agency: Anomaly

nextwall
Agency: Jung von Matt
Creative directors: Simone Ashoff, Sven Loskill
Designers: Janine Hoffmann, David Neumann
Concept: Timo Wilks, Leif Abraham, Christian Behrendt, Felix Schulz
Artists: Mirko Reisser, Gerrit Peters, Benjamin Dressel, Claus Winkler, Heiko Zahlmann
Copywriters: Henning Korb, Robert Ehlers
Programming: Frederik Mellert, Ralf Lechner, Nils Doehring, Christoph Maeschig, Nina Borrusch, Sven Herrmann
Account managers: Mirja Rudau, Jana Purucker

W+ K Tokyo Lab
Agency: Wieden + Kennedy Tokyo
Artists: Erica Dorn, Toshiko Kimura, Takagi Masakatsu, Kosai Sekine

Index

Contacts

4 Creative
11 Francis House, Francis Street
London SW1P 1DE, UK
Tel: +44 20 7306 6414
www.channel4.com/4creative

72andSunny
6300 Arizona Circle
Los Angeles, CA 90045, USA
Tel: +1 310 215 9009
www.72andsunny.com

180 Amsterdam
Herengracht 506
1017 CB, Amsterdam, The Netherlands
Tel: +31 20 422 2180
www.180amsterdam.com

180 LA
1424 2nd Street, 3rd Floor
Santa Monica, CA 90401, USA
Tel: +1 310 382 1400
www.180la.com

Absolut
www.absolut.com

ACNE
Lilla Nygatan 23,
Box 2327, SE-103 18
Stockholm, Sweden
Tel: +46 8 555 799 00
www.acne.se

Agency Republic
1 Battersea Bridge Road
London SW11 3BZ, UK
Tel: +44 20 7942 0000
www.agencyrepublic.com

AKQA
1 St. John's Lane
London EC1M 4BL, UK
Tel: +44 20 7780 4786
www.akqa.com

Amalgamated
145 West 30th Street, 7th Floor
New York, NY 10001, USA
Tel: +1 646 878 1700
www.amalgamatednyc.com

Amsterdam Worldwide
Keizersgracht 121
1015 CJ Amsterdam, The Netherlands
Tel: +31 20 5300 400
www.amsterdamworldwide.com

Anomaly
536 Broadway, 11th Floor
New York, NY 10012, USA
Tel: +1 917 595 2200
www.anomaly.com

BBDO Argentina
Arenales 495
Vicente Lopez, Buenos Aires, Argentina
Tel: +54 11 6091 2700
www.bbdo.com

BBDO New York
1285 Avenue of the Americas
New York, NY 10019, USA
Tel: +1 212 459 5000
www.bbdo.com

BETC Euro RSCG
85–87 rue du Faubourg St. Martin
Paris 75010, France
Tel: +33 1 56 41 35 00
www.betc.eurorscg.fr

Big Spaceship
45 Main Street, Suite 716
Brooklyn, NY 11201, USA
Tel: +1 718 222 0281
www.bigspaceship.com

Campfire
www.campfirenyc.com

Clemenger BBDO
8 Kent Terrace
Wellington, New Zealand
Tel: +64 4 802 3333
www.clemengerbbdo.co.nz

Coudal Partners
400 North May Street
Chicago, IL 60642, USA
Tel: +1 312 243 1107
www.coudal.com

Crispin Porter + Bogusky
www.cpbgroup.com

Crush
439 Wellington St West, 3rd Floor
Toronto, ON, M5V 1E7, Canada
Tel: +1 416 345 1936
www.crushinc.com

Dare
13–14 Margaret Street
London W1W 8RN, UK
Tel: +44 20 7299 3000
www.daredigital.com

Dentsu
www.dentsu.com

Droga5
400 Lafayette, 5th Floor
New York, NY 10003, USA
Tel: +1 917 237 8888
www.droga5.com

Fallon
Elsley Court, 20–22 Great Titchfield Street
London W1W 8BE, UK
Tel: +44 20 7494 9120
www.fallon.co.uk

The Glue Society
Tel: +61 2 9211 7977
www.gluesociety.com

Goodby, Silverstein & Partners
720 California Street
San Francisco, CA 94108, USA
Tel: +1 415 392 0669
www.goodbysilverstein.com

GT Tokyo
www.gtinc.jp

Herraiz & Soto
www.herraizsoto.com

Hill Holliday
www.hhcc.com

Host
Ground Floor, 63–73 Ann Street,
Surry Hills, Sydney NSW 2010
Australia
Tel: +61 2 9281 0333
www.hostville.com.au

Idealogue
28 Howard Street
New York, NY 10013, USA
Tel: +1 212 680 1044
www.idealogue.com

Jeh United
2nd Floor, The Third Place Bld.
Thonglor 10, Sukhumvit 55
Bangkok, Thailand

Jung von Matt
Glashüttenstrasse 38
20357 Hamburg, Germany
Tel: +49 40 43210
www.jvm.de

JWT Paris
155 rue Anatole France Levallois Perret
Cedex, Paris 92593, France
Tel: +33 1 41 05 8000
www.jwt.com

KesselsKramer
Lauriergracht 39
1016 RG, Amsterdam, The Netherlands
Tel: +31 20 5301060
www.kesselskramer.com

LBi
Vermundsgade 40A
2100 Copenhagen, Denmark
Tel: +45 3916 2929
www.lbicph.com

Leo Burnett Worldwide
www.leoburnett.com

less rain
201B, IID 2-4-5 Ikejiri
Setagaya-ku 154–0001
Tokyo, Japan
Tel: +81 3 6277 3340/1
www.lessrain.com

McCann
600 Battery Street
San Francisco, CA 94111, USA
Tel: +1 415 262 5600
www.mccann.com

McKinney
318 Blackwell Street
Durham, NC 27701, USA
Tel: +1 919 313 0802
www.mckinney-silver.com

Madre
Rodney 234, Capital Federal
Buenos Aires, Argentina
Tel: +54 11 4857 4010
www.madrebuenosaires.com

Vincent Morisset
3710 St-Laurent, #1
Montréal, Québec H2X2V4, Canada
Tel: +1 514 497 9786
www.vincentmorisset.com

Mother
Biscuit Building
10 Redchurch Street
London E2 7DD, UK
Tel: +44 20 7012 1999
www.motherlondon.com

Netthink
c/ Gral. Álvarez de Castro, 26
28010 Madrid, Spain
Tel: +34 915 938 367
www.netthink.es

Ogilvy & Mather
33 Yonge Street
Toronto, ON, M5E 1X6, Canada
Tel: +1 416 367 3573
www.ogilvy.com

The Partners
Albion Courtyard, Greenhill Rents
Smithfield, London EC1M 6PQ, UK
Tel: +44 20 7608 0051
www.thepartners.co.uk

Pitch
8825 National Boulevard
Culver City, CA 90232, USA
Tel: +1 310 838 7300
www.thepitchagency.com

Poke
4th Floor, Biscuit Building
10 Redchurch Street
London E2 7DD, UK
Tel: +44 20 7749 5353
www.pokelondon.com

Projector
Taiyo Mansion 5F
5–38–8 Jingumae
Shibuya-ku, Tokyo 150–001, Japan
Tel: +81 3 5466 3061
www.projector.jp

Publicis Mojo
Level 4, Textile Centre
Kenwyn Street, Parnell
Auckland, New Zealand
Tel: +64 9 915 6656
www.publicismojo.co.nz

R/GA
350 West 39th Street
New York, NY 10018, USA
Tel: +1 212 946 4000
www.rga.com

Smuggler
1715 North Gower Street
Hollywood, CA 90028, USA
Tel: +1 323 817 3300
www.smugglersite.com

StrawberryFrog
60 Madison Avenue, Penthouse
New York, NY 10010, USA
Tel: +1 212 366 0500
www.strawberryfrog.com

T.A.G.
215 Leidesdorff Street, 4th Floor
San Francisco, CA 94111, USA
Tel: +1 415 262 3500
www.tagsf.com

Vegaolmosponce
Avenida del Libertador 14.950
C1641ANS Buenos Aires, Argentina
Tel: +54 11 473 351 00
www.vegaolmoponce.com.ar

Wieden + Kennedy China
5th Floor, No.1035 ChangLe Rd
Shanghai, 200031, China
Tel: +86 21 5158 3900
www.wk.com

Wieden + Kennedy London
16 Hanbury Street
London E1 6QR, UK
Tel: +44 20 7194 7000
www.wk.com

Wieden + Kennedy Tokyo
7–5–6 Roppongi, Minato-ku
Tokyo, Japan 106–0032
Tel: + 81 3 5771 2900
www.wk.com